DYLAN THOMAS
IN AMERICA

Prion Lost Treasures

The Bourbons of Naples • Harold Acton

Disraeli • Robert Blake

The River War • Winston S. Churchill

Poets in a Landscape • Gilbert Highet

The Dilessi Murders • Romilly Jenkins

Mozart • Annette Kolb

Napoleon and his Marshals • A G Macdonell

Byron—The Last Journey • Harold Nicolson

The Atrocities of the Pirates • Aaron Smith

Conversations with Wellington • Earl Stanhope

Napoleon's Letters • J M Thompson

A King's Story • H. R. H. the Duke of Windsor

Memoirs Vol I• Duc de Saint-Simon

Memoirs Vol II• Duc de Saint-Simon

Memoirs Vol III• Duc de Saint-Simon

DYLAN THOMAS
IN AMERICA

by

JOHN MALCOLM BRINNIN

With a new introduction by
DREW MILNE

PRION

This edition published in 2000 in Great Britain by
Prion Books Limited
Imperial Works, Perren Street,
London NW5 3ED
www.prionbooks.com

British Library Cataloguing in Publication Data
A catalogue record for this book is available from the
British Library

ISBN 1-85375-378-5

Cover design by Bob Eames
Cover image courtesy of Rollie McKenna

Printed and bound in Great Britain
by Creative Print & Design, Wales

Acknowledgments

Readers of this book will understand why my debts of gratitude for many kinds of help are far greater than those most authors are moved to acknowledge. To Caitlin Thomas, above all, I owe thanks for having allowed me to record, from my own point of view, the story of those few years of Dylan Thomas's life in which I participated, and to publish personal letters without which my account would have little documentation.

No formal acknowledgment would adequately discharge the debt, or express the gratitude, I owe to Elizabeth Reitell, Howard Moss, Patrick Boland, Herb Hannum, Rollie McKenna, Bill Read, Pearl Kazin, Joseph Everingham, Dame Edith Sitwell and Sir Osbert Sitwell, and Seymour Lawrence. Each of these friends, of Dylan's as well as of mine, knows his part in the often torturous and discouraging progress of this book.

JOHN MALCOLM BRINNIN
1956

Contents

Introduction		ix
I	1950: February—June	01
II	1950: June—September	65
III	September 1950—July 1951	73
IV	July 1951—June 1952	77
V	1952: June—September	139
VI	September 1952—June 1953	147
VII	1953: June—September	179
VIII	1953: September—November	199
Appendices:		
	I Statement by Caitlin Thomas	239
	II Introduction to the 1988 edition by the author	240
	III Afterword to the 1988 edition by the author	242

INTRODUCTION

'Tell this for legend in America...' So begins John Malcolm Brinnin's sequence of poems on the life of Abraham Lincoln, entitled *The Lincoln Lyrics* and published by New Directions in 1942. Brinnin's interest in the poetic artifice of legends combined a concern for public virtue with more unconventional and decidedly private morals. In seeking to bring Dylan Thomas to the American public, he was predisposed, even before he met Thomas, to turn life into poetic legend. Thomas's own lust for notoriety found an ally in Brinnin. But the combination of their different interests and personalities proved toxic, if not tragic.

Among the fascinations of reading *Dylan Thomas in America* is trying to discern the responsibilities and interests of Thomas and Brinnin. The continual but defensively veiled sub-text is Brinnin's own mediating role, both as Thomas's American literary agent and as his narrator. Like any good legend, the separation of fact from fiction in their relations is a continual question of interpretation. They were both poets and literary dissemblers, writers whose daily life was informed by a sense of its literary significance. Thomas made his life as a poet into a performance, while Brinnin kept detailed journals and combined a sensibility haunted by Henry James with a Proustian capacity for the literary fictions of recollection.

Brinnin's account, although he confesses himself an almost Messianic admirer of Thomas's poetry, is also critical. It provided an influential myth of Thomas's life which deflected attention away from his poetry. There has been much talk of a 'Dylan industry', but the bulk of it is mired in biographical controversy. In *The Redress of Poetry* (1995) Seamus Heaney has recently attempted to suggest the durability of Thomas's poetry. But it remains difficult to explain how Thomas's fame rests on more than what has become familiar as the machinery of hype. Literary history has not been much kinder to Thomas's contemporaries, poets such as J F Hendry, Nicholas Moore, George Barker and W S Graham, who were in part nurtured by Thomas's intimations of poetic possibility. The conservative entrenchment of British poetry after 1945 somehow succeeded in linking the supposed decadence of such possibilities to the mythic decadence of Thomas's life.

Thomas's concern not to embrace academic respectability and scholarly explanation should not, however, be taken at face value. Beneath the bardic bluff of booze, sex and song, Thomas was mediating a wide range of literary predecessors such as William Blake, Walt Whitman, D H Lawrence and surrealism. His poetry sought to combine the comic invention of Joyce, the metaphysical wit of John Donne, and the fluid and sonorously intellectual syntax of the later Yeats. However flawed by a preference for resonant phrasing over the mettle of content, his poetics were beginning to find audiences in America that might have heralded a wider transformation in public taste. The myth of Thomas as a drunken womaniser helped to interrupt the mediation of Thomas's modernism, reviving that media death-wish by which lyrical creativity has to be combined with alcohol, drugs, a flawed constitution and an early death. Thomas partic-ipated in this myth, but it is time his bluff was called.

If Thomas's poetry has yet to recover from the shift of attention instigated in part by Brinnin, the fate of Brinnin's own literary aspirations is also poignant. Brinnin was an early admirer of Gertrude Stein. He published several volumes of poetry, edited an edition of Emily Dickinson and various poetic anthologies, wrote critical studies and biographical memoirs of T S Eliot, Truman Capote, Elizabeth Bowen and Edith Sitwell. *Dylan Thomas in America* nevertheless remains his best known and most important book. There is some irony, then, in Brin-nin's account of his role as a literary agent in the service of another writer. This book not only marks the summit of his literary achievement, but deflected attention away from the literary achievement of the subject it purports to admire, the writer for whose premature death he was at least indirectly responsible. As such, Brinnin's account makes compulsive reading as a glittering novel of doomed fame, something like a post-war version of *The Great Gatsby*, with Thomas as the bardic precursor of what became the beat culture of Allen Ginsberg and Bob Dylan. The story is indeed dramatic, drawing in many of the literary characters of the 'age', from W H Auden to Charlie Chaplin, from e e cummings to William Faulkner. But the real drama is Brinnin's fictional persona as the well-meaning Nick Carraway of this story, posing as the sympathetic observer reluctantly drawn into the unfolding tragedy.

From dazzled admirer to supportive friend, however, this fictional persona also overlaps with the man who brought Thomas to the America in which he died. Brinnin's honest concern to provide a true and faithful record inevitably comes into tension with his own interests. Like many an engaging but ultimately unreliable narrator, his own interests remain intriguingly veiled. There have always been detractors ready to suggest that Brinnin besmirched Thomas's character or that he exploited the life and death of Thomas for financial gain. His account often seeks to defend himself against such charges, but the limits of his rectitude in his dealings with Thomas are evident. Such rectitude was no match for Thomas's studied performance as a less respectable and more spontaneously gregarious character than any dreamt of in Brinnin's philosophy.

The fictional role Thomas devised and performed still stands as an allegory of the resistance to poetry in the twentieth century and the extreme lengths necessary to generate a public audience for a young poet. Prime among such resistances is the desire to romanticise the relation between poetry and the life of the poet, a desire evident in the pathos of authenticity attached to the poet's voice. Thomas had a remarkable poetic 'voice', and became a skilled performer. This gave Thomas's poetry the rare status of an apparently immediate intimacy with his audiences. He was not allowed, however, to rest on his laurels as a performer, but forced to play his role to excess. Alcohol was part of the mask. Thomas himself often said that he would not live to

40, all too conscious of the public death wish inflicted on the romantic figure of the poet, but also secretive about the medical advice he had been given early in his life.

Brinnin's book is ostensibly a critical account of this tragic stardom. But for all Brinnin's distaste for sensationalism, he relishes revealing the lovable rogue behind the rapturously received professional performances. Brinnin is critical of the stories made up about Thomas, but his own account is often dependent on second-hand gossip that subsequent invest-igations have contested. Apparently unbeknownst to Brinnin, for example, Thomas also sought out the company of what became known as the New York School of artists and poets. Brinnin seems out of sympathy with the possibility of connections with groupings that might have been more congenial to Thomas the Fitzrovian. Hints of Thomas's independence are confirmed by Thomas's own often quite lengthy accounts in the *Collected Letters* edited by Paul Ferris. Responses to Brinnin's book when it was first published, however, suggest that many readers were all too ready to imagine that this was the true story. Brinnin's personal involve-ment, along with his evident if occasionally clumsy literariness, ought to have alerted readers to awkward narrative tensions.

This, perhaps, is the implication that Caitlin Thomas sought to highlight in her prefatory letter [see Appendix I], though the effect was to invite open season on what would otherwise have been a series of libel cases. Caitlin Thomas also wrote some extraordinary pen portraits of Brinnin. In *Leftover Life to Kill* (1957) she suggested that Brinnin was 'a creature, certainly not from this world, and not formed of mortal clay, but from some prehistoric planet, undiscovered by men, and of a translucent liquor, solidified into moon-opaque, cloud-gargoyled shape.' She goes on to say that he: 'lived in a purely artificially-stimulated vatican city of his own, which to us radiated serenity. He carried with him everywhere a suitcase of magic tablets, without which, he assured us, taken in ordered rotation, he would magically fall apart and disintegrate. No doubt, as he intimated, he seethed underneath, and his private life was fraught with excruciating, unprintable dramas...' In *Dylan the Bard*, Andrew Sinclair claims that Brinnin 'was both puritanical and gay', and Caitlin herself accused Brinnin of being in love with her husband. It is also clear that Brinnin was uncomfortable with Caitlin and more sympathetic to Liz Reitell. Given that Brinnin depended on Liz Reitell's account of Thomas's last days, the reader needs here to be especially alert to possible elisions and omissions.

Part of the formal sophistication of Brinnin's narrative is its underlying sense of Thomas's hubris and doomed journey to self-destruction. There is a tangible hostility to the fragility of poetic extremity. Health seems to be sacrificed to the gods of fast living. Despite his best intentions, Brinnin somehow shares in the tragic catharsis his aesthetically shaped account provides his readers. His suggestions that by the end of his life both Thomas's health and his abilities as a poet were failing are contradicted by his account of the success of Thomas's work on *Under Milk Wood*. Early on Brinnin suggests that: 'No poet can live wholly in his poetry, or by it—yet the disciplines of art and the consolations of liquor, bar-room garrulity, encounters with strangers, and endless questing for meaningless experience, confounded and alarmed me.' Brinnin and Thomas clearly had very different conceptions of poetry and meaningful experience. There is a persistent comedy of misrecognition in their relations which Brinnin reveals almost as if unaware of being a potential butt of Thomas's mischief. Photographs of the two together speak volumes as to their differences. But this comedy also suggests further sub-texts which Brinnin avoids discussing. Recent accounts, most notably *The Death of Dylan Thomas* (1977) by George Tremlett and James Nashold, suggest alternative interpretations. They argue that Thomas died not of excessive alcohol, but of medical errors and malpractice based on the misdiagnosis of Thomas's diabetic condition. Thomas did not disclose what he knew about his diabetes and ignored the advice of doctors to change his life-style. It nevertheless appears that Thomas died unnecessarily and that there was a medical cover-up. Tremlett and Nashold suggest a plausible medical narrative for the peculiar physical states recorded by Brinnin, while further complicating the web of substance abuse and morality.

Even those most concerned to discredit *Dylan Thomas in America* concede that it remains among the most important biographical documents about Thomas. The literary quality of Brinnin's book has less often been recognised. Read simply as a novel, it works as an engaging kind of moral thriller. That Brinnin's defensive literary persona is that of a real person out of his depth, gives an edge to the book's sense of moral complicity and tragic naivety. *Dylan Thomas in America* can be compared with a range of dramatic misrecognitions between Europeans and Americans in this period. One thinks of Bertolt Brecht in America. Such experiences of migration and misrecognition can be traced through the novels of Henry James into the heart of the American novel. The narrator's complicity in *Dylan Thomas in America* sometimes reads like a combination of Truman Capote's *Breakfast at Tiffany's* (1958) and Vladimir Nabokov's *Pale Fire* (1962). Capote, according to Brinnin's memoir, was a close acquaintance of Brinnin. It is hard not to see Nabokov's work as a sustained reflection on the literary misrecognitions between Europe and American that Brinnin so vividly dramatises. The flaws in *Dylan Thomas in America* are all the more interesting for the way the desire to live out the poetic artifice of legend combines the sensibilities of the novel with the difficulty of being true to a poet's life.

DREW MILNE
Lecturer in Poetry and Drama,
University of Cambridge

I

1950: February—June

Bundled like an immigrant in a shapeless rough woollen parka, his hair as tangled as a nest from which the bird has flown, his eyes wide, scared, as if they sought the whole dreadful truth of America at once, he came into the zero cold of a frosty bright morning at Idlewild Airport. The date was 21st February 1950. Among a dozen other strangers waiting to welcome their friends, I stood pressed against a rope barrier keeping prominently in sight so that he might identify me. As he stood about in a sort of disconsolate huddle of himself waiting for his bags to be carted in from the plane to the customs room, suddenly he walked, pigeon-proud, to a point where through an open doorway he could study the waiting group. When I waved, he lifted a tentative hand and showed a quick uncertain smile that seemed at once a greeting and an apology. In the ensuing forty minutes or so we smiled often again, a little foolishly now, and shrugged our shoulders against the officialdom that was keeping us apart.

I had never seen him before, yet he had been part of my consciousness for sixteen years. When he was twenty and I was eighteen, I had read some of the first few poems he had published in English magazines, particularly those in *New Verse*. Since then I had watched his career with a concern, essentially literary, which nevertheless registered as a personal devotion fired by the Messianic enthusiasm of which perhaps only very young poets are capable, or culpable. I had published articles about his work, lectured upon it extensively in the colleges and universities where I was employed, and generally celebrated it as the most remarkable literary accomplishment to come out of my generation—so that when critics began to point out telling echoes of Dylan Thomas in my own books of poetry, I could only assent to the marks of an influence I could in no way have

1

avoided. While we had had no personal contact, I had learned, about five years previous to this morning's meeting, that he was hopeful of finding someone who might sponsor the American visit to which he had long looked forward. Without his knowledge I had made a number of attempts to have him invited to America by certain colleges and universities, and to enlist for him the support of wealthy individuals who might be willing to become his patrons. But all of these efforts were unsuccessful. When, in 1949, I was offered the directorship of the Poetry Center of the Y.M.– Y.W.H.A. (Young Men's and Young Women's Hebrew Association) in New York, I accepted this position with one thought foremost in mind: at last I could myself invite Dylan Thomas to come to America. My first act in my new position was to write to him. His reply was an immediate warm acceptance, not only of my official invitation, but of my offer to do whatever I could to make his American visit a success. When I had discussed with his American literary agents the possibility that they might act also as his lecture agents, I found them reluctant to undertake duties beyond their ken. With the bravado of complete inexperience, I had then suggested that I would be willing to arrange a series of engagements for him myself. Now, in a moment that was the culmination of knowing Dylan Thomas only through his poetry, I was about to meet him as a potential friend and—a development strange and a little confounding—as the person to whom, for the duration of his American tour, he had already entrusted his physical and financial well-being.

But all consciousness of this personal history had dissolved in a moment of recognition: Dylan Thomas walked on American soil and by a thousand mysterious little events I had somehow become the one to greet him. When finally he was processed through customs, he came jauntily toward me; we shook hands gingerly, picked up his string-tied bundles of luggage, and went straight into the airport bar for a breakfast of double Scotch and soda. He had nearly suffocated on the flight, he told me, it had been 'so bloody hot.' The passengers were a grim and forbidding lot of 'gnomes, international spies, and Presbyterians.' Since

2

there was not a soul among them he could bring himself to speak to, his only conversation was with the stewardess who served him long and well in the lounge-bar beneath the main cabin. The hermetic bar we stood in now was temperature-controlled, according to a gold-lettered sign, but even this was too hot. He seemed unable to shake off some massive discomfort when, within half an hour, we dragged his luggage out into the razor-cold morning and crossed a roadway to the parking lot where I had left my small black Studebaker. 'What posh cars American poets have,' he said, and within a few minutes we were speeding through the wastes of Queens. He stared silently at the endlessly ramshackle streets, the junk-yards, and the sad cluttered fields full of weeds and debris, held this morning in a strict pall of frost. 'I k*new* America would be just like this,' he said.

It was still no later than eight o'clock; the sun was rising in a solid ball, putting disks in the windows of geometrical rows of semi-detached houses, fake Spanish, fake Tudor, fake modern; smoke from hundreds of chimneys went straight up in thin lines, then drifted out wide in a barely moving veil. Glancing about this ashen wilderness with bloodshot eyes, he said that it must be obvious from the looks of him that he had still not wholly recovered from the rigours of a farewell party in London that had gone on for days. Friends more sober than he had rushed him to the airport and pushed him aboard his plane mere minutes before its departure. He had brought a volume of Max Beerbohm's to read in flight, but found he could not, and so solaced himself in the bar.

Approaching Manhattan, we shot into a long dimly lighted tunnel. 'I can never help shuddering a little when I have to go through one of these passages,' I said. 'Do you suppose it has something to do with the memories of birth trauma?' Dylan snorted, and as we came from darkness into icy light made a high cooing sound: 'Ee-ee-EE—it *does* remind one of Mummy,' he said. Now we could see Manhattan and the skyscrapers, as formal and white in the sun as an island of the dead, and Dylan stared and said nothing.

We were speeding toward a room I had engaged for him at

the Beekman Tower Hotel, which overlooks the Fast River and Queens on one side and all of mid-Manhattan on the other. We had hardly arrived when I realized I had made a vast mistake. His room was a high one, looking out upon the whole charged centre of the city—a powerful but oppressive view, certainly not the landscape with which to confront a man who saw himself as a mendicant poet come to America in a fear that he might lose everything, including his identity. As soon as we were ushered into the room, he stood at the window and took in the whole dazzling panorama. But the shock of it all made another drink imperative. We had room service send us a beer for Dylan and a Scotch for me. He shaved then, making piteous groans and profane little cries as he nicked himself a dozen times with a new razor-blade. When he had changed from his rough tweed suit into a shiny blue serge one, we set out on foot along 50th Street toward mid-town.

Third Avenue would surely appeal to him, I felt. Inside the first Irish bar we came to, as he climbed on to a stool and made a quick *farouche*-eyed inventory of his surroundings, I sensed his relief. *This* was a part of America he had not counted on. It was as homely and dingy as many a London pub, and perhaps just as old. From one darkly mirrored bar-room to the other we went then, Dylan brightening visibly in the run-down familiarity of each new place and in the congenial indifference of the many faces lined up along bars in the middle of the morning.

When finally he seemed comfortable with himself, with New York, and perhaps with me, he loosened his bulky tent of a coat, called to the bartender to replenish his beer and my whisky-and-milk, and spread out on the bar a handful of American coins which he asked me to identify and evaluate. I could not for the life of me explain how a quarter had come to be 'two bits' and did not do too well in impressing Dylan with the worth of other coins either. He had already begun a practice he continued for weeks: whenever he wanted to buy anything costing less than a dollar, he simply handed over a bill and waited to see what his change would look like. His pockets were soon bulging like money-bags. He accepted one of my Pall Malls and gave me in

4

exchange the remains of a ragged packet of Woodbines. Inconsequential as they were, these little gestures showed him newly at ease, I felt, ready to test for himself the ways of the world into which he had stepped. The first American writer he asked about was Theodore Roethke, and this was happy chance. Long an admirer of Roethke's work, I felt relieved to know that, without having to go exploring for it, Dylan and I had already met upon a subject for which we shared enthusiasm. As I talked to him about Roethke, an old friend, I found myself moving away from the scattered personal reminiscence, with which I began, toward analytical assertions far more detailed and vehement than the occasion demanded. I wanted to seem knowledgeable, I suppose, ready to move into discourse and literary high-talk at the mention of a name. I had no way of knowing that Dylan abhorred such determinedly literary conversation as much as I did, and that he would soon be attempting to flee its purveyors from one end of the country to the other. But since Roethke's recent poetry was still somewhat controversial, and we had met together upon its virtues so warmly, this was a good start, the beginning of a wide and easy mutual confidence established within a few hours and, it pleases me to think, sustained by affection through the rollicking and tragic turmoil of the final four years of his life.

Deserting Third Avenue for a little while, we walked to Radio City and took an elevator to the observation roof of the R.C.A. (Radio Corporation of America) building. North and south through the hyaline sunlight Manhattan Island glittered, austere and inhuman, a jewel in the hand. Dylan stared into the strangely far-away silence of the streets directly below and out into the Bay where through shining mist he could see the spiked head and lifted torch of Liberty. To break the spell that all the city's grandeur, point-blank, had exerted, I said: 'Of course it's all a mistake, but you and I are too late to do anything about it.' Dylan laughed, pulled his head into his coat like a turtle. We hurried back into the elevator, dropped sixty-five storeys as our stomachs turned to vacuums, and fled toward Third Avenue as if to our only refuge.

Several times already that morning he had fitfully broken into spells of coughing that racked the whole length of his body, brought tears to his eyes, and left him momentarily speechless. When, in some alarm, I had asked him what the matter was, he said it was a liver condition, adding, as if to dismiss it, 'I think it's called cirrhosis of the liver.' Whether he really thought this to be true, whether it had even been suggested to him, I never knew. But, as I later found out, it was not true. Yet such shattering fits of coughing, often followed by frightful retching and vomiting, went on through all the time I was to know him. These attacks were as a rule brief, did not seem to alarm him, and he recovered always within a few minutes, seemingly undisturbed by a collapse that would have sent almost anyone else to bed.

Early afternoon, after our methodical tour of bars had brought us to one in which Dylan felt particularly happy, he settled down to easy talk over a succession of beers and had a lunch of hot pastrami sandwiches. But I had business matters to attend to now, and told Dylan I would have to leave him for a couple of hours. He said he would like to stay right where he was until we could meet later. Before I left, I learned from a phone call (someone had made a good guess as to just which bar we were now visiting) that news of our pub-crawl had travelled; Ruthven Todd, an old friend of Dylan's from London who lived now in New York, was on his way to join us and other English friends would soon be following him. After several hurried appointments concerned with details incidental to Dylan's first reading, for which, I was pleased to learn, all tickets had already been sold, I dropped by at the apartment of my close friend, Howard Moss, a poet and an editor of the *New Yorker*, with whom I was staying. There I found a message informing me that Patrick Boland, a young poet from Detroit whom I had never met, but whose work I found remarkable, would be coming to see me at four o'clock. Within a few minutes I opened the door to the palest, most fragile, and soft-spoken young man I had ever seen. He reminded me of faded photographs of the young Gerard Manley Hopkins, and, at the moment, seemed just as unreal. Still somewhat tensed-up and dizzy after my first hours with Dylan,

6

and pretty well worn out from having tried to keep pace with him on our sorties along Third Avenue, I could barely manage to keep conversation alive. Since Patrick had nothing to say either, I thought I would conclude our almost speechless interview by taking him back with me to rejoin Dylan, who would by now have gone to await me in the penthouse bar of the Beekman Tower. We found him there with Allen Curnow, a New Zealand poet in New York for a time, who had visited him in Wales only a month before. Here is Patrick's report of this meeting: 'I had seen a recent photograph of him and so I was not one of those who could have been disappointed not to see the Augustus John portrait come alive; and actually he looked much better than that recent photograph and anyway I could not have been disappointed myself if he had looked like *Danny* Thomas. After we had been introduced and he had taken (not his curtsy but) his courteous courtly little step backwards, we all sat down and wondered momentarily what to say and even what to drink. You explained how I happened to be there: I had won a big prize and I was going to read some of my prize-winning poems a month later—"All that for poems?"—but I had come a month early to hear him read—"Did you really come all that way to hear me?" This latter question he asked me not as if I were a crackpot but as if I were the credible proof of a creditable proposition...He seemed quite sober just then (though he held his head when he mentioned the farewell party he had been given just before he left England and said he could not clearly remember having left), and he seemed calm, though alert, and occasionally extra pensive. I noticed too that he tried never to laugh too heartily: that he would purse his lips and dilate his nostrils and snort and snozzle and chuckle and nearly choke before he would open his mouth wide. Maybe he wished (but vainly) to hide his broken teeth—but he was not vain; or maybe he wished to protect his stomach; or maybe he only wished to attract less attention...It was my impression that his gaiety was not perfectly spontaneous: that there was behind it not force or effort but some premeditation: that it was first a matter of choice and then of abandon.'

Leaving our sky-room, we headed for the Village and

Julius's, where the *décor* consists mainly of wistaria-like drapings of dust and sacred photographs of racehorses and pugilists. Dylan seemed pleased to have come across Curnow, another stranger in bewildering New York; and in his deference to the still impenetrably silent Patrick, I felt he showed an instinctive understanding of the boy's pale astonishment at being, within twenty-four hours, out of Detroit and into the presence of Dylan Thomas.

We walked across Washington Square to have dinner at a popular Italian place, the Grand Ticino, where Patrick, prompted into speech by several martinis, caused us all to look at him anew as he spoke long, meticulously accurate quotations from eighteenth- and nineteenth-century poets almost everyone else had forgotten. Howard Moss had joined us by this time and we went on to Bleecker Street and the San Remo, which was then the restlessly crowded hang-out of the intellectual hipster and catch-all for whatever survived of dedicated Bohemianism in Greenwich Village. There Dylan was ogled, and intruded upon, and recognized with surliness or awe, but the life of his drinks was his strength now and he seemed unruffled by the many attentions directed toward him. For the most part he talked with the now irrepressible Patrick, turning away from him only when some wide- or sheep-eyed stranger pushed forward to ask if he were really Dylan Thomas. When the late crowd at the San Remo developed into such a press that we could no longer keep even remotely together, we stumbled on toward Howard's apartment for what, I had reasonably expected, would be a night-cap. There I fell into a deep sleep almost immediately; when I could not be awakened, Dylan led Patrick and Allen out to explore new areas of the Village.

Dylan was up and out of the Beekman Tower when I called there for him the next morning, but had left a note: 'Dear John, Gone to 3rd Avenue. See you at Costello's. Come at once. (I like this peremptory tone.) Ever, Dylan.' This was fine, since we had made an appointment with Harvey Breit of the *New York Times* to meet there for lunch. But he was not at Costello's, and I fought the wind and sleet of Third Avenue until eventually I found him standing at the bar in Murphy's, which he already referred to as 'Moiphy's,' and guided him back. Ruthven Todd and Len Lye, another English friend of Dylan's, joined our luncheon party and the smoky air was soon loud with Rabelaisian reminiscence—of prodigious drinking bouts that had laid everyone under the table, of literary parties that had not so much ended as disintegrated, of pub-room ribaldries that had shocked the fatuous and famous, of escapades that had brought wives, mothers, and the London police running.

Harvey Breit had taken on the assignment of interviewing Dylan for the Sunday book section of his paper. While not, outwardly, the least bit uncooperative, Dylan made playful evasions of Breit's questions and the result was very little that could be shaped for the public print without extensive censoring. Nevertheless, he did quotably commit himself on two subjects: New York and American poetry. 'I love Third Avenue. I don't believe New York. It's obvious to anyone why. All the same, I believe in New Yorkers. Whether they've ever questioned the dream in which they live, I wouldn't know, because I won't ever dare ask that question.' Asked if he ever read American poetry, Dylan replied: 'Whenever the day is dull and the rain is falling and the feet of the heron are battering against my window, and whenever the Garnetts (who are a literary family) or the gannets (who I believe are a bird) are gossiping in the bay, then what do I do but count my beads and then: a volume of American verse edited by Oscar Williams. I suddenly have the death wish, which is what I started with. And then I have to read the poetry again and then I like it. And then it all begins again: the melancholy, gay, euphoric roundabout.' But these were but accidental moments of sense in a monologue that wonderfully made no sense; Harvey Breit had finally to resort to telling Dylan more or less what he was going to say, and to ask for his blanket approval. When the interview appeared in the *Sunday Times Book Review* some months later, the scandalously gnomic material of which it was made had been dry-cleaned and tailored to a fine-fitting blandness. Yet it was a technical triumph on Harvey's part to have been able to make any sort of feature of the chimerical interview at all.

When Len Lye's wife, Jane, came to join us, she took one dismayed look at Dylan, whom she had not seen in ten years, and said in a sinking voice: 'Oh, Dylan—the last time I saw you you were an angel.' As Dylan winced, his face darkening in a way that put all of his expression into his big rueful eyes, I knew that I had seen the first real evidence that the derogatory remarks he continually made about his appearance were based on his own painful recognition of how profoundly he had changed. Crowded into a booth, his hair a matted aureole, his crooked teeth brown with tobacco stains, his paunchy flesh bunched into fuzzy tweeds, he was not even a memory of the seraphic young artist Augustus John had painted some fifteen years before.

As, one by one, our companions left to go back to their advertising offices and newspaper desks, Dylan, undaunted by the dwindling company, continued to elaborate fanciful statements and whimsical opinions for an imaginary interview with the press: 'a description of a typical day in my Welsh bog'; the report of a poetry reading by 'Dylan Thomas—the poor man's Charles Laughton'; 'a bard's-eye view of New York by a dollar-mad nightingale'; and, supposing someone would ask him why he had come to America, he would reply: 'To continue my life-long search for naked women in wet mackintoshes.' But Harvey Breit was gone now, and no one else was interested in making copy of what he said. We left Costello's to plod up Third Avenue through the increasingly foul weather. But he was stricken with a fit of coughing in the first shamrock-festooned bar in which we stopped, and, as the retching and vomiting began, had to go quickly to the men's room. Unable, at last, not to assert myself, I urged him back to his hotel and put him to bed, but only after having had to assure him, almost solemnly, that I would not leave the room before he had awakened. He slept, breathing heavily, as I fingered through some English magazines he had brought with him and watched the early lights of Manhattan come on through the sleet. As I contemplated Dylan's deep sleep, I tried first to comprehend and then to accept the quality (it was too early to know the dimensions) of my assignment, whether it be that of reluctant guardian angel, brother's keeper, nursemaid, amanuensis, or bar-companion; no one term would serve to define a relationship which had overwhelmed my expectations and already forced upon me a personal concern that was constantly puzzled, increasingly solicitous, and, I knew well by now, impossible to escape.

Our engagement for the evening was with a young academic critic who had published a perceptive essay on Dylan's work and who had been one of the first people to ask me to persuade Dylan to come to dinner. Refreshed, apparently, by two hours of sleep, Dylan was quite himself again when we arrived at the apartment on 12th Street. We bounced into a fourth-floor room where we were introduced to a group of scholar-teachers and their wives, among them two men who were expert dissectors of the works of James Joyce. Dylan accepted a drink but would have nothing to eat. On this first social occasion in New York, he grew alarmingly bold and assertive—telling bawdy, scatological stories, making preposterous suggestions to the ladies, answering serious questions about certain of his poems with straight-faced obscenity. His one-sentence explanation of the central meaning of his *Ballad of the Long-legged Bait* was so lewd and searing as to stop conversation altogether. That may very well have been his intention. He had come for a good time; instead, he was being cornered by scholars and critics as if he were their quarry. One of the wives had even gone so far as to sit with a note-book, pencil in hand, to take down whatever might fall from the lips of this bardic clown. Whether Dylan noticed this, or understood what the note-book was about, I was never sure. It was the sort of well-meaning affront that never failed to touch off his drive to quench any show of a sacred-flame attitude toward him.

Harvey Breit was that same evening giving a welcoming party for Dylan at his apartment in the east Fifties. We got away from the dinner party with a sense of relief—on Dylan's part because the company had caged him, on my part because it had been painful to see him caricature the worst version of himself before people who were likely to see no other. As we floundered uptown in my car through piled-up snow and ice, he began to

11

fall asleep. He had drunk too fast and too much, and while by now I needed no further evidence of his incredible capacity, I could see that he was feeling the effects of this evening's bout more sharply than those of any other since he had arrived. His chin fell on to his chest as we ploughed along, and he slept until his cigarette burned his fingers, jerking him awake. Since he had had no more than three or four hours in bed since he had stepped from the plane two days before, I suggested that we give up the party and return to the hotel. But he would not hear of this. Muttering that he would be all right in a moment, he slumped back into sleep. Parked on a mound of slush in front of Harvey Breit's apartment, with the motor running and the car-heater on, we sat for more than an hour. Dylan snored, as I wondered to myself just what to do about so recalcitrant a bundle of manhood. Speculation was useless; but since he was at last getting some sleep, I was determined to make no move to awaken him even if we had to sit right where we were until dawn. The 'purest lyrical poet of the twentieth century,' here he was, sadly crumpled in drunken exhaustion, 'Black-tongued and tipsy from salvation's bottle,' unable to think for himself, to face himself, or to face, for what they were, the insatiable attentions that could only destroy him. No poet can live wholly in his poetry, or by it—yet the already apparent discrepancy in Dylan's life between the disciplines of art and the consolations of liquor, bar-room garrulity, encounters with strangers, and endless questing for meaningless experience, confounded and alarmed me. I knew that, above all now, I wanted to take care of him, against my will to impose my notions of sanity on his; even, inadmissibly, to protect him from himself. Just as certainly, I knew that I wanted to get rid of him, to save myself from having to be party to his self-devouring miseries and to forestall any further waiting upon his inevitable collapses. Yet I could do neither. This weakness, this ability neither to reject nor to accept, neither wholly to go nor to stay, troubled the air through which now I had to witness the phenomenon of Dylan Thomas.

Oblivious to pelting hail and the sloshing of traffic, Dylan slept on. Then, bolt upright, he came awake all at once in the way which I soon came to know was characteristic. He was all for the party now. What were we doing just sitting here? We went up into a room buzzing with writers and editors, some of whom were old friends of mine. Wystan Auden was there, James Agee, Louis Kronenberger, and the Trillings, Lionel and Diana, and James and Tania Stern, and Charles Rolo, Katherine Anne Porter, and many others. As Dylan, by a loud and awkward entrance, seemed to demand considerably more attention than the party was disposed to grant him, becoming again the very figure of the wine-soaked poet, I looked at Auden and winced inwardly. I could not help feeling that his eyes showed more than a hint of accusation, that before the evening was out he would somehow say: 'I told you so.' Weeks before, I had run into him at a subway stop. He had questioned me about Dylan's announced coming, and in view of his London reputation for roaring behaviour, wondered whether it were wise. I had told him that I had no way of knowing whether it were wise or not; all that I knew was that Dylan had shown himself most anxious to come, had written me that he had hoped for years that someone would sponsor a visit, and that he was at the moment ticketed, visaed, and just about ready to depart.

The first woman on whom Dylan's glazed eyes fell was Ruth Ford, the actress, who had just come from her night's performance. She knew Dylan's work well, and told him she kept a 'pin-up boy' picture of him in her dressing-room. This was far more encouragement than he needed, and while his approach toward her was a lurching one, it was otherwise direct and not without crudity. With considerable art and charm which, under the circumstances, were rather more than he deserved, she kept him at a respectable distance. He seemed neither offended nor encouraged; if, presumably, he was still capable of reacting to any influence. On later occasions, when other shocked, petrified, or merely astonished girls found themselves the objects of such straightforward intentions, I often remembered Ruth Ford's handling of this episode, and wished others could, with as much grace, either save or ignore a situation that too often ended in outrage and social disaster.

13

His sudden waking in the car, I could see now, was not the bouncing back into life I had thought. Confronting him as he floundered blind drunk through some corner of the party, I asked him as firmly as I dared and as gently as I could to come along with me to the hotel. He said he would but, even after I had repeated my suggestion several times, made no move to join me. I debated with myself. Should I somehow force him to leave? By what right could I force him to do anything? I did not know it then, but I was in the dead centre of a dilemma that was to recur a hundred times. It had become impossible for me to carry on conversation with anyone. To turn my eyes from Dylan was but to encounter faces the spectacle of him made sad and uncomfortable, eyes that implored me to do something. Goaded by them and by my new ill-fitting sense of responsibility, I still could do nothing but loathe my indecision and wish that I were miles away. When Katherine Anne Porter, toward whom Dylan had made mumbling, fumbling, and gently rebuffed overtures through the course of the party, was about to leave, he approached her again, to suggest that they make a date for a drink on the following day, and to announce that he was going to accompany her home right then. As she was politely refusing both of his notions, Dylan held her hands in his and, in his most engaging baby-owl manner, told her how glad he was to have met her, then suddenly, as if she had no more weight than a doll, lifted her in her coat and gloves until her head was within an inch of the ceiling, and kept her there. Indecision left me at this point; through a little group of half-amused, half-appalled witnesses I stepped forward to indicate to Dylan that the party was over. In greater composure than any of us, in spite of her unexpected elevation, Katherine Anne was able to say a final good night to Dylan, though not until he had followed her half-way down the stairs. When I helped him into his coat, he was all at once the most docile of literary lions and quite willing to be led away.

I took him to his hotel and wanted to see him to his room, but he insisted that he was quite all right. Surprisingly now, he *looked* all right. I bid him good night in the lobby, and went off through the sleet. My own vision and sense of things must have been badly impaired. As I learned two days later, Dylan's progress toward his room, which could hardly have involved more than an elevator ride and a few steps along a corridor, was nevertheless so spectacular that the management suggested he find quarters elsewhere.

After sleeping until noon, I found Dylan on Third Avenue, morosely having a drink by himself in a bar where, hours before, he had been the morning's first customer. Since he was scheduled to give his first American reading that evening at the Poetry Center, I persuaded him to go back to the hotel for a few more hours of sleep. He said he felt 'like death itself,' and seemed, again, quite willing to lean on my direction. Meanwhile, I had heard from Patrick Boland, whose silence of two days had puzzled both Dylan and me. The last lap of Dylan's first marathon day in America, I learned, had been too much for him. As their night about the Village had continued into morning, he found he could not leave, and that he could not stay without literally holding on to the bar. When, finally, he had coaxed himself away from Dylan and a charmed circle of new companions, he fared homeward through a nightmare of driving sleet and snow. After nearly an hour of confused wandering, he hailed a taxi, collapsed on the street in front of it, and got to his hotel covered with bruises and trailing blood. He had been in bed ever since, doctors and bell-boys turning his hotel into a hospital room.

When I told Dylan what had happened, he said we must absolutely visit Patrick before the day was out. He slept for a couple of hours then, and awoke announcing that it was time for us to make our sick-bed call. Wan and alone with his bruises and quite the saddest mid-westerner in New York, Patrick picked up under Dylan's affectionate concern and decided that perhaps he could get out of bed to have dinner with us…especially when Dylan had made our visit the occasion of his American début, private though it was, as a reader. The poems he chose to read to hasten Patrick's recovery were selections from James Stephens, Andrew Lang, W. H. Davies, and W. H. Auden. 'He loved the

15

poems he read,' Patrick wrote later, 'and he loved reading them; and I think that it was while, nervous and sick as he was, he went through his special rehearsal and showed such great good nature that I first loved him as a person above the poet...Nervous and sick he was. You remember that he started to vomit and called us into the bath-room after him to see "some more of that bloody blood." I know now (since I had my own) that he must have had an ulcer but when I asked you what he had you said he had told you he had cirrhosis of the liver. I wanted to call a doctor but he would not let me. He took his chair again, and a swallow of beer which he immediately coughed back against the window; and then he took another swallow and began gaily to read again.'

We phoned Howard Moss, who joined us at the hotel, and started to walk to dinner at a Broadway restaurant, the Blue Ribbon. Dylan had another sick spell, vomited on the street between parked cars, then had to borrow Howard's handkerchief to wipe the tears from his eyes. When we were settled at our table, Dylan said he could not eat a thing, but I persuaded him into allowing me to order a dozen oysters which, surprisingly, he downed in a couple of minutes. Since I had been attempting, without any success, to get him to eat at least one full meal a day, I took inordinate satisfaction even in this. He was completely sober during the meal, and I hardly knew to what to attribute the change. Later I knew that it was my first experience of the bone-chilling anxiety that gripped him before almost every one of his public appearances. His appetite went away altogether, alcohol seemed only to make him more sober. During these times his face would become sepulchral, his whole body sag in a doomed sort of resignation. Nevertheless, he would continue to talk to entertain himself and the company. But beneath the social demeanour he was apprehensive and cold to the marrow. Each of us felt the change in him, and tried to divert him or encourage him to divert himself. He took up our conversational leads, told us scandalous stories about members of Parliament and English royalty. But this was all talk just to keep things going, and we could see that he was not diverted.

In the taxi uptown—the first of many doomed last miles

16

along which I was to accompany him toward that moment when he would come face to face with his public—he was alternately morbid and self-pitying, talkative and gay. One minute, as if he had no care in the world, he was singing

> 'She went to the city
> To be on a committee,
> But someone touched her—
> And she went back home.'

And the next minute he was bemoaning, as he always did, the events that had led him to this present pass, wishing he were 'lost and proud' instead of 'found and humble' and bracing himself spiritually against the terrors of his first American audience. The Kaufmann Auditorium of the Y.M.–Y.W.H.A. was filled to capacity, with many standees; more than a thousand people were waiting for him. Back-stage, he asked for a cold glass of beer and this was quickly brought. Then, barely five minutes before he was to go on stage, he was overtaken by a coughing attack so violent I had to hold him to enable him to keep his feet. While I tried to help in a helpless situation, he retched into a basin as if he would never stop. Yet at the appointed time he walked on to the stage, shoulders straight, chest out in his staunch and pouter-pigeon advance, and proceeded to give the first of those performances which were to bring to America a whole new conception of poetry reading. The enormous range and organ-deep resonance of his voice as he read from Yeats, Hardy, Auden, Lawrence, MacNeice, Alun Lewis, and Edith Sitwell gave new music to familiar cadences and, at times, revealed values in the poems never disclosed on the page. When he concluded the evening with a selection of his own works—encompassing both tenderly lyrical and oratorical passages with absolute authority, it was difficult to know which gave the greater pleasure; the music or the meaning. Some of his listeners were moved by the almost sacred sense of his approach to language; some by the bravado of a modern poet whose themes dealt directly and unapologetically with birth and death and the presence of God;

17

some were entertained merely by the plangent virtuosity of an actor with a great voice. In every case the response was one of delight. Ovations greeting him as he came on and as he went off were tremendous, but the sweat on his brow flowed no less copiously either time. It was my first full and striking knowledge of the fact that Dylan was alone, that he had been born into a loneliness beyond the comprehension of those of us who feel we live in loneliness, and that those recognitions of success or failure by which we can survive meant nothing to him.

An editor of a leading literary magazine was giving a party for Dylan at his Park Avenue apartment after the reading. As soon as I could diplomatically extricate Dylan from the enveloping crowd of autograph-seekers and 'ardents,' as he called them, we started to walk the few blocks toward the apartment. But the first bar in sight was, inevitably, our first stop. He ordered a beer, sipped it once, then, staring into a tinted mirror in a sort of momentary trance, hoarsely whispered the last lines of Yeats's *Lapis Lazuli*:

> '...their eyes,
> Their ancient glittering eyes, are gay.'

As we moved on, he became ill again and began to cough in a spasm so binding it seemed he would break asunder. After he had vomited in the street, he was leaning, faint with exhaustion, against the side of a brick building, yet still not ready to give up the party, when I hailed a cab and took him to the hotel, persuaded him to take a sedative, and put him to bed. Feeling the need of a solid night's sleep myself, I took the twelve-thirty train to Westport where I lived, and was back in New York just after noon on the following day.

Dylan was in bed, brooding over his just having been told that he would have to leave the hotel at once. His orders for beer were being refused crossly when he phoned Bar Service, and he was wretchedly depressed and sobered by the whole situation. Allen Curnow, the New Zealander, had stopped by. While Dylan writhed on his sick-bed, cursing the Beekman Tower Hotel and all its 'rat-faced' staff, we packed his things and then removed him and them to Midston House, on 39th Street at Madison Avenue, where Allen was staying. It was now late afternoon. Though he had had nothing to eat all day, Dylan refused any suggestion of food. I went out to a drug store and brought back an enormous milk-shake. He drank this, and said it was wonderful. I went out and got him another one and he drank that. At last I had come upon a way to keep him nourished. But he continued to feel ill, groaned in misery and impatience as he lay on his bed, and turned his face to the wall. Oscar Williams had come by to visit, bringing news of offers from magazine editors for new poems of Dylan's, but Dylan was in no condition to discuss such matters. A doctor was called. He prescribed medications which soon put Dylan into a deep sleep.

While his first real night's rest in New York was an artificially induced one, it served to restore him to a state of well-being he had probably last felt in England. I found him cheerily dressing himself the next morning, combed, crisp, and bright-eyed and—something I would never have predicted—frankly interested in seeing something of New York City. We got in my car and headed for Harlem. When we had crossed back and forth through the area from Sugar Hill to Lexington Avenue, we parked the car near Lenox Avenue and wandered about on foot. At an outdoor news-stand Dylan bought several copies of Negro picture-magazines, saying that he wanted to send them to English friends, who would be sure to find them amazing. We had a light sea-food lunch and a single glass of beer in an almost empty restaurant on 125th Street, then drove leisurely around the edge of Manhattan in the misty quiet of a grey Saturday afternoon. As I pointed out landmarks, Dylan seemed to have settled back comfortably to take in everything, yet had very little to say. Sober or not sober, he was as observant as anyone, but it was often puzzling to know just what had impressed him about a place or a situation until, sometimes months later, he would make a remark proving he had noted everything in detail.

When our circle tour had taken us all the way from the Bronx down to the Battery and back up to the Village, we stopped at a desolate little bar on Christopher Street just because it was in the basement of an old brick house and looked sadly in need of patronage. Since we were still at leisure, with no appointment to be concerned about for hours, I asked Dylan if there were anyone in New York he might like to visit. When he mentioned that he had hoped to meet E. E. Cummings, I phoned Marion Morehouse (Mrs Cummings), who said they would be delighted to have us come over right away. We walked the few blocks to Patchin Place where one apartment house holds Cummings's living quarters and his studio. Once they had overcome a brief, exploratory, and mutual shyness, Dylan and Cummings seemed happily at ease and intimately sympathetic as they came upon ways to express the curiously double-edged iconoclasm that marks the work and character of each of them. As our tea-time conversation ranged lightly over literary terrain, it seemed to me that some of their judgments showed the acerb, profound, and confident insights of artists who in their work have defined a world within the world, and that some showed merely the conspiratorial naughtiness of gleefully clever school-boys. Cummings's poetry, both Dylan and I knew, had for years met with determined or outraged resistance in England; often with but a puzzled and tentative interest. Introducing this subject himself, Cummings told us of recent instances when a book of his had been returned to its English publisher by wary reviewers who suspected a literary hoax. In distinction to this reaction, Cummings was touched, I felt, to have been paid the first respect of a British poet whose work he regarded so highly. He had been so moved by Dylan's reading the previous Thursday evening, his wife told me, that he had left the auditorium to walk the streets alone for hours.

Dylan was to go to dinner that evening with the painter William Stanley Hayter and his wife at their apartment on Central Park West. Back at Midston House, still in the glow of his visit with Cummings, whose simplicity and easy humour had quite disarmed him, Dylan changed into the blue suit and polka-dot bow tie that had now become his conventional reading costume, fussed for a while over the order of his poems for his second Poetry Center recital that evening, gathered up the several books and papers from which he would read, then went off by taxi. A few hours later I joined him at the Hayter's. Dinner was over, and he had begun to sink into the coils of his pre-reading *angst*. Slumped into the corner of a taxi, begging for any sign of reprieve, he was the doomed man again as I went with him towards his place of execution. But once on the stage he seemed to rise up out of himself to give another ringing performance. This time he was hale enough afterwards to attend a small party at the apartment of Lloyd Frankenberg, the poet, and his wife, the painter Loren McIver, and later to drink through the long night on the itinerary of Village bars that would shortly become standard.

With two resonant performances behind him he was now scheduled to be away from New York for almost two months, during which he would journey as far west as San Francisco, as far north as Vancouver, as far south as Florida. In his first four days in America he had exhibited himself at his worst and at his best. His readings were more wonderful than anyone had anticipated; his personal behaviour had already led to the cancellation of a number of parties and receptions planned in his honour. My own affection for him, transformed from an impersonal devotion into an almost hourly concern, had grown steadily, perhaps just a little faster than my fears for the consequences of his obsessive drinking and my increasingly biting anxiety about the responsibility his dependence had imposed. He seemed to count upon my help in every way, and to take me for granted in terms for which I was still not prepared; yet beyond our busy engagement in those matters for which he had come to America and the often absurdly intimate situations they entailed, I felt no conviction that I was personally one whit more important to him than any of a dozen others he had met and found congenial. One of the most beguiling things about Dylan's social character was the spell-like illusion of intimacy he would cast upon anyone who came near. The greatest of his gifts was the human touch—an exercise of sympathy so natural, effortless, and constant that his life seemed sometimes to be the furious denial of a saintliness he could not hide. He was instinctively and helplessly drawn to

21

innocence in all its forms; he could detect malice, meanness, and perversion of spirit as if they were odours. Since it was no trouble at all to make a friend of Dylan, many people, most of whom he would not even recognize on a second encounter, blithely claimed him as an intimate. While their claims, like all claims upon Dylan's goodness, were valid, they could never lead to preference. Everyone, it seemed, could command his intimate attention; yet he had bestowed it on no one.

Since his first stop outside of New York was to be a brief visit with me at home, on Sunday afternoon we drove to Westport on the Merritt Parkway. At last he found excitement in one of those American phenomena all visitors are supposed to find remarkable. Shining lines of chromium-plated cars visible almost bumper to bumper from the parkway hill-tops struck him as incredible and he said so. As we drove leisurely into Connecticut he drew me out about my poetry, pleasing me by knowing far more about it than I had any reason to expect, and then he somewhat coyly indicated that he knew more about me personally than my limited correspondence with him could have revealed. He explained that, before accepting my invitation to come to America, he had written for information about me to his publisher, James Laughlin of New Directions. My fifteen-year acquaintance with Laughlin had apparently provided sufficient knowledge to reassure Dylan and to encourage him to proceed. And as we confessed the fanciful pictures of one another we had carried to the moment of our meeting at Idlewild—pictures that had since been quite obliterated or dissolved—I remembered the two letters I had received from Dylan before his coming. The first had been brief, simply expressing his pleasure in 'the honour you have paid me,' and his intention to come to New York as soon as he could put his affairs in order. The second was far less formal—leading me to believe that either my interim letter to him or some other relaxing influence had penetrated the reserve in which he had composed the first:

Dear John Malcolm Brinnin,

First of all: many apologies for this month-long delay in

answering your extremely nice and helpful letter. My lying cable said, 'Letter in mail.' And I did intend to write at once, but had to go away, felt suddenly ill, clean forgot, put it off for a rainy day, was struck by lightning, any or all of these.

Thank you profoundly for your letter. I can't tell you how pleased I am that you should have suggested you look after my readings. I can think of nothing more sensibly pleasant. What an abominable phrase! Nothing I have ever enjoyed has been sensibly pleasant. I mean, I can think of nothing better. I was very nervous about my visit: that is, about the arranging of readings to make some money. I should have made a mess of things. My life here, in the deep country, is incredibly complicated; but in a city, I spin like a top. And procrastination is an element in which I live. Thank you, very much indeed, for having, in the first place, made my visit possible, and for wishing to work with me. Naturally, I couldn't allow you to work with me if you did not take a percentage for all the troublesome work you'll have to do. I feel relieved now, and can face the whole undertaking with only quite minor paralysis.

As to the number of readings: you say that you will be able, you think, 'to arrange for, at least, fifteen engagements, and, very likely, considerably more.' How many jobs do *you* think I should do? I don't want to work my head off, but, on the other hand, I *do* want to return to England with some dollars in my pocket. And, of course, I want to get around the States a bit. I'll have to leave this to you. I hand the baby over, with bewildered gratitude.

About the readings themselves: Is there any strong reason why my readings should all be devoted to my own work? I most sincerely hope not. What I should like to do, more than anything else, is to read from a number of contemporary British poets, including myself. I far prefer reading other chaps' work to my own: I find it clearer. An hour of me aloud is hell, and produces large burning spots in front of the mind.

Will you be seeing Laughlin? He wrote to me about the same time you did, saying that 'to make any real money for you, things will have to be done hard and tough and business-like.' I hope you're an adamantine tartar. Laughlin also suggests that 'it might be well to get up a variant program in which you would read the classic English poets.' What do you think? Personally, I shall be glad to read *anything*—and will certainly do my best to make it entertaining—except poems in dialect, hymns to Stalin, anything over 500 lines. Dare I, in my Welsh-English voice, read any American poets to American audiences? Over here, when I give broadcast readings,

23

I quite often read some Ransom. But I do very much want to read from *other* contemporary British poets. At the mere thought of reading only myself, I begin to feel hunted, invisible trolls shake hands with my Adam's apple.

Very many thanks again, for what you have done and will do, for all the friendliness.

Laughlin says there will be a party for me at the Gothan Book Mart as soon as I get there: I shall polish up my glass belly.

With best wishes,

Yours sincerely,

DYLAN THOMAS.

As we filed along in the heavy Sunday traffic, we began to speak of political trends here and in Great Britain. He had signed the Stockholm Peace Petition in the previous year, he said, had been attacked for it in the press along with many other prominent Britons, and wondered what effect that publicity might have on his American appearances. When he had applied in London for an American visa, he had been subject to questions which had made him angry, but also apprehensive. He had been asked, for instance, whether he would attend a song-recital of Paul Robeson's. He had answered in the affirmative. Then his interrogator had rather portentously queried him about a literary conference in Prague which Dylan had recently attended and he had to admit that his expenses were paid by his hosts behind the Iron Curtain. But finally suspicions were allayed and he had received the official approval that designated him as politically harmless. This was certainly applicable. Dylan's political naïveté, it seemed to me, was a consequence of his promiscuous affection for humanity and of his need for emotional identification with the lowest stratum of society. His socialism was basically Tolstoyan, the attempt of the spiritual aristocrat to hold in one embrace the good heart of mankind, a gesture and a purpose uncontaminated by the *realpolitik* of the twentieth century. While he expressed himself strongly on political matters and tended indiscriminately to support the far left, his attitude was a kind of stance unsupported by knowledge, almost in defiance of knowledge. As long as, anywhere in the world, there existed groups of men pilloried by the forces of propertied power, Dylan wanted to be counted among their sympathizers. And yet no political manifestations of this ever showed in his poetry. Americans who had celebrated him as the romantic liberator—as the poet who had broken the domination of the once politically minded generation of Auden, Spender, MacNeice, and Lewis, would have been perplexed to find that he was actually far more censorious of the *status quo* than any of the other British poets. As far as America was concerned, this was Dylan's unguarded secret—a secret in which no one showed the least interest.

We turned off the Parkway at Westport and drove to the small, severely modern house in which I then lived—an aseptic sort of structure of planes and coloured surfaces that seemed more like a city apartment set down on a rocky crag than like a house. We made a light supper together, reminiscing about the four phrenetic days of his visit as if they were four bygone years. By early evening the country silence had become a little oppressive. Perhaps because I was feeling inadequate to entertain Dylan now that we were alone and quite removed from everything that had entertained him in New York, or perhaps because I noticed signs of restlessness in him, I suggested we make a sort of suburban pub-crawl along the Post Road. It was a crackling cold night, with few people in any of the neon-lighted roadstands. But Dylan soon learned the pleasures of the juke-box and the pin-ball machine and we played them all the way to Bridgeport. He was curious about the Polish-speaking family groups, wanted to know what was in the mixed drinks with the fancy names, and talked now and then to lonely people who had come this bleak night to look at themselves in bar-room mirrors. By late evening it had become too cold even for Dylan's comfort, and we fled out of the howling wind to visit Peter DeVries, the novelist and *New Yorker* editor who lived not far from me. He and his wife, Katinka, made easy good company and served us proper drinks until well after midnight.

Next morning came a letter for Dylan from his wife, Caitlin. He had been waiting for this every day, yet now that it had

25

arrived he seemed reluctant to open it. He kept the letter in his pocket for an hour or so, then went out into the foggy cold morning and sat on a rock to open and read it. Draped in a voluminous tweed overcoat I had given him, lumpishly Byronic on his stony perch, he was the only figure in the landscape. He sat there in still contemplation until a new event made his position ludicrous. My poodle, Nana, was in heat, a condition in which her outings were usually made on a leash. But this morning she had somehow escaped surveillance and had disappeared for hours. When she returned, panting and notably dishevelled, some twelve or fifteen other dogs of many breeds followed in her wake. Nana was let into the house and absurdly scolded for her wantonness. The other dogs, patient and immovable as the granite on which they crouched, settled themselves at observation points around the house to wait for her next gala appearance. With the open letter in his hand, Dylan sat in a landscape of dogs—dogs behind him, in front of him, dogs under trees and bushes, dogs on the rocks. From indoors I could make out only snatches of what he said, but as he began to lecture them in tones of commiseration, I did hear him tell them he knew just how they felt. They looked at him blankly, keeping their distance on other rocks, and paid no attention at all.

He came into the house to read me passages of the letter— phrases and images which, I felt, had the quality of folk poetry. 'She's a better poet than I am,' he said, and read me further passages, including one about their infant, Colm, who was 'sweet as a bee.' He put the letter into his pocket, saying: 'Oh, she's the only one for me. I adored her the day I married her and now after fourteen years I adore her more than ever. When I was little she could carry me across a brook. She's stronger than I am *now*.' And then, saying that she really had no patience with him ever, he mimicked her scoldings: 'Mumble, mumble, mumble— all you ever do is mumble. I haven't understood a word you've said since the day you married me.' But while the letter had provided this much release, it did not otherwise make him happy, and I sensed that his reluctance to open it had been a foreboding of what he would find. He pored over magazines and

26

lounged about the house all day, not very talkative except once when, picking up at random some poems of students I was annotating, he spotted phrases he liked and read whole poems aloud. The respect he showed for some of these efforts would have transported my students into happy delirium.

Stanley Edgar Hyman, the critic, and his novelist wife, Shirley Jackson, who lived in a big Victorian house in nearby Saugatuck, had asked us to come over in the late afternoon. Their children roared through our cocktail hour until they were bribed off with television. We went out for spaghetti at an Italian restaurant, and returned to an evening given over to tele-vised boxing matches, of which both of the Hymans were knowing devotees, and, eventually to some literary talk that led to the co-operative plotting of a series of gruesomely pathologi-cal murder mysteries, in the details of which Dylan and Shirley tried to outdo one another. Finally, Dylan gave a rather heavy-tongued reading from books of his the Hymans took down from their shelves. As usual, we stayed too late and drank too much and the evening ended gracelessly, with some of us out in the snow, and some of us silent before a dead television set. When finally we got back to my house about three, the steep icy steps in the rock-face leading up to it seemed insurmountable. Liter-ally pushing Dylan ahead of me, stopping to catch my breath or to pull him out of the snow when I lost control of him, I even-tually got him to within arm's length of the door. But he would not go in. 'Now,' he said lugubriously, 'now you know exactly what you've brought to America.'

Just before I fell asleep, as I glanced across the room, Dylan was sitting up with a paper-backed mystery story, his bedclothes littered with wrapped and unwrapped nickel candy bars he had been secretly collecting for days. I dozed off as he contentedly fingered through his hoard of Tootsie Rolls, Milky Ways, Baby Ruths, and Bit-O-Honeys.

He awoke singing and Nana leaped into bed with him. As I prepared breakfast two rooms away, I could hear him giving her fatherly advice as to proper conduct in her present situation, fol-lowed by what I supposed were peals of Welsh song. After a full

27

breakfast, which he ate without protest and without beer, I had errands to do in Norwalk, a drive of three miles. Dylan came with me, and said he would wait in a bar until I had completed them. When I rejoined him in less than an hour, his face was sunken and he spoke in an almost inaudible mutter. He had been insulted: someone had made a remark about his speech and called him a foreigner—someone in working clothes, and that made it even worse. He would not speak further about it except to say: 'Let's leave this pigsty of a town.' I could not tell whether the real or imagined offence had depressed him as deeply as it seemed to, or whether he were finally feeling the effects of his roaring days in New York. We drove back to Westport, packed his ragged baggage, and set out after lunch for New Haven, where he was to read in the late afternoon at Yale.

But his depression, I could see now, was profound; no word of mine could lift it. Slumped in the front seat beside me, he slept every mile of the way to New Haven, where I awakened him in front of the house of friends of mine with whom we were to stay overnight. Dylan wanted to buy nylon stockings for Caitlin and for his friend Ivy Williams who keeps Browns Hotel in his village. We went to a department store where an obliging salesgirl assured us they would be sent off directly. Then we joined Norman Holmes Pearson in the Provost's Office at the Yale Graduate School. He escorted us to the lecture hall, where a rather modest crowd awaited Dylan's first American college appearance.

Pearson had arranged a dinner party at Mory's in one of the upstairs dining-rooms for after the reading. There we were introduced into a group of seven or eight English professors, most of whom seemed confoundingly ill at ease and indisposed toward conversation during the hurried few minutes in which we gulped Manhattans before settling ourselves about a circular table. For reasons we never understood, certainly not as the result of any provocation by Dylan, who came into the wary-eyed group in the mildest and most ingratiating humour, this occasion at Yale—his introduction to academic life in America—was so grim and stultifying as to become the standard against

28

which he would measure every awkward and unhappy event. With the exception of Cleanth Brooks, who conveyed by his presence more than by anything he said a sympathetic recognition of Dylan's dilemma, and of Norman Pearson, who was the talkative host to the party, all the professors sat around in a brooding druidic circle apparently awaiting an oracle. Perhaps they were offended by Dylan's generally dishevelled appearance, or put off by his obvious disdain for the unremittingly scholarly talk of scholars. Perhaps the volubility of so live a poet was too much for those who fingered habitually the bones of dead ones. In any case, an uneasy sense of waiting, a feeling that nothing was happening, turned the meal into a ritual of politeness in which the passing of a plate of celery was an event of magnitude. Across the table from me Dylan looked trapped and forlorn— there was no relief to his right or to his left. But when coffee was brought in, finally, and somebody handed him a cigar, he moved to break the spell. He told a bawdy story—something about Edward VII and what he had said at the dedication of a tunnel. This was received with a feint at muffled, grudging laughter. He told other stories; uneasiness in the room became palpable. While he was in the middle of an anecdote about Oscar Wilde and a jockey, the party began swiftly to break up. There were mumbled excuses about evening appointments, theses to read, wives waiting—a general sense of retreat at once and at all costs. Within five minutes the professors had fled into the night, leaving Dylan with his unfinished story and a burned-out cigar.

As Dylan moaned and fumed and I tried to put conviction in my assurances that it wouldn't *all* be like that, we drove to a party to which my friends had invited five or six of the younger Yale faculty. The wife of one of them was Welsh, knew Dylan's part of Wales intimately, and was extraordinarily pretty. Ignoring her husband's presence as he made quite clear the precise nature of his interest in her, Dylan drank steadily, released his pent-up high spirits in a flow of talk and told every story that came into his head. He was still the loud life of the party when, about two o'clock, I went to bed. When I awoke at eight in the morning the bed across from me had not been slept in. In a few

29

minutes I heard our hostess coming downstairs. She spoke a greeting to Dylan who, groaning and sighing, was fighting his way out of sleep on the living-room couch. 'I expect I was a pretty bad boy last night, wasn't I?' he said. 'Oh, Dylan, you were fine, we all had a wonderful time.' 'No, I wasn't,' he said. 'And do you know what the trouble is? I'm going to do the very same thing to-night!'

Mid morning we drove him to the railroad station and waved him off to Boston, where he was to read that afternoon at Harvard. Thinking of my friends in Cambridge, above all of F. O. Matthiessen, who would have him in charge, I shuddered a little bit and drove back to Westport.

So began a relationship of four years which, except for brief occasions abroad and a few plateau-like days in this country, was a busy matter of greeting Dylan on arrival, processing him through the hundreds of official and unofficial engagements he counted on me to oversee, then bidding him the farewells that always came like interruptions and, in spite of the anxieties and trouble his presence guaranteed, always too soon. Since I handled all of his lecture engagements, and all of his finances, we were always in touch and always together in matters having to do with his career. His sensitivity to every nuance of human exchange, his hilarious self-deprecating wit, along with his great generosity of mind and soul—qualities that kept him above and apart from the damning, dubious, or scurrilous things that were already said about him—had within the mere space of a week made him the most exhausting, exasperating, and most completely endearing human being I had ever encountered. When I realized that to know Dylan was to know a personality having the power of a natural force—with all the thoughtless, self-driven, and predestined vitality that the term implies—I determined to keep our relationship on a strict professional basis, and so be relieved of having to grant the endless indulgence he expected and the sort of nursing attendance he demanded. But these impulses and the resolutions they engendered simply dissolved whenever he turned up. Like almost everyone else who came close to Dylan, I assumed that he was far more helpless

30

than actually he was. To be a part of his erratic and abnormal life was to be drawn into prolonged states of anxiety which, in my case at least, threatened to reach more or less to the edge of breakdown. Only after having known him for two full years did I realize and begin to act upon a conviction that, when he fell, he fell on his own two feet.

To make sure that he would not lack information about his next reading, and that he would have the names of people who might help him to get about, I had in rather naïve confidence prepared for Dylan a diary which told him how he would travel, how long it would take to get from one place to another, who would meet him, where he would stay, and what to do if anything went amiss. This, of course, was in addition to arrangements I followed daily by wire and telephone. While he largely ignored his diary, often left people waiting at appointed places, and sometimes disappeared altogether, he almost invariably got to the scenes of his readings at the right time and was seldom very far off schedule in his sometimes highly complicated travels. Fortunately, there were always as many people to look after him as there were those who wanted only to keep him talking in a bar.

His reading at Harvard went well, I gathered from him and others, but at Matthiessen's party on Louisburg Square afterwards he dismayed his host and a number of guests by behaviour that threatened the solidity of antique furniture and the virtue of girls from Radcliffe. On the following day, after he had made recordings of his poems for John L. Sweeney's collection in Lamont Library, he was to be driven to Mt Holyoke College by my friend, Gray Burr. In order to have them at the College in time for dinner with the faculty committee, I had strongly advised, by underlinings and exclamation points in the diary, that he and Gray leave Cambridge no later than one o'clock. But Dylan disappeared from the vicinity of Harvard Square for hours; hastily organized searching parties kept meeting one another in likely places. When finally he was spotted and taken in tow, he cajoled his captors into having further drinks with him and the journey to Mt Holyoke did not begin until four. *En route* he insisted on stopping at every neon sign that offered beer, and then on playing every pin-ball machine. As the students of Mt Holyoke were happily trooping into the lecture hall, Dylan, many miles away, was attempting, with the sort of tipsy lep-rechaun-like blandishments with which he tended to meet Authority, to placate a traffic cop who had flagged Gray for speeding. The cop did his duty and handed in a ticket, but did not, as Gray had reasonably expected, haul them away to jail for erratic driving. After twice running into snow banks, they got to Mt Holyoke, where Dylan rewarded the long patience of the audience with a fine full reading.

Afterwards there was a reception—one of those occasions at which a whole harem of college girls in blue jeans and Ber-muda shorts sprawl on the floor about the feet of the visiting celebrity. Within this budding grove, Dylan was bewildered, shocked by the proximity of so much bare flesh carelessly displayed, and incautious in some of his remarks. The elder ladies of the faculty, distressed and fidgety, hurried in the name of decency to bring the evening to a respectable conclusion. As I later learned, they lost no time in sending out warning signals from Eastport to Block Island. On his visits to other women's colleges Dylan was protected from the student body by a cordon of vigilantes passing itself off as a guard of honour.

Peter Viereck, the poet who teaches history at Mt Holyoke, and his wife entertained Dylan the following day and helped him to get to his next engagement, at Amherst, from which he returned to New York by a late train. When I went to see him at Midston House I found him limp and sore, unable to shake off a daylong hang-over. Allen Curnow dropped in, followed short-ly by Oscar Williams. Dylan ordered beer to be sent up and we sat about in commiseration while he tried to pull himself togeth-er. The editors of a literary journal had invited him and me to go to dinner uptown, and Dylan had accepted. Oscar came with us to a Viennese restaurant on upper Third Avenue, where our hosts were waiting. The dinner was not a happy one. Dylan con-fided to me later that he felt he had been needled into making

32

statements which were then turned against him in support or defence of the editors' Roman Catholic point of view. Under this suspicion, he made indiscreet and foolish attacks on the Church which, actually, had little basis in his thinking. Everything was at sixes and sevens when I had to leave to catch a train, Dylan being ebullient and rude, his hosts obviously uncomfortable but politely making the most of an unexpected situation. I was relieved to learn later that *rapprochement* had come about, and that the evening had ended in considerably better feeling and in the sale, for a generous price, of one of Dylan's unpublished new poems.

Much has been said of Dylan's rudeness to people whom he had no cause to offend, but in my association with him I rarely saw evidence of it. If he sensed he was being held in disapproval, or that he was being attacked, especially if the attack was veiled, his way of response was often to refuse to talk seriously, to irritate those who sought his opinions by lampooning their questions. While drunken carelessness sometimes led him to assume a childishly minatory face and manner, these were whimsical rather than malicious or aggressive gestures. What impressed me always, and on far more numerous occasions, was his kindly response to people whose only concern with him was arrantly self-interested, as well as to those whose stupidity or dullness of mind led them to make tedious demands on his attention. The friends he most cherished in America were, by and large, of no literary or academic importance. It was inevitable in his travels that he meet national and local celebrities, and be the guest of literary and academic cliques, but he flew all their nets and chose his real friends by instinct.

By this time, even far from Third Avenue, he had come to feel quite at home in New York. While he refused to learn the comparative values of American coins, and threw them away in lavish tips with a fine free hand, he bungled busily about the city on his own, and, nearly always, managed to get to his destinations. He had became most fond of Greenwich Village, and every few days or so a new bar would serve as headquarters—the Minetta Tavern (where he made good friends with, and played

Maecenas to, Joe Gould, 'Professor Seagull'), the San Remo and, later, Goody's on Sixth Avenue. He continued to drink through the days and to take nourishment only by whim or accident—an egg in brandy for breakfast, perhaps, or a hamburger someone would set down before him.

I next saw him on 7th March, when I turned up in my convertible (Dylan called it 'the incontrovertible'), in which we were going to drive to Philadelphia for his evening's reading at Bryn Mawr. We started off well enough in sunny weather, but the trip was punctuated by several bad coughing spells, the last of which occurred just before we turned into the campus. But when this spasm was broken and he straightened up in his miraculous way, he wanted an ice-cold beer and a cigar. After we had stopped for these, he arrived at the College looking like a Celtic business man. I put him into the hands of Professor Mary Woodworth, who had arranged his visit. Our bags were taken up to the famous guest-room in the Deanery—a sort of 'Turkish corner' of canopied beds, oriental lattice-work, and brass whatnots from the days of Ella Wheeler Wilcox. When Professor Woodworth took Dylan off to the chapel, where nine hundred students awaited him, I drove back into Philadelphia to see a pre-Broadway performance of a musical comedy in which a friend had her first starring role. When I came back late to the Deanery, Dylan was sleeping beatifically in his Byzantine surroundings and I did not wake him.

He was ill and downcast again in the morning as he coughed and flushed his way through breakfast and, later, sat for a student interview. As we drove through heavy traffic toward Washington he stared with a glum interest at passing landscapes and had little to say. But after a few stops at roadside taverns, his talk and manner brightened and he came to Washington in ruminative good humour. When he said he would first like to do a bit of sightseeing, we drove about rather aimlessly, circling Capitol Hill and eventually getting as far as the newly completed Jefferson Monument. He commented on the incongruity of vistas of heavy Roman architecture in this twentieth-century capital, and was not otherwise moved by its advertised beauties. Some while later he told an interviewer: 'Washington isn't a city, it's an abstraction.' We drove on to Georgetown where Robert Richman, sponsor of his Washington reading, awaited us at his home on Q Street. There we learned that Dylan was to be the guest, for part of the week-end at least, of Francis and Katherine Biddle, whose big house was just half a block away. After leaving him on the Biddles' doorstep, I returned to have dinner with Richman and his wife. Dylan's reading that evening was at the Institute of Contemporary Arts, located just a few steps from the White House. Karl Shapiro, the poet and editor who, with his wife, Evalyn, had come from Baltimore for the event, joined us afterwards when we returned to the Biddles' for a large reception for the literati of Washington. In the glow of burning fireplaces and the mellowing aura of Georgian elegance, Dylan was a model of deportment, the most volatile and charming conversationalist in the room. He could accept his surroundings sometimes with as much grace as, at other times, he would defy them.

Next morning he was scheduled to make recordings of his poems at the Library of Congress. When I joined him and the Biddles for a lingering breakfast, I found him again on his best behaviour—modest, gracious, yet spirited as he took part in a rambling discussion, mostly on the state of liberalism here and in England. I could see that the Biddles had somehow allayed the fear and suspicion of 'people in high places' that lay behind his sometimes inexplicable behaviour. On the way to the Library we stopped for a mid-morning glass of beer. As we sat in a dark booth, Dylan took his wallet from his vest pocket and began to finger through its somewhat flimsy contents. He did not seem to be looking for anything in particular, but then he unfolded a yellowed newspaper clipping. It was a photograph, very dim and hazy, of a thin little boy dressed in a droopy sort of gymkhana costume. His curly hair hung unevenly on his forehead, his face was serious, his eyes upturned, no hint of a smile on his lips. The caption beneath read: 'Dylan Marlais Thomas, aged 12, son of Mr and Mrs D. J. Thomas of Swansea,' and went on to report that he had been the victor in the 220-yard dash at the annual games of some grammar-school competition. Dylan had carried this grimy scrap of a photograph with him for more than twenty years. As he studied it somewhat sadly now, his affection for that very thin and very little boy seemed to have opened in a moment a world of nostalgia. Very carefully he folded the clipping and inserted it into his wallet.

At the Library of Congress I introduced him to Elizabeth Bishop. In her capacity as Incumbent of the Chair of Poetry, she gave him official greetings and took him off to the recording studios. I went back to the car to set out for Sweet Briar College in Virginia, where I was to take part in a week-end 'festival of the arts.' I drove back to Washington early Sunday with two passengers: John Cage, the composer, and Merce Cunningham, the modern dancer. They had also taken part in the week-end festival.

Meanwhile, the Biddles had gone to Bermuda, leaving Dylan alone in the big house except for servants. Their absence was an advantage he could not resist. Before leaving his room he opened the drawer of a high-boy, lifted out several shirts belonging to one of the male Biddles, and stuffed them in his bag. As he came downstairs grandly smoking a cigar, the Biddles' housekeeper, who had taken a special fancy to him, waited to say good-bye. 'Well,' Dylan said, 'here goes another one of your rich visitors.' 'You are not a rich man,' she said. 'Oh, *aren't* I!' said Dylan. 'Just what makes you think that?' 'Because,' she said quietly, 'I did your laundry.' As we got into the car, Dylan made no secret of the purloined shirts. I told him it was absurd to steal from the Biddles, that we could buy him other shirts to-morrow or the next day, and that the whole thing was silly and childish. But no, the shirts stayed in his bag. When, inevitably, his theft was found out some weeks later, the Biddles told one of my Washington friends that they hoped only that the shirts he had taken were of a proper fit.

The journey north along U.S. 1 was tediously slowed by heavy traffic, but Dylan was in fine fettle. His Washington visit had been unexpectedly pleasant, he had especially enjoyed dinner and a long evening with Huntington Cairns, the art critic and official of the National Gallery, and he had been delighted

36

to encounter a number of British friends who were correspondents for London newspapers or who had posts in the Embassy. We stopped for a single beer outside of Baltimore, and he and John Cage began to weave a zany, pointless, and disconnected conversation that lasted all day. It was as if Dylan found Cage's contrary views on anything conventional, or, for that matter, on anything remotely human, an irresistible goad to flights of his own. Merce and I were far more audience than they needed in this mood, and the trip was entertained by hilariously insane discourses on life in America. It was on this occasion when I first became aware of a fact about Dylan for which I still cannot account—the fact that, without liquor at all, or with but a glass or two of beer, he would often move into a state of euphoria precisely like that state of uninhibited gaiety common to people who depend upon liquor. His talk all that day was wildly fanciful, funny, and drunken, and yet he had had nothing to drink but two small glasses of beer. This observation made me feel that my first and most obvious suspicion was a true one: that Dylan drank primarily in defence, out of a need for a barrier between his guilt and his laughter, between himself and the world around him, even between himself and one other person. When he felt this need—and I had begun to understand by now that his coming to America had been undertaken in nothing short of terror—intoxication was a kind of licence by which he was able to participate in, and at the same time keep himself responsibly removed from, situations he could not control. When his imagination was free and he was at ease with his surroundings, liquor became but an incidental amenity and not the centre of interest. His poems were always written when he was sober—a fact which emphasizes, partly, his respect for his art, but more significantly allows of careful discrimination between Dylan and the conventional alcoholic. His drinking was not a means of denying or fleeing life, not a way of making it tolerable, but of fiercely embracing it. When he was creatively alive, his genius was his whole stimulant. On this occasion, John and Merce were sensitive and easy companions and, like not too many other passing acquaintances, offered Dylan no challenge as a person, put him

37

on no guard as an intellect, or as a foreigner, but simply accepted him with a human respect he could instantly recognize. The result was a sort of drunken spree without drunkenness.

He read his poems at Columbia University the next day. I did not see him until Tuesday afternoon when I turned up with a fistful of plane and train tickets, and written directions I hoped would successfully launch him on his junket to the west coast. He had been out on the town until after 4 a.m., had spent a dreadful day with a pounding hang-over, and had not turned a hand to packing. We quickly put basic things into the one bag he was going to take and hurried to an airline office from which he would leave for Ithaca and his reading that evening at Cornell. Looking rather more like an unhappy child being sent off to school than like a poet on a triumphal tour, he waved from a window of the bus and went off for six crowded weeks of travelling and reading.

In that time he roared across the continent creating the legend that still grows and changes and threatens altogether to becloud the personality of the man who wrote the poems of Dylan Thomas. At first it was a legend at least tenuously related to plausible actions and conversations in plausible places. But soon, like all legends, it snowballed through fact and fancy alike, and became too big and complicated to allow for the separation of truth from malice, fantasy from the easier forms of hyperbole. If Dylan had done and said all that was reported as truth, he would not have been tolerated in even the most liberal of surroundings; if his rumoured carousals and lecheries had been as outrageous and consistent as they were said to be he would have been hauled off to jail or committed to an asylum. It was as if Dylan were the vehicle by which imagination might ride out of academic doldrums. Since he was expected always to say and do shocking things, and since he very often failed to do either, certain elements of his public, determined to keep Dylan as their poet-clown, made up stories of what he *should* have done and said. In the long run, of course, this became more of a comment on his public than on him.

Beginning with his stop-over at Cornell, he went on by train to Kenyon College in Ohio, the University of Chicago, Notre Dame, the University of Illinois, the State University of Iowa. After a few days in Iowa City, he flew to San Francisco to read, first at the University of California, and later at the University of British Columbia. A report of his reading which appeared in the Vancouver *News-Herald* was typical of the tributes he gathered: 'Within this generation, there has been no equally impressive and delightful poetry recital in Vancouver and audiences were scarcely prepared for the powerful emotional experience with which they were presented.' In Seattle a few days later he read at the University of Washington, then flew south for visits to the University of California at Los Angeles, Pomona College, the Santa Barbara Museum and Santa Barbara College, and finally to Mills College and San Francisco State College. In San Francisco, after stopping for a few days at the old Palace Hotel, he was the house guest of Ruth Witt-Diamant, a teacher at San Francisco State, who became Dylan's close friend and, later, a close friend of his wife.

I next saw him on 24th April in his room at the Hotel Earle on Waverley Place in the Village, where we talked for two pleasantly unhurried hours over a bottle of Grand Marnier someone had given him. Dylan seemed remarkably hale, in quiet command of himself and his many affairs, said he had had a marvellous time seeing America, but that coming back to New York was like coming home to the most wonderful place of all. The City which, he wrote later, had first struck him as 'all of a sheepish never-sleeping heap,' now, 'after the ulcerous rigours of a lecturer's spring,' seemed to be 'a haven as cosy as toast, cool as an icebox, and safe as skyscrapers.' The worst thing he had had to put up with was travel itself; he wished his wanderings were over and done with. Of all the cities he had visited, he was most warmly impressed with San Francisco, then Chicago and Hollywood. What he meant, I thought, was that these were the places where he was most congenially entertained, or where, in the company of one or two unconventional or maverick spirits, he could break away from reception committees and faculty teas to

39

put his foot on a brass rail. Dylan was a sightseer only by whim or entrapment. For him the flavour of a town was apparent largely in the kind and number of its pub-like bars, and in the degree of accessibility to them. His ideal metropolis, I sometimes felt, would have been an interminable skid row. Probably sensing this, Nelson Algren, the Chicago novelist, for whom Dylan had developed enthusiastic affection, introduced him to people and places he could never have uncovered without a knowing guide who was himself *persona grata* in the dives of the South Side.

For part of his Hollywood visit he had been the guest of Christopher Isherwood. His report of the British novelist's life which, to Dylan, seemed to be all of a sun-baked ambience on the sands of southern California, was not without acid or without envy. When Isherwood had asked him what he wanted to do and whom he wanted to see, Dylan had told him that all his life long he had wanted to come to Hollywood for two reasons: to meet Charles Chaplin, and to have a date with an 'ash-blonde' movie star. These wishes were both granted in one evening.

The 'ash-blonde' who became his partner at dinner with Isherwood and a small group of friends, was Shelley Winters. While Dylan had not previously heard of her, she surprised him by remarks that showed she knew not only of him, but that she was acquainted with his work. Nevertheless, Dylan refused to address her by her given name—because, he told her, that would be odd and upsetting. Shortly after they had met, they had sat down for drinks somewhere and, according to Dylan, talked mostly of baseball, of which he knew nothing. Eventually the conversation changed, becoming centred in Dylan's appreciative enumeration of Miss Winters's more obvious physical attractions, which he had wanted to measure for himself. But he was rebuffed, he said, in language which was as direct as a stevedore's and notably more colourful.

When they joined the dinner party at a Hollywood restaurant, Frank Taylor, the well-known New York editor who was then working with one of the movie studios, phoned Charles Chaplin to tell him of Dylan's great hope of meeting him. This resulted in an invitation to come to Chaplin's home for the evening. When the group arrived, they were greeted with an impromptu *commedia del arte* performance in which, with a grace and skill at which Dylan marvelled, Chaplin travestied the manners of a perfect host, a butler, and a cloak-room maid. Shaken by his *contretemps* with Miss Winters, who herself had been made morose by the behaviour of this tipsy poet from Wales, Dylan was at first not wholly in command of himself. But, before long, exhilarated to hear Chaplin laughing at *his* jokes, Dylan had bounced back. When he told his host that no one back in Laugharne would believe him when eventually he would tell of the visit, Chaplin delighted him again by composing a cable and sending it off directly to Caitlin.

In San Francisco he was much taken with a college girl who, she said, would on her twenty-first birthday come into several millions of dollars. Since she was only eighteen, they would have to be patient for three years but, if he would marry her, she said, they could then live anywhere in the world and in any fashion that might appeal to him. Her only concern was for Dylan's patience. Could he really wait three long years for her? In his telling of the incident, I sensed that he was amused, but also that he could not make up his mind about just how serious a proposition had been made to him. For the girl herself he felt great respect; she was, he said, beautiful, intelligent, used to life among horses and dogs, and wonderfully entertaining as she drove him about the slopes of sunny California in a yellow convertible.

Throughout the tour he had somehow managed to keep all of his many reading engagements. Against evidence of so many other failures, this gave me a conviction that behind the irresponsible façade of Dylan Thomas there lay a core of responsibility few people would ever see. But while the engagements were all met, troubles attending them were endless, and many fidgety sponsors wished they had never heard of this particular Welsh poet. I had become quite inured to such telegrams as the following: 'Contact with Thomas re-established after lapse. Will do all I can but cannot assume responsibility since he is indis-

41

posed to keep appointments. Trust he will meet engagement Tuesday. He says Vancouver plane reservations made.' Surly letters and other distressed telegrams came to me almost daily, some of them blaming me for having foisted Dylan upon them, a few of them making careful distinctions between a great poet and an impossible man. Dylan did not go into detail, although I felt certain he could have if only he were rid of the onus of guilt, but I gathered that in San Francisco and Los Angeles there were a number of critical mishaps. Usually these were his fault, and he knew it; at other times he was justifiably annoyed and uncooperative in the face of overzealous attentions and day-long schedules of appearances that would have taxed the Queen of England.

He was about to set off again now, first to Hobart College in upstate New York, then by plane to Florida, to read at the University in Gainesville. While we were discussing finances and details of the next engagements, Loren McIver and Lloyd Frankenberg came by to take him to a Marx Brothers movie. I said good-bye, and promised to meet his plane in Boston a week later.

In Florida he made an affectionate friend of Marjorie Kinnan Rawlings, who offered him the use of her country house at Cross Creek for the following winter. It was a serious offer and Dylan accepted it gratefully. But while he later referred to the possibility on a number of occasions, and thought that he would like to spend the winter months there with Caitlin and the children, nothing came of it.

On the following Sunday morning I awaited his plane at the Boston airport. Richard Eberhart, the poet, at whose house Dylan was to stay, had invited fifteen or twenty people to a day-long garden party to which he was to be escorted immediately. But one plane after another landed, and Dylan was not on any of them. I went back to the Eberharts', waited hopefully for a wire or a phone call, but there was no news and the party, like so many others for Dylan, had to carry on and conclude without its guest of honour.

Next morning came a telegram from Dylan saying he would

arrive in the early afternoon. It was a cloudy day and his plane had to circle the airport for almost an hour before it was given clearance to land in the heavy weather. We had barely enough time to drive to Wellesley College for his late afternoon reading. There he gave a good performance, but was carefully kept from inflammatory contact with the delectable students in blue jeans. Vivid accounts of his behaviour at Mt Holyoke had come through to Wellesley directly. The reading had hardly been concluded before he was hustled off the campus for ever. A few members of the English department took us away to a faculty house for drinks and later drove us to a steak place before we returned to Cambridge and the Eberharts'.

On the drive back he was unusually sober and disposed to talk. American academic people were still a great puzzle to him, he said; in his months of travel he had met thousands of them and they were all so much alike as they milled about in cloistered classrooms and banal, well-lighted houses furnished with television sets, electric mixers, and twin beds. As for women professors, he found them either sweet, dry, and sad, or loud, overgrown, and forbidding. He could not understand what poetry meant to them, most of all the sort of poetry he wrote, since he could see no evidence that they were able to face the living experience from which it sprang or, for that matter, any vital experience at all. There was no unkindness in these sentiments of Dylan's, I felt, but a genuine and persistent bewilderment—as if he were trying to find an explanation for its success in relation to the people who had been responsible for it. He had visited academic couples in over-heated houses on innumerable Faculty Rows, and the sterility of such marriages appalled him. He said he was certain that a great number of the husbands were sexually abnormal—some of the wives had told him so, and, oddly enough, some of the husbands. In any case, they were frightened or ambiguous men given marital haven by women stronger than themselves. When I asked him what the enormous show of interest in him and his work had meant to him, he said, simply, that it was all wonderful, wonderful; that it not only made him feel good but that, in spite of unfriendly for-

43

eign critics and widespread anti-American bias he had encountered in Britain and Europe, it was a sign of this country's
really impressive interest in literature. But as much as he liked
attention, he was always aware of that romantic disposition
which led so many people to underestimate the sheer pleasant
ordinariness of the lives and characters of dead poets and to
overestimate that of living poets; especially of a poet like himself
who, pushed into the limelight ready or not, could say no
phrase or make no gesture which was not regarded as part of an
endless public performance. And he knew that, after having
been introduced to him—perhaps on some occasion when he
was barely able to keep his balance on a bar stool, or perhaps
when, sick and sullen, he glowered through the depths of a
drunken party—many people found if difficult to connect him
with the poems he wrote. But, as he said, they would have felt
the same sort of consternation— 'how could such a man have
written such marvellous devotional poems, I saw him fall downstairs in his suspenders' —had they met some of the famous
dead. He went on to say that, against all the dull, inaccessible,
or blustering people he had met, it would be only fair to point,
for balance, to the many brilliant, charming, and commanding
individuals who existed, like uncharted islands, in the most
unexpected places everywhere. While he was weary to death of
parties where bright, well-dressed young people crowded
around him to ask not, What do you think? but, Whom do you
know?—these were the expected burdens of the literary man.
His happier and far more frequent memories concerned the
'lovely' people—individuals who had not been dehumanized by
academicism or depersonalized by Bohemianism. These were
his friends—a word Dylan never used without discrimination—
and as he named them I could sense that they had succeeded in
giving him more confidence in himself than the great chorus of
public praise and public applause could ever give him. While
some of them were college presidents, men of letters, business
tycoons, and some were truck drivers, impoverished graduate
students, or bar-flies, they had each shown themselves capable
of accepting Dylan's first condition for friendship—a bed-rock

conviction, beyond every personal or social judgment of character, behaviour, or position, that no one was one iota better than
anyone else.

When I called at the Eberhart's for him early the next afternoon I found him still in bed. He had awakened early, called for
beer in lieu of breakfast, and then had gone back to sleep. But
soon after I had arrived he was combed, bow-tied, and ready for
an afternoon we had planned together in downtown Boston.
Convinced that architecture, monuments, and swan boats would
only bore him, I took him into Scollay Square. We had a few
beers in the midday blackness of several honky-tonk places, then
took in a matinée performance of burlesque at the Old Howard.
A long-time devotee of London music-halls, Dylan chuckled
with enthusiasm about everything—the long-limbed Petty
girls whose bumps and grinds ended finally in statuesque nudi-
ty and the flip of a G-string, the sleazy leering comedians who
belted one another with inflated bladders, the dead-on-its-feet
chorus line slouching through zombie-like routines, while a desperately smiling juvenile in a double-breasted suit sang selections from *Rio Rita*. Whenever he came to Boston afterwards,
we always went back to the Old Howard.

The Eberharts had asked in a large number of people for
drinks and a buffet supper before Dylan's reading that night
at Brandeis University in nearby Waltham. We sat on the floor
with plates in our laps and beer stains beside us. At some point,
Dylan took out a large silver watch he carried hanging on a
safety-pin just inside the waist of his trousers. It was an elegant
old Victorian timepiece his father had given him and everyone
wanted to examine it. While it was being passed about, it
suddenly slipped from someone's grasp, made a little loop across
the room, and gurgled down to the bottom of a stein of beer.
Fished out still ticking, it shortly afterwards stopped. Someone
offered to have it fixed in New York. When Dylan sailed for
home it was still in a repair shop, and may even now be waiting
to be claimed.

I did not accompany the group that drove out with him to
Brandeis and thereby missed, with little regret, another post-

45

reading party, and a later one back at the Eberharts'. Dylan stayed up most of the night and took a plane the next morning for Ann Arbor.

Readings at the University of Michigan, Wayne University, and Indiana University would keep him away from New York until the following week-end. In Detroit he was looked after by Patrick Boland, who enlisted his whole family, including his father who once pitched for the Detroit *Tigers*, in helping to get Dylan housed, his clothes mended, and his appointments kept. Patrick later wrote of this visit in terms that allow of no paraphrase. Shortly after Dylan's plane from Boston had landed at Willow Run, they stopped at a bar in Ypsilanti *en route* to Ann Arbor. 'When we had got inside and got our beers,' wrote Patrick, 'Dylan found that he was quite warm and so removed his sweater. The struggle left his hair (which was really very fine and soft though curly) high like a wiry headdress—electrified perhaps by friction. He looked not so much like a maestro or a bird as like Elsa Lanchester as the Bride of Frankenstein and showed a similar toothy grin. He asked me to lend him my comb, which was not (I warned him) a clean one; and this he dipped deftly into his beer and therewith unravelled and settled his knotty problem—ouch—the fast hard way and politely returned it...That book (a sort of symposium) which had recently been given T. S. Eliot upon the occasion of his sixtieth birthday was mentioned. Had I wondered why he was not amongst the contributors? Well: he had offered the editors a poem but—could I imagine?—they had rejected it! It was only a couplet but a quite appropriate one. It was:

> He who once gave us the silver plate
> Now passes the collection.'

After his reading at the University of Michigan, he was driven to Detroit for his engagement the following day at Wayne University. 'When we had gone perhaps ten miles,' wrote Patrick, 'I said that I smelled smoke. Then the others sniffed and we all smelled smoke and wondered if the engine was afire. No;

it was Dylan, I discovered. Something other than his new money was burning a hole in his pocket. We all jumped and I started beating him (beating a great poet: it seemed terrible) with the only thing I had except my bare hand—my handkerchief. This was not as futile as it sounds: it extinguished him although it caught fire itself and I threw it wildly out the window. There was oil and gasoline all over the ground (we had pulled into a gas station) but we did not explode. Dylan closed his eyes again and we continued our journey. One of the party recalled that as he had got into the car he had put a cigarette butt into his pocket.'

In a letter to Patrick which I had asked Dylan to deliver, I said I hoped that they might find time to buy him another of the cord suits which he found most comfortable in the spring climate. Patrick accepted this commission and escorted Dylan to an enormous department store. 'I shall never forget the sight of him as the clock-faced tailor and clerk cried Shabby and Shorten around him. Upon his little pedestal, pliant and plump as putty, he looked almost pathetic. He had fumbled and bumbled around inside one of those little dressing booths a long while but he had finally stumbled (or flipflopped) forth and there they had him. I remembered that when he had dressed he had omitted his underwear and now when they asked him to let his arms and his over-large over-long pants hang free I pretended that some other sight compelled me to walk away. I walked only a few feet away and gazed into a less apprehensible span of space, but soon I heard him call me: "Patrick. Where are you?" The scene shames me differently now—especially when I remember that he said gently but somewhat fretfully when I reappeared: "I thought you had deserted me." Whether his attendants dropped their stitches and/or he dropped his breeches I shall never know.'

After his evening reading at Wayne University they were invited to a party at the Park Sheraton Hotel where New York editors were showing off a ballad singer whose book was about to be published. 'Upstairs there was a great press of people sitting in chairs and on the floor of the one room around the "star" of the evening (theirs, not mine). Dylan was probably glad, but

I was somewhat indignant, that he did not share the spotlight—
or steal it. However it was not his party—and the men who gave
it were quite affable and affluent: two ardent spirits dispensing
ardent spirits, shot after shot, like rapid-fire hawkers. The guest
of honour sang ballad after ballad very very loudly, one foot bobbing up and down; and sometimes everybody sang, their feet
bobbing up and down and their hands clapping; so that the joint
really jumped. I have never properly appreciated community
songs—much less, community sings—but I became impatient
only when Dylan had his polite requests politely ignored once or
twice. Perhaps he asked too softly: "Do you know She went to
the city to be on a committee?" But once he sang alone (since no
one else knew the song) *Miss Twye* (that quatrain by Gavin
Ewart)—without accompaniment but not without good effect.
Also he sang *Molly Malone* so sweetly that everybody else
seemed to hush—except the guest of honour (who had the loud-
er voice, but not the better).'

From Detroit, Dylan was to fly to Indianapolis, where he
would be met and driven to his next engagement at Indiana University, in Bloomington. When he and Patrick got to the Willow
Run air terminal early in the morning, wrote Patrick: 'Just outside I stopped him: a prominent sign read NO DOGS ALLOWED.
He understood and smiled. Then I read the smaller print:
"Except Seeing Eye Dogs"; and I said, "I guess that lets you
through."

'We went through—and we checked his baggage "through"
—and he browsed around the news-stand and he bought some
magazines and candy and he said: "The only reason I am going
is that I want to meet John Crowe Ransom. If I thought I would
not meet him I certainly would not go." I said that he would
have to go: he had already promised. He said: "Well surely I will
see you again soon," and I said that I doubted very much that I
would ever travel as far as Wales, though there was now far more
reason than ever to wish that I could. But he meant: within a
month, before he went home. I explained that I had spent all but
the last of my money; and he argued as he searched his pockets
again: "Here. But I have money." (I often think that he held an

uncannily sane and saintly view of property, and that he was as glad to give as to take whatever seemed necessary and just; and that he trusted—much more than any economic order or orderliness—some superhuman providence of simple, ordinary, divine human charity or even some blind shuffle or reshuffle of it all to redistribute fairly the wealth of the world: he took no thought of the morrow except when necessary, and he doubted that anything wholly could ever be lost.) I said that I could not take it (it had cost him so much) and he said: "Well then I will send it to you."...I need not have told you that I thought he was a great man as well as a great poet—one of the finest I shall ever meet. He practised and promoted joy like a virtue, and he showed not only a wide, deep, general human compassion but a very special consideration of persons he met and liked. (I doubt that he was ever forgetful of matters that mattered: I see now that he often followed certain trends of thought over a period of time when I myself had abandoned them.)'

At Indiana University he not only gave a reading but lectured to students in a motion picture course on his work with various British documentary film units. Back in New York, he took up bar life in the old Village routine and might be found, momentarily alone or eternally surrounded, at almost any hour except for those few occasions when acquaintances took him away to make other acquaintances, or to be seen with him at some literary gathering. While Dylan as a rule had but hazy recollections of where he had been and what he had done, his impressions of people were always quick and definite. Carl Sandburg's brusque manners and salty talk entertained him enormously; Thornton Wilder, whose work, he thought, had been insensitively dismissed by many high-brow critics, struck him as one of the most endearing men he had ever met; Dwight D. Eisenhower was 'nice enough,' but I gathered that their interview had taken place in a crowded room and in a drunken mist, exuding, of course, from Dylan and not from the General who would soon be President.

When I called for him at the Earle a few days after he had returned from the mid-west he was in bed, sick and exhausted from days of his own brand of dissipation, and reluctant, or temporarily unable, to move. His engagement for that evening was at Vassar College, where I had once taught in the English department for a period of five years. Most anxious that Dylan keep this date, I was disturbed to find him so pale and low-spirited. After I had sat with him for a while, trying to convey some sympathy for the miseries of his hang-over as he alternately dozed and waked, I went out and brought in a bag full of food. He sat up in bed, ate the delicatessen buffet I had selected, and drank a vanilla milk-shake. By four o'clock or so he had brightened but, feeling as though I were bent on injecting life into a corpse, I decided that the wiser course would be to let Dylan remain where he was. Yet I knew that when evening came on the 'corpse' would walk straight to the nearest bar. Since I was used to his quick false recoveries and the sudden collapses that often followed them, I had little faith in his being able to make the transition from sick-bed to lecture platform in a matter of hours. If he could possibly keep his Vassar engagement I very much wanted him to. But I could see that his earlier moanings and groanings were signs of real anguish, and that it would be unkind to urge him to heed a responsibility for which, in this case, I was perhaps over-zealous. When I said I would phone Vassar to report that he was too ill to come, I felt certain that he was at last going to forgo a scheduled engagement. But I was wrong. He said he was quite ready to go, got up, put on his blue suit and his polka-dot tie. We got into my car, headed for the parkway, and were punctually in Poughkeepsie about seven. There we checked in with friends of mine in their house on Faculty Row.

No sign of his day-long indisposition showed as he read to a large audience that evening or when he stayed up, after I had gone to bed, to talk and drink with our hosts until after three. But as we drove back to New York through heavy rains the next morning, his head sank on to his chest and he slept nearly all the way. By mid afternoon he was off by train to Princeton for another reading and, as it turned out, a night-long bull session with a congenial crowd of undergraduates.

I found him at the San Remo the next afternoon. We had a drink or two and, in our unconventional way, reviewed financial matters and discussed plans for his remaining appearances. The reading dates were easily accounted for—I simply put details in Dylan's now dog-eared and beer-soaked diary, gave him plane or train tickets, or noted where he could buy them and how much they would cost. But to try to enlist Dylan's interest in details of his financial situation was to attempt the impossible. I had kept a record of every penny he had earned from the time he had arrived; while I had no strict record of what he had spent, or given away, or lost, I knew of course how much I had turned over to him from his earnings, and the exact costs of transportation fees I had provided. Engagements I made for him had brought him fees between one hundred and fifty dollars and five hundred dollars. But we had also made a professionally unorthodox agreement whereby he was free to accept engagements he might be offered without my representation. While I was unhappy to learn—not for my sake, but for his—that he would sometimes accept offers to read for no more than fifty dollars, I made little point of this except to warn him that widespread knowledge of such small fees would seriously hamper my efforts to get him large ones. As agent for Dylan's first tour, I retained ten per cent of his earnings. Actually, this amounted only to a token payment. While it had been agreed that I would be recompensed for time spent in arranging dates and in supervising his travels, out of this remuneration was to come telephone and telegraph costs incidental to such arrangements. Very early in the course of my dealings I came to understand why professional lecture agents feel it necessary to retain thirty-three to fifty per cent of the earnings of their clients.

While Dylan had already earned thousands of dollars in the United States, his bank account was dwindling at an alarming rate. In spite of my determination to keep free of such concern, his relentless need for money had led me to becoming miserly about his funds and painfully reluctant to meet his requests for new amounts. I could not understand why he carelessly spent fifty and sixty dollars every day, or why, with Caitlin continually requesting money for household accounts, he paid no heed to my warnings that unless he cut down on his spending he would return to Wales empty-handed. He did send modest amounts to his wife now and then, but when I suggested that we deposit in his local bank in Carmarthen for safe keeping all the money except what he would need for basic expenses, he balked. At the onset of his travels it had seemed reasonable to estimate that he might be able to go home with about three thousand dollars in cash. Soon this figure was revised to two thousand dollars. When, day by day, it became apparent that even this amount was too much to hope for, I despaired of his returning with anything at all. In our talk at the San Remo, I showed him his accounts, but he looked at these only, it seemed, by way of politely thanking me for my trouble, and turned away to order another drink. Dylan could not have known it, but his indifference to the accounts over which I had worked many hours left me dispirited and hopeless. While I had tried to make clear from the first that I was no business man, Dylan had said that he wouldn't *want* a business man to be taking care of his affairs. Secretly, I wanted to be a good business man, and to have him recognize beyond good will and friendship the clarity and order of accounts, which, normally, were as unfamiliar to me as to him. But as far as Dylan was concerned, I could play at being bookkeeper as much as I cared; he was just not interested. My only moment of satisfaction came later, when we went to the income tax office in order to get his sailing permit. When questions about his earnings, expenditures, and living expenses were put to him, I whipped out my shining columns of figures and supplied a hundred small and pertinent details. Because of these records, especially those involving his travelling and living expenses, Dylan's American income tax was far below the amount we had been told it would be; I felt, finally, that he had recognized my labours and, perhaps, found some excuse for my immoderate concern.

A few nights later he read a selection from *Portrait of the Artist as a Young Dog* at the Poetry Center, the first full recital of prose he had given. An unusually intense and uncompromisingly sophomoric group of 'ardents' took him out to a bar afterwards; against my will, but to please Dylan I went along. One of these young admirers kept announcing with bravado, and to a rather unlikely band of prospective buyers, that he was ready to sell his body to the first man or woman who would offer him ten thousand dollars. When I caught the late train for Westport, I could see that Dylan had an audience, juvenile though it might be, that would stay by him to the end of the night.

Early next morning I was awakened by a phone call from New York. A baby-voiced woman said that she was Anita Loos, that she had heard the reading at the Poetry Center the night before, and that she wondered if Dylan might be interested in taking the leading role in a new comedy by Garson Kanin that was shortly scheduled for Broadway. I said I would speak to Dylan about the notion and have him report his reactions to her. In a letter to his parents written about this time, the only one he wrote during the length of his visit and which, for some reason, he never posted, he makes simple expressions of feeling and tells simple bits of information, among them the possibility of his becoming an actor. This letter turned up long after Dylan's death among papers he had left with me and was forwarded to his mother, with whose permission it is quoted here.

(Printed) Hotel Earle
Washington Square, N.W.
New York 11, N.Y.
May 22, 1950

My Dear Mother and Dad,

How are you both? How, especially, is Dad? I think a great deal of you both, and very often, though I know you would hardly think so from my not-writing for so very long. But indeed, you are constantly in my mind; I worry very much about Dad's health, or lack of it; and, though I hear about you quite often from Caitlin, I still do not really get a clear picture of how you are. Is Dad in bed all the time? Oh, I do hope not. And he doesn't still have to have injections, does he? And how is Mother walking now?

I am sailing for home on June the first, on the *Queen Elizabeth*. It will take four and a half days. So, somewhere in the first

53

week of June, I shall be seeing you. And I am looking forward to it terribly.

At last my tour is at an end. I have visited over forty universities, schools, and colleges, from Vancouver, in British Columbia, to southern Florida. I have travelled right through the Middle West, the North West, and on to the western coast of California. After a reading in Indianapolis, a man came up to me and said, in a strong Swansea accent, 'How's D. J. these days? He used to teach me English before the last war. I've been an American citizen now for 25 years.' And he sounded as if he'd just stepped out from Morriston. I didn't get his name, because just then I was captured by some one else. I've met Welsh people after every public reading I've given, several of them from Swansea, Carmarthen, and Pembrokeshire, and all of whom knew Laugharne—or, at least, Pendine. And was, in nearly every case, offered the hospitality of their homes: which I never had time to accept. It has been the time element in this tour that has been most tiring: and the reason, too, I have hardly written any letters at all. I have almost never had a moment to myself, except in bed and then I was too exhausted to do anything. And the varying kinds of climates and temperatures have lessened my energy, too. In Chicago, it was bitterly snowing; a few days later, in Florida, the temperature was ninety. And New York itself never has the same sort of weather 2 days running. So one of my greatest troubles has been to know what to wear; my second greatest trouble, as I flashed around the continent, was that of laundry and cleaners. Sometimes I have to buy a new shirt in each new town.

I am writing this in bed, at about seven in the morning, in my hotel bedroom, which is right in Washington Square, a beautiful Square, which is right in the middle of Greenwich Village, the artists' quarter of New York. To-day I have lunch with my American literary agent, and supper with Anita Loos, who wrote a best-seller years ago called *Gentlemen Prefer Blondes*. She is interested in a play in which I might appear, as an actor, sometime, though of course it is all very much up in the air.

I am longing to come home. How is Caitlin *really*? And Aeron and Colm?

Excuse this very bad pencil, and scrappy letter.

Love to you both,
DYLAN.

While Dylan did for a time seem genuinely intrigued by the possibilities of a professional acting début, nothing came of his

talks with Anita Loos. When Kanin's play, *The Rat Race*, was produced in the following autumn, its run was limited to a matter of days. Meanwhile, I was touched to learn from Dylan that his only regret was not for himself but for me—if he really did become a high-salaried Broadway actor, he said, he would insist that I be his manager so that, with no work to do, I would at last make money for all my trouble in taking care of him.

One evening Dylan came to a poetry writing class I conducted as one of the activities of the Poetry Center. To a group of twenty adult students he explained aspects of his more difficult poems with great care, answered all questions—even the foolish ones—with respectful consideration, was soberly self-critical, precisely discriminating, and thoroughly beguiling as a personality. Yet this role as guide through his collected works was one he despised, when he played it, and when others played it. While such an attitude may seem incongruous in relation to many of his activities and may seem to undermine the conviction with which he often spoke, he had an obsessive antipathy to poetry as a public forum activity. To Dylan poetry was something that happened, that had been happening for a long time, and would go on happening; it was not something to meet upon, to debate, or to fix into hierarchical tables. It is hard to say just what the basis of this antipathy was. For one thing, he had a very shaky sense of himself as a critic. He knew just enough about the perspectives and the jargon of the new critics of poetry to use them in discussion and, as a rule, tended to disparage the more rigid applications of the approach they represent. But while he distrusted official or sectarian approaches to poetry, his own approach was often whimsical, hasty, and impressionistic. More than once I had heard him say that he preferred to judge poetry by the character of the poet. While this was most likely facetious evasion, it was evident that Dylan was never quite sure of just what poetry he could say he liked. His judgments shifted rapidly and were often influenced by opinions quite at variance with his own.

I can remember one occasion when I found him carrying a volume of poetry by a young American who was at the time receiving much flattering attention. In my opinion the value of this poet's work was negligible, and the breadth of acclaim attending it absurd. But I wanted Dylan's reaction and, without betraying my own low regard, asked him what he thought of the book. He answered that he thought it was fine, that it was just about the best new book of American poetry he had come across in fifteen years. I was so taken aback that I could say nothing. Five or six weeks later, however, having absorbed Dylan's reaction, having re-read the poet's work, and having been unable to find a line of poetry in his whole wretched volume, I brought up the subject again. 'Look,' I said, 'you'll remember my asking you about X's poetry. When you said how much you liked it, I went back and read it page by page. I think it's lousy and I want you to tell me why it isn't.' Dylan turned to me with a slow, sheepish part of a smile, then concentrated on his drink. 'Well?' I said. 'Don't,' he said. 'No one likes to be told just how wrong they were. I've read it again myself. It's just no good.'

There were opportunities for me to see Dylan on many days during the latter part of his visit but, in spite of his expectation that I would naturally choose to be with him when I could, I found myself avoiding them. I had come to despise the press and onerous involvement of lectures and sponsors and plans for dinners with committees, and could not save myself from becoming irritable when, attempting to gain his attention or his commitment on some request made to me, I had always to approach him, almost to importune him, in the centre of some new group of free souls, bar-flies, poetry lovers, or people who had not yet given up last night's party. To his companions, who sometimes looked at me as though I were trying to sell him an insurance policy, I must have seemed like a death's head at the banquet table, soberly standing by for an opportunity to break in upon the general merriment and force Dylan to tell me what to do about half a dozen matters I could not execute without his consideration. I enjoyed his company as much as ever, but half-drunken palaver was too often the only substance of these random meetings. The hangers-on who seemed to make up his interminable retinue depressed me, and I refused to be counted among them. If I could not see him at leisure, I would not see him at all. I had accepted the alcoholic tenor of his life, but it still appalled and saddened me; his protracted states of nausea and spells of retching made me want to risk seeming presumptuous in order to direct him firmly toward medical help and all the limitation on his freedom that would probably entail; yet I knew that Dylan's sickness was only partially physical, that he had become resigned to it as the normal burden of his days and nights, and that I could in any case effectively influence only that part of his career he had put into my hands. I had become ill-tempered, insomnious for the first time in my life, neglectful of my friends—some of whom, barely acquainted with Dylan, looked upon him as a monster—and unable to concentrate upon my work. When all of these factors led to a grating distress that became daily more acute and seemed continually farther away from any chance of relief, I resolved to stay out of Dylan's orbit except when professional matters forced us together. If I could do nothing to stop his largely self-inflicted agonies, at least I did not have to suffer the helpless anxiety of watching them. Curbing a hundred impulses to phone him, to drop by at his hotel, or to join him casually at one or another of his Village haunts, I succeeded in living by this resolution for about ten days.

When next I saw him it was by chance, at a garrulous party in the steaming-hot studio of an abstractionist painter on 8th Street. Dylan and Delmore Schwartz, the poet, were in the centre of a crowd within a crowd when I spotted him. Approaching from behind, I touched him on the arm. When he turned and saw me his face stiffened as if he had been touched on the quick. Assuming a pouting, wounded look—his head on his chest, his dark eyes looking up—he rushed to the nearest window as though he were going to throw himself out. I asked him what the matter was. 'You've deserted me,' he said, almost fiercely. Ignoring the truth, I tried to explain how busy I had been. He was neither convinced nor placated by my earnest evasions, but gradually we made a kind of peace and went back to the party. Yet, when I said good night, his expression was rueful, single, and piercing, and I could see he had not forgiven me. His

57

wounded eyes followed me for days. They may have been the skilled eyes of an actor, or the eyes of a man genuinely hurt. In either case, it did not matter now. Unable to dismiss their pointed accusation, or the realization that he may have been more deeply hurt by my neglect than I could imagine, I felt my dilemma had become unanswerable.

In just one more week Dylan would be gone. I resolved to ignore the frustrations spoiling the pleasure we might have taken in one another's company. They were my frustrations, after all, and by allowing them to keep us apart I would only be denying myself a friend I cherished. I decided to see him whenever I could, and to put aside the feeling that my appearances were necessarily intrusions upon the little peace of mind that bar-room existence could grant him. Since an inability to express our emotions in spoken words was a characteristic we shared, we had by this time found a way to make a sort of left-handed recognition of the affection that kept us together. When we met, even after but a day's separation, our greetings would take the form of a joke capable of endless variations. I would say something to the effect that it was good to see him but that suddenly I was nauseous and dizzy, and he would reply that it was lovely to see me but that he was probably going to be sick on the spot. In spite of these hazards we were frequently together in the last days of his visit, and I came to know a part of his life of which I had had no previous knowledge.

The sexual life of Dylan Thomas was already as much a source of legend as was his fabulous capacity for alcohol. Reports from Boston to Los Angeles suggested he lived by lechery, fondling girl sophomores and the wives of deans with an obsessive disregard for anything but his own insatiable desires. The tumescence of his poems fed such rumours and supported them; uncovering sexual imagery in the poems of Dylan Thomas had already become a national undergraduate pastime. The precise, obscene references and the four-letter ejaculations of his drunken talk, his often lascivious retorts to civil questions, and his lewd attentions to details of the female anatomy were repeated and embellished. In California, it was reported, he had suffered through an intolerably long and dull dinner party with a group of male professors. When cigars were passed around, Dylan, refusing to sink into the general stupor, addressed the company: 'Gentlemen, I wish we were all hermaphrodites!' 'Why,' said one of the professors politely, 'why do you wish that, Mr Thomas?' 'Because, gentlemen, then we could all —— ourselves!' Similar stories cropped up everywhere, along with rumours of fantastic sexual prowess and a sexual preoccupation indicating satyriasis. While the extravagance of Dylan's social behaviour made these true in tenor, in their details they were almost always spurious, and often so debasing that they seemed to have come not out of amusement but out of malice. Contributing to the unhappier part of the legend of Dylan, they continued until his death and, morbidly enough, were to be renewed by that event.

Up to this time, all that I knew of Dylan's sexual interests were his continual, and by now rather tiresome, references to 'naked girls in wet mackintoshes' and his often-expressed desire for 'a little woman, one just my size.' At parties his inevitable approaches to pretty women showed not so much sexual aggression as a kind of puppy-dog appreciation for the physical attractions he might snuggle up to. Since his addresses to women were made publicly, they were almost always answered by public rebuff. This little vaudeville show of Dylan's sometimes occurred in situations where it could only register as being in the most heinous bad taste. But on other occasions, in more emancipated company, neither the women so addressed nor the men escorting them took him seriously. Yet, when he had suffered a rebuff, he would seldom dismiss it. The little boy doing penance in a corner, he would end up sulking about his ugliness and mumbling about the cruelty of women as he drank on into the night. More than one of the women who had humoured him through such episodes told me that there was nothing clearer than the fact that he did not really want them to respond, at least not to the point of commitment. His act was a mere *divertissement*, a matter of words, four-lettered though they might be, and of easily tamed ferocity.

In spite of actions that belie the thought, and may even make it seem ridiculous, I came early to understand that Dylan loved his wife with a singleness of passion and a serenity of heart which his other passions could never confuse. The women who loved him instinctively knew this, and protected him from having to explain, even to himself, the causes of his infidelity. To love Dylan was to have recognized in the first place the weaknesses that made him need the love which the same weaknesses would inevitably destroy or shut out. The more understanding among the women he allowed to love him, or whom he loved, knew that they had to protect him from their demands, to preserve for him his belief that he was never really involved, and consequently never really responsible.

Since his temperament was predominantly passive, Dylan waited for women to come to him or, under the neurotic solicitude of one particularly busy acquaintance, to be procured for him. While there may have been hasty amorous encounters in the course of his tour or during the intervals in New York, I knew nothing about them. But in the last few days of his visit, he told me of affairs with three women. The first was a poet, a small somewhat boyish girl, shy and charming, a writer of high talent well known in *avant garde* circles. But this affair was short-lived, and Dylan seemed regretful when he spoke of it. Since he referred to her always with affection and with a kind of distant nostalgia—as though some unforeseen act of God had taken her from him—I had the feeling that he had neglected her not by intention but by default, which, in his case, was allowing other women to pre-empt all of his time. Dylan could be led anywhere; his sins were nearly always sins of omission, his failures in human relations a series of defaultings he would eventually recognize yet could never halt. In any case, the girl poet's place was now wholly taken over by Doris and by Sarah. Doris was frankly a passing fancy, but with Sarah he fell in love, with consequences that were to disturb him profoundly for more than a year.

Doris had a light, talkative, bird-like manner that made her seem considerably sillier than she was. A professional model, she had a foreign car, and more money and time than she could use-fully spend. While she was an avid reader of modern poetry and was well versed in literary movements and personalities, one had the feeling that her true interests were statistical and documentary. She could name the poetic reputations of the twenties and thirties just as quickly as an old movie-fan might pinpoint the careers of Richard Barthelmess and John Gilbert. In her new hierarchy, one felt, Dylan was as significant as Marlon Brando. Dylan said little about the affair, but through many casual confidences Doris drew me into their relationship and I began to find myself absurdly mixed up with her and Dylan in a series of clandestine afternoons, missed appointments, telephoned excuses, debates about Dylan's true temperament, and proprietary discussions about his poetry. As a critic of his poetry, Doris was most worried that Dylan was going to begin to repeat himself; she had seen ominous signs of this in his latest works, she said, and she was going to take him to task for them. But her concern for Dylan himself was deeper. 'That kid is going to kill himself,' she would say. 'You can't live the way he does and not pay for it. What's eatin' him?' Like every woman he knew, Doris became maternally solicitous of Dylan's drinking and eating habits, scolded him, shooed him about as if he were a wayward child, and sang to him when he felt depressed. Meanwhile, she fed him pills and capsules for everything that did or might ail him, sent his dirty clothes to the cleaners and bought him new clothes, expensive liquors, a portable radio for his bedside, and came to his hotel whenever he lifted the phone.

Sarah was vastly different in manner, substance, and background. She held an important job in publishing to which she brought extraordinary intelligence, an executive sense of responsibility, and that air of professional sophistication governed by the Madison Avenue fashion journals. She had been highly educated, had taught for several years at one of the leading women's colleges, and was knowledgeably devoted to Dylan's work from the time of its earliest publication. These qualities, combined with her dark handsomeness and social poise, made her precisely the sort of woman from whom one would expect

Dylan only to flee. How deeply he felt about her I did not then know, since neither he nor Sarah confided in me except to let me know that they were lovers.

Having learned of these two simultaneous affairs, I realized I knew nothing of Dylan's real needs or of the quality of his emotional experience. A normally curious person, I had no curiosity at all about these involvements, and simply accepted them as facts pertinent to the phenomenon of Dylan Thomas. I had, I suppose, come to a total acceptance of him, so that what in someone else might have struck me as weak, or wrong, or self-indulgent, made no register. But I could not help wondering how he managed to keep his two loves apart. By circumstance to which I was neither committed or indifferent, I found myself one day literally in the centre of a dilemma I had previously known only as a matter of conjecture.

Dylan was to sail for home on the *Queen Elizabeth* at mid-night on 31st May. Farewell parties that eventually seemed to be all one party, dentist appointments, income tax interviews, punctuated by frequent romantic interludes either with Sarah or with Doris, occupied the final days of his visit. On the afternoon of his sailing day I did some shopping for him, bought my own presents for Caitlin and his children, then joined him in his hotel room. He had packed not even a toothbrush; the room was strewn with clothes, manuscripts, empty beer bottles, candy wrappers, Mickey Spillanes, and wilted flowers. I volunteered to lay out his frowzy luggage and began to pack a mountain of dirty shirts. (Dylan had eventually found it easier to buy a shirt every other day or so than to send what he had to a laundry.) As I was attempting to be systematic about where to fit in suits and manuscripts and books, there came a knock at the door. Doris swooped in with a trill of greeting, followed by bell-boys loaded with packages in tottering piles. There were fifths of Scotch in gift cartons and we opened these and sent down for ice. As we drank our highballs, Doris took the elegant wrappings off her purchases one by one. There were presents for Dylan—a new tweed jacket, cigars, neckties—and presents for his children—lollipops tied with ribbons, a space suit, a cowboy outfit complete with pistols, T-shirts, an archery set, a monkey that climbed up a string. Getting on with the packing, wondering how I was going to squeeze in this toyland windfall, I was entertained by Dylan and by Doris as they sang songs from recent musicals which she had taught him. Doris had brought him some sort of perfumed air-purifier which she began to squirt throughout the room and all over Dylan's stuffy effects. He was in the middle of a solo about a train that went to New York saying toot-toot when the telephone rang. Dylan answered. It was Sarah, come to say good-bye. I looked at Dylan mutely and, wildly, he looked back at me. It was all too late; there was nothing to be done. I whispered to Dylan that I would wait downstairs in the lobby, but he begged me to stay and I went on with the packing. I was attempting to appear exclusively engrossed in this when Sarah came into the room, took one look at Doris, of whom I was sure now she had long been aware, and said acidly: 'What is that *frightful* odour?' Doris went on airily squirting everything in sight with her noisome attar. 'I *like* this odour,' she said. 'Don't *you* like it, Dylan?'

I cannot remember the ensuing conversation, if it can be termed conversation, but the atmosphere was strait-jacketed with tensions relieved only when three or four more drinks were downed. By that time the room had filled up with others who had come to say *bon voyage*, and the war of the rose-water that had seemed imminent was never joined.

We went out to dinner *en masse* but were rejected from the first place we entered because Dylan refused to wear a jacket. We trapsed through the Village to an Italian place, spoke our orders, and were about to lay into enormous platters of anti-pasto when, bursting into tears, Doris rushed from the table and out of the restaurant into the street. As someone rose to follow her and bring her back, Sarah wondered aloud what she was doing there, anyway, and everyone tried to ignore new scenes of excessive passion by bolting his food. Finally, in a caravan of three cars, we converged on Pier 90 and escorted Dylan up the gangplank of the *Queen Elizabeth*. We crowded his Cabin Class cabin to the walls, tried to allay the undisguised alarm of his aged

63

cabin-mates by offering them tumblers of whisky, and stayed far beyond the visitors' limit. Stewards kept trying to herd us back on to the pier, but no one would leave. Everyone was secretly scheming to be the last to say good-bye. When a representative of the Cunard Line came to present the Company's compliments to Dylan as a distinguished passenger, we felt even more boldly entitled to the privilege of remaining until the very last minute. Finally, we said farewell to Dylan, now gone glazed and babyish with drink and exhaustion, and went Indian file through narrow gangways back to the pier. The last visitor off the ship was Doris. She had outwitted us all.

When the abysmal whistle blew and the gang-plank was hauled up, I stood alone in a dim corner of Pier 90, feeling not only parting sadness but a suddenly overwhelming wave of desolation. As the ship began to move away, I noticed Sarah standing quite by herself not far away from me, quietly weeping. When she ran toward me, we embraced in an absurd and wordless flood of tears as the *Queen Elizabeth* backed into the wash of her propellors and began to slide out to sea.

Dylan Thomas had come to America. The meaning of his voyage was incalculable for those of us who had come to know him intimately and for those thousands who had been electrified by his gifts and the sense of genius rampant he had recovered for an age disposed to assign genius only to the past, or to the psychiatric case-book. I had no real notion of what America had meant to him. I could not tell with what he was returning. But there were, at least, eight hundred American dollars carefully secreted in a hand-bag I had put in his luggage as a present for his wife. It was a risky and foolish thing to do, but I could think of no other certain way of getting the money to her. Had Dylan knowledge of it, who knows how many hundreds of dollars would have been left in the ship's bar? But, of course, that would have been his privilege, and I remained troubled.

II

1950: June—September

The only direct news I had of Dylan during the following summer came not from him but from his wife. The first of many
unhappy letters, it served to introduce me at once to the incor-
rigible realities of Dylan's domestic life. She felt that her husband had been 'spoiled' in America and expressed the opinion
that, while he did not say so, he must be finding it very difficult
to come back 'to the cold hard English after all the warmth and
welcome and presents, unheard of over here, and his numerous
new friends.' But the worst trial, she felt, would be to get him to
work on projects that would bring in money for family necessi-
ties—especially when all that Dylan wanted to do was to work
on 'his own non paying poetry slowly and peacefully.' Since this
problem had become a permanent one, she wondered whether,
in America, there might be wider opportunity for 'combining, or
rather segregating, the commercial from the personal.' Her letter was affectionately cordial, and I was more than a little
warmed to learn that Dylan had spoken of me in terms that
made her consider me a close friend of hers as well. Having
often speculated, in the grimmer moments of our association,
upon what it must mean to be married to Dylan and dependent
upon him, I was also impressed by the insight and intelligence
with which she had stated her dilemma.

I went to Europe late in August, disembarking at Plymouth
where I found a wire from Dylan saying he would be waiting
for me when the boat-train pulled into Paddington station. My
first sight of him showed me a new man: his clothes were new
and well-matched, his shoes glinted with a high shine, his face
was serene and ruddy, and he was smoking a cigar—not one of
the little cigarette-sized ones of which he had become so fond
in America—but a Rotarian-size stogie with which he imperi-

ously hailed a taxi. As he ordered porters to take care of my luggage and escorted me into the cab, he might have been a glad-handed representative of the London Chamber of Commerce come to greet an American out for a good time. We trundled into the dizzying miniature traffic of London and drove directly to his club, the Savage, on Carlton House Terrace. He had found a room for me 'in a great jail of a hotel' just off Russell Square, he said, but first we had to have a drink. While awaiting my train he had gone to see Gloria Swanson in *Sunset Boulevard* and now he was as dry as a camel. The Savage Club was precisely what one would expect an Englishman's club to be—shabby, hushed, brushed, polished, and eternal. My new picture of Dylan as an affluent reception committee-of-one was furthered in the firm manner in which he piloted me about, introducing me to club members in galleries and on the stairs, showing me the history of the place in its fading group photographs, enscrolled plaques, and heroic-sized paintings dim with age. Somewhat overcome by my first hours in Europe—I had not been there since I was nineteen—and unused to this reversal of roles between us, I had little to say. But Dylan was full of reminiscence about people and places in America and, over warmish whiskies and sodas, we had a happy hour of fragmentary conversation. I was most conscious of the fact that we had met so warmly without any matter of engagements or appointments to make the meeting necessary. He seemed as happy to see me as I was to see him, and his heart-ily expansive manner made the occasion buoyant, relieving me of all those troubling, unresolved feelings that had dogged our association in America. In the late afternoon, Dylan had an appointment to meet at Broadcasting House, and so we parted *en route* to my hotel.

Early evening I rejoined him at one of his favourite pubs, the flamboyantly Victorian Salisbury, in St Martin's Lane. He was standing at the bar among a number of friends and acquain-tances, none of whose names I remember, all of whom pressed drinks upon me and fed me dry little sandwiches from a rack. As usual, Dylan could not abide the thought of dinner, and I was myself quite willing to settle for another pint of bitter and more titbits from the cold buffet. When our companions began to drift off toward their evening appointments, Dylan suggested that he and I take in a Marx Brothers movie, *Duck Soup*, then playing in Oxford Street. During the movie, Dylan got shushed continually for fussing with matches as he lighted one cigarette after another, and then he fell asleep and got shushed for snoring. Afterwards he wanted to go on to another of his clubs for a drink. But, too weary to stand straight, I said good night and walked to my hotel.

Early next afternoon I joined Dylan at El Vino in Fleet Street, a journalists' rendezvous also frequented by younger members of Parliament. He was drinking at a table with three friends, to whom he introduced me with a proprietary affection that was as unexpected as it was touching. We stayed there talking about American novelists, especially about William Faulkner, for whom Dylan held a deep regard, and Truman Capote, about whom he expressed an amused curiosity, until we were shooed out at the three-o'clock closing time, when we piled into a taxi and went on to the Mandrake Club. This was the place Dylan frequented most, and where people in search of him usually looked first. He was treated with no special deference in the Mandrake, as far as I could see, but with an almost calculated indifference. Still unused to being with him when he was not the object of everyone's attention, I could not understand why, as he moved among chess players, newspaper readers, and little conversational groups, he was allowed to pass not only without a greeting but even without recognition. I made a point of this when, later in the afternoon, I was introduced to Margaret Taylor, a long-standing friend and patron of Dylan's. She said I was quite wrong, that he was really treated with enormous deference, but that the ways in which this happened were perhaps not quickly apparent to the eyes of an American. Behind the little bar at the club was a Nell Gwyn sort of barmaid who maintained toward Dylan a noticeably distant and guarded air of wariness and amusement, as if his requests for drinks were really euphemisms for other requests. His attitude toward her seemed somehow gnomish, somewhat sheepish. I had the feeling that

67

earlier encounters between them had resulted in this unspoken truce. We lingered on at the Mandrake until early evening, nibbling at items from the *smörgåsbord*, moving in and out of new groupings of people, none of whom I remember clearly except Margaret Taylor, who stayed constantly with Dylan and me, and an iron-grey woman with the face of a sea-captain who tapped me brusquely on the back. 'Do you know Henry Miller?' she roared. I said no, but that I had once spent a few hours with him at his home in Big Sur. 'Hah!' she said, and turned away.

Thinking, surely, more of my appetite than of his, Dylan decided we would have dinner at Wheeler's in Old Compton Street—very smart, he said, very expensive, and crawling with literary and theatrical celebrities. We dined there on what, to my New England palate, seemed extraordinarily tasteless oysters and lobster, gossiped anew about our American acquaintances, and saw no celebrities. Then, on Dylan's suggestion, we went to the London Casino near by, where Les Compagnons de la Chanson were the star attraction. Because Dylan insisted on paying for the best seats in the house, we were too close to the stage for comfort. Before the loud, lavish revue was half over, he had slumped asleep and was snoring in an easy rhythm, just quietly enough to be unnoticed in the din of the show. The production was stultifying in every way, but this was my first taste of English theatre in fifteen years and I was prepared to enjoy it for novelty if for nothing else. But, with Dylan asleep beside me, I was conscious mainly of him, and sentimentally amused by the care he had taken to receive me. For some reason he had got it into his head that I should be entertained. He had on this score already done far more than he need have, and now, it was apparent, the effort was proving to be too great. But he came awake at the intermission and we went to the foyer to have champagne at the bar. While we were sipping it, the theatre's resident photographer came along and took a flashlight photograph. Dylan paid her for the results and copied his address on a card she handed to him. Many months later he sent me the photograph, which turned out to be a fine portrait of him and a caricature of me. Dylan's comment came in a letter accompanying it, the first

I received from him after my London visit: 'How nice, nice, nice! Oh, my conscience, I had feared that you left London breathing—no, I can't possibly mean that—had left London saying: "No more of that coarsened booby and his backstairs drizzling town. Foul enough in America, feebly lascivious in his pigsty at the Earle, puking in Philadelphia, burgling the Biddles, blackmailing physicists' mistakes for radiosets and trousers, hounding poor Oscar, but there! there in that English sink, intolerable, dribbly, lost. And, oh, his so-called friends! toadying slaves of the licensing laws, rats on a drinking ship!"—or didn't we meet any friends? I can't remember. I remember I liked, very much, our being together, though you were in that jail and I in my false bonhomous club. I remember meeting you at the station, and that was fine. And the London frowsty Casino, a memento of which I enclose: who are those perhaps-men, one bluebottle-bloated, one villainously simpering, with floral and yachting ties, so untrustworthily neat and prosperous with their flat champagne?'

The pubs were closed by the time the show was over. We taxied to the Savage Club, but the liquor cabinets there were shut against the late hour. We stood disconsolately in the lobby while Dylan tried to cajole the aged night porter into giving us just one little drink. Kindly but adamant, the porter was attempting to ease us gracefully out of the club when the hall phone rang. Someone was asking for Dylan. We were invited to join a party given by the American Negro actress, Hilda Simms, at her house near Regent's Park. Our evening was saved. We skimmed over wet streets and were in the middle of the party within fifteen minutes. People kept coming and going, and I remember few of them except George Barker, the poet, whom I had known in New York; Betty Smart, a Canadian girl who worked on the London *Vogue*; Lennie Hayton and his wife, Lena Horne. I chatted mostly with George Barker about many mutual acquaintances and Dylan spent most of his time with Lena Horne whom, I found, he had known before. I joined them at one point and was not particularly surprised to find Dylan in the same sort of party mood that had caused so much comment in America. His approach to Lena Horne was alternately boyish-bashful and straightforward, but I could see that she was comfortably aware of his proclivities. She fended him off with great charm, without for a moment losing an affectionate and smiling sense of him. Then we all settled down to listen to an old record. We put shillings in a hat, and the first one correctly to guess the singer would collect the jackpot. Dismal, lovesick, and determined, the voice stumped everyone until, correctly identifying the record, Lena Horne said: 'O for heaven's sake, it's Tallu!'

All the next day I wandered about by myself, becoming reacquainted with my favourite city in Europe. Dylan had wanted me to spend it with him but, even in his company, another day of drinking struck me as a waste of time, and I had made excuses that I hoped would not offend him. Early in the evening I went to the Mandrake, where he was waiting for me. He had been alone and on the loose all day and was now lumpish and unsteady on his feet. Margaret Taylor and another friend were with him, but he wanted to get away from the Mandrake. Oddly enough, he had an urge to see a movie, *Destination Moon*, then playing at one of the big houses in Leicester Square. Margaret and I consented to go with him, but only if he would stop for something to eat on the way to the theatre. The friend left, and Margaret and I escorted a very tipsy Dylan to a counter supper of sea food at the House of Hamburger before going on to a late showing of the movie. The only available seats were high up, where the atmosphere was suffocatingly stuffy and smoky, but Dylan remained awake through the picture and, by chuckles, sighs, and squeals of fright and amusement, seemed delighted with the boys'-book adventure story of men in space suits who ride a rocket ship to the moon. After the movie, as if he had suddenly downed a double Scotch, his sobriety instantly vanished and we had to support him in the midst of a crowd as we went down the stairs of the theatre. Margaret seemed to want to take charge of him, said she would see him to his club, and would not allow me to come along.

The next day was a grey, silent, and furtively oppressive London Sunday. Friends of Dylan's were holding a sort of open house in their basement flat, and I dropped by around mid afternoon. Everyone was already well armed against the desolation of the day. I stayed for a drink or two, talked with the Scottish painters, MacBryde and Colquhoun, and was annoyed by someone who kept insisting drunkenly, and to my face, that I was 'a nice American'; he had, he said inscrutably, met only one other and that was Vera-Ellen, the dancer. Dylan was drinking heavily, being sloppy about his person, but enjoying himself loudly when I left to keep an appointment with some English friends.

Sarah was now at sea on her way to England from New York, having cabled Dylan that she would arrive in London on 4th September. He asked me to come to lunch with them as soon as her boat-train pulled in. I went to Wheeler's, the appointed place, at one o'clock, but neither Dylan nor Sarah turned up. As I waited about, I encountered Harry Thornton Moore, the American critic whom, I learned, Dylan had also asked to lunch at that time. After an hour or so of watching the door, Moore and I had lunch together. Later in the afternoon I went to have tea with T. S. Eliot in his office in Russell Square and, when I returned to my hotel, found a telephoned note from Dylan asking me to join him and Sarah at the Café Royale. 1 hurried to Piccadilly and found them in a gilt and plush bar. Dylan seemed very happy to see Sarah again, treated her with the same welcoming committee eagerness to please with which he had greeted me, but was obviously most interested in being alone with her. I left after one drink.

Next afternoon we met, all three, at the Salisbury, drank gins and limes and strolled through crowded streets toward the Embankment. There, on Dylan's suggestion, we took a river bus down the Thames to a point beyond Greenwich. It was a grey day on the busy river and Sarah and I enjoyed being tourists and asking Dylan to identify all the domes and towers we saw. There was a little bar on the river-boat; we took our drinks out on deck as we chugged among outgoing tramp-steamers, coal-laden barges, and puffing tugboats. We took snapshots, some of which resulted in fine characteristic portraits of Dylan. It was a festive little excursion, but in spite of outbursts of his high explosive laughter, Dylan was most of the time gloomy and troubled. At one point, when Sarah had gone to fetch us drinks from the bar, he turned to me: 'John, what am I going to do?' His face, suddenly sober, showed bewilderment and his eyes were set upon something far away. 'About what?' 'I'm in love with Sarah, and I'm in love with my wife. I don't know what to do.' It was a question no one could have answered save himself, and I did not attempt to. But this was a new confidence, and my first experience of seeing Dylan wrestling with a problem rather than seeking out means to circumvent it.

We disembarked at Waterloo Bridge and walked through Trafalgar Square back up to St Martin's Lane where in the midst of passing traffic we stopped to say good-bye. Like the illicit lovers of a thousand English novels, they were going off to Brighton for a day or two; I was flying to Paris in the morning. Dylan and I spoke of meeting in London again when I should have returned from travels on the Continent, but these plans fell through when I decided to sail from Le Havre. I did not see him again until I visited him in Wales in the following July.

III

September 1950—July 1951

I wrote to Dylan now and then but, unable to evoke an answer, was out of direct touch with him for nearly seven months. The only news of him I had came from Sarah, who was spending most of the winter in Greece. After I had left them in London together, she had stayed on for a few days and then gone to France, expecting to return to England to be with Dylan for a week or so in October. But when she returned to London he was nowhere to be found. Her letters and messages sent to the club where he normally received all of his London mail were never answered. She stayed in London for some weeks, learned that Dylan was ill and could not be seen, and finally, in the continued absence of any word from him at all, left for Greece feeling betrayed and unwanted. When she wrote to me expressing incomprehension at Dylan's neglect of her, I wrote to say that I was convinced there had been some large misunderstanding. I was sure that Dylan could not intentionally be unkind, especially toward her, and asked her to stave off disillusion until the facts could be known. To remind her of the day on which Dylan had declared to me his love for her, I enclosed some of the snapshots we had taken on our river-bus excursion.

Sarah wrote back early in January: 'Your letter gave me as much delight as anything that's happened to me recently. Thank you, so much more than I can begin to say here, and just now, for writing as you did. And the pictures, which in my happily time-less suspension here seem to have been taken centuries ago, are wonderful to have, and help eradicate the woes of my second London quite entirely. For you are quite right, and neither of us needs, thank God, to contemplate any disillusion. I wrote you a whining little note last week, which crossed your fine envelope packed with the best, and I spoke in that of a letter from Dylan.

73

And the explanation did lie, as he discovered only when he got my letters from here, and as I suspected all the time, in the fine Italian hand of the grey lady,—— I won't attempt to tell it all here, and there's no need, but Dylan was ill first with pleurisy and then pneumonia all the weeks I was in London, and she collected his mail for him at his club every morning. What she did with them neither of us will probably ever know, but he saw none of my messages and my letters, nothing. She came to see me off at the air station when I finally did give up and go back to France, laden with her flowers and dulcet doom, and even now she sends me poisonously cheerful letters about how lucky I am to be out of England. But that's the end of it now, with all its soap-opera bubbles broken, finally.'

This last sentence was Sarah's epitaph for a romance which, as time would tell, had irrevocably foundered, partly through plotted intervention, partly through Dylan's inability to deal maturely with his feelings or to recognize their consequences. Soon, I learned from Sarah, he had gone off to Persia, to gather material for a film-script on commission from the Anglo-Iranian oil company. When I wrote to him in April I was again able to tender an invitation for him to read at the Poetry Center and to assure him that, should he care to undertake a second reading tour, I would be happy to begin planning for it at once. His reply contained the passage about our London Casino evening quoted earlier, and went on: 'I remember the Thames and old Sarah —whom I saw something of later but who, I imagine, left London, as I imagined you had done, rasping to herself: "No more of that beer-cheapened hoddy-noddy, snoring, paunched, his corn, his sick, his fibs, I'm off to Greece where you know where you are; oh, his sodden bounce, his mis-theatrical-demeanour, the boastful tuppence!" I haven't heard from her since she went away...I am so glad, indeed, that you will be here in July; and I shall be less revolting than last time, whatever the sacrifice. And let us meet the truly great for tea, and go to Oxford where I know a human being. Caitlin will be in London in July, which will not make things any quieter. We both will probably be living there for some time: I am about to take on a new job: co-writing with the best gagman in England—he is an Irishman from New Zealand—a new comic series for the radio. I have already thought of two jokes, both quite unusable. And may I come to Edith Sitwell's party for you?

'Give my love, if ever you see them or believe it, to Sarah, Lloyd and Loren, Marion and Cummings, Stanley Moss, Jean Garrigue, Gene Baro, Doris, David Lougée, Howard, Patrick Boland, and any ugly stranger in the street. Have a thousand boilermakers for me, and send me your stomach: I'll put it under my pillow.

'I have written three new poems, one alright, which I will, if you like, send you when I can find them.

'I have no news at all. 1 am broke and in debt. Now, next time: I would very much like (I'd adore it) to be imported to the States next year, 1952. The Poetry Center paying my passage and the first fee. I would bring Caitlin with me, if by that time I have made, as I intend to do, much money from my ha ha scripts. And would you, *could* you, act as Agent or Christ knows what for me again? I do not think I would wish to go through the Middle West, excepting Chicago, again, but anywhere, everywhere else, unless I have quite ruined myself in all those places where you were not with me. Could you put out feelers, spin wheels, grow wings for me? I am so deadly sick of it here. I would bring great packages of new poems to read, and much more pre-written prose to pad them in. I would be much better than I was; I mean, sick less often. I mean, I would so much like to come. Could you write to any friends or acquaintances I might have made and see if they would help. Would you, now?

'No, Persia wasn't all depressing. Beautiful Ispahan and Shiraz. Wicked, pompous, oily British. Nervous, cunning, corrupt and delightful Persian bloody bastards. Opium no good. Persian vodka, made of beetroot, like stimulating sockjuice, very enjoyable. Beer full of glycerine and pips. Women veiled, or unveiled ugly, or beautiful and entirely inaccessible, or hungry. The lovely camels who sit on their necks and smile. I shan't go there again.'

75

IV

July 1951—June 1952

With my friend Bill Read from Boston, I sailed for England in July. When I phoned Dylan from London he asked us to come to Laugharne immediately, and we promised to arrive at the beginning of the next week-end. Taking the rickety night-sleeper of the Red Dragon from Paddington station at midnight, we got off at Cardiff just after sunrise. Through the kindness of the British poet, Henry Treece, whom I had met in New York, I had been invited to give a lecture for the B.B.C. by Aneirin Talfan Davies, a friend of Dylan's who was in charge of the Welsh Home Service; our stop-over in Cardiff was for the purpose of discussing with Talfan Davies the nature of remarks I would make. My best notion was to speak on 'Dylan Thomas in America.' This pleased Talfan Davies and we made an appointment to meet a week later in London, when I would have my script ready.

Our train from Cardiff to Carmarthen was slow and over-crowded with bulky children in scout uniforms. We watched the landscape change abruptly from the ravaged, begrimed valleys and sooty towns of the mining country to the electric green of the estuary region where sheep lay still as stones on hill-sides and little picture-book castles were perched on promontories above inlets and the mouths of rivers. Pulling into Carmarthen in a hiss of steam, we sighted Dylan, the most important and impatient man on the platform. He was handsomely turned out in new tweeds, a bright silk ascot around his neck, a cap sitting rakishly over his protruding curls. Once more, I could see, he was The Host. Puffing a cigar, he peremptorily took us in charge, ordered porters to see to our luggage, led us out to a waiting car he had hired in Laugharne, and introduced us to his chauffeur, Billy Williams. We got in, settled back for the ride to

77

Laugharne, drove about three hundred yards, and stopped at a pub. Some two hours and six or seven roadside pubs later, we had covered the brief thirteen miles to Laugharne. Entering the village at the beginning of the long Welsh twilight, we drove through crooked streets lined with grey stuccoed houses, caught sight of the jaunty little town clock-tower with its weathercock sitting in the wind, passed by the wooden turnstile leading to the castle, and stopped in the seaside bottom of the village at the Cross House, the pub where Caitlin was to join us.

After a drink there, I told Dylan I most wanted to see the castle. Bill and I had toured Cardiff Castle that morning, but its restored towers and brightly painted interiors had struck us as mere Victorian approximations of the medieval and we had already become disillusioned about castles in general. Dylan led us outside and around a cobble-stone corner. There in the sea-heavy gloaming floated ivy-walled Laugharne Castle—a crumbling, dignified thrust of stone that seemed to organize the whole village about itself. Little boats with toothpick masts sat lopsided on the mud-flats under its eight-hundred-year-old walls, from which nearly horizontal trees leaned on the water. It was all that we could have hoped for in a castle.

Back in the Cross House, we found the little pub beginning to fill up with villagers and Welsh song, the first notes of which struck us as curiously unmelodic and definitely off key. Through the din of rising choruses, Caitlin arrived, bringing with her two friends, the Leishmans, who had driven over from Swansea to have dinner with us. I was quite taken aback by her Celtic blonde beauty, first, and then by the puzzling combination in her manner and bearing of the primitive and the *svelte*. She was fashionably dressed in a wide-skirted red coat, her loosely combed flaxen hair falling brightly over her shoulders. Struck by her sharp, exquisitely fine-boned features, her composed, seldom-changing expression, her observant yet frightened or distrustful eyes, I mentioned to Dylan that he had not prepared me for her at all. I had expected a country girl. Minutes later, I noticed Dylan whispering to Caitlin. 'Didn't I *tell* you?' I heard him say, and he came toward me. 'Caitlin says you're just as nice as I said you were, but she never believes anything I tell her.'

Someone passed around a jar of pickled cockles and we ate these with our bitters as the pub became more crowded, smoky, and boisterous. A grimy man in a cap began to sing the Welsh national anthem. This was uproariously taken up all around, and we departed from the Cross House on a loud cracked crescendo of Welsh pride. There were, we learned, two ways of going to the Boat House, where the Thomas's lived. Over Caitlin's protest, Dylan decided that we should go, not through village streets and lanes, but by the seaside path which the tide washed over twice a day. First we had to cross a deceptively narrow rivulet. In attempting to make this in one leap, most of us came down ankle deep in mud. Bill, carrying Caitlin, lost his footing, and they landed, sprawling, in marsh-grass. We pulled them upright, but Bill's glasses had jumped from his pocket and had already been washed out to sea. Duck-footed, we picked our way along the oozing paths leading under the walls of the castle and got to the Boat House through an opening in the breakwater that fenced in the small backyard.

We were deep in the misty gloaming by now, so that our first sense of the house was but a partially true one. Not until daylight could we understand that it was as much given to the sea as sequestered against it. Beginning with the terrace, on which stood a few old weather-beaten chairs and a knob-kneed table, there were four ascending levels. Advancing into the house by the back door, you stepped on to the second level, and found yourself at the foot of a stairwell from which a dark genie's cavern of a kitchen led off to your left, and a shining ship-cosy dining-room to your right. The stairs were as steep as those on shipboard, but you could keep your balance by hanging on to a rope railing as you ascended. At the head of the stairs, on the third level, you came to the front door. Opening this, you would find yourself at the bottom of a wild garden through which a stony, muddy path wound steeply upward through blackthorns and wild roses to a sort of promenade paralleling a mossy wall running along the property on which the Boat House stood.

Leading off from the front door to the left was the bedroom of the oldest child, Llewelyn; to the right was the sitting-room with an adjoining bath-room. To reach the fourth level of the house you had to pass through the sitting-room.

While Caitlin prepared our meal downstairs, we talked in the sitting-room as the wireless crackled with Light Programme music from London, and went out to take the air on the little widow's-walk that ran around two sides of the house. Walking on this was like walking on deck. Lights in the distance that seemed as though they might belong to passing ships were really lights in farmhouses across the mouth of the River Taf where it flowed into the estuary. The sitting-room itself was informal, with a coal-burning grate over which stood a collection of china objects on the mantelpiece and, except for a series of unframed Renoir prints Caitlin had tacked on the walls, wholly mid Victorian in feeling. The night was warm enough to allow doors and windows to remain open; sleepy bird-calls and the wash of tidal waters filled the silences in our conversation.

Downstairs, the six of us crowded the dining-table in a room so tiny that anyone could touch a wall just by reaching out. We were talkative as Caitlin served us a good dinner of baked ham and steaming greens, but most of the conversation was initiated by the Leishmans, who wanted to exchange with Dylan news of old friends they shared in Swansea, where Dylan had lived until he was nearly twenty. Caitlin had very little to say throughout the meal, and I again had the feeling that she was meticulously observant but, for some reason, also suspicious. Her physical radiance which, because she had no awareness of it, showed with a special charm, was a natural attribute; but within it, one felt, there was a spirit alternately caged and restless, quiescent and removed.

It had been a long day for Bill and me, and our pub-crawl along the road from Carmarthen had made us sleepy. When the Leishmans left soon after dinner, we were glad to retire. I was put in the sitting-room, which, in the nature of things, was a thoroughfare for the whole Thomas family as they went to or from their bedrooms, and, since Llewelyn was still away at

school, Bill was given his room, which was decorated with drawings and photographs of airplanes and battleships, and had a
library of boys' adventure books. Dylan and Caitlin retired to
the fourth level, where Aeron and Colm, the younger children,
in an adjoining room, were already long asleep.

The soft sing-song voices of children and the dazzle of the
sea in every window woke me early. The whole family, except for
Dylan, had passed alongside my day-bed as I slept out of doors
on the terrace, soundly; now Caitlin was calling us to breakfast.
As we ate fried eggs in the sweet morning air, Dylan struggled
out to join us, groaning, dishevelled, but in his characteristically good morning temper, and began his meal with a plate of
fried kippers. Aeron, getting ready for school in the village, came
to ask her mother to comb tangles out of her hair. Physically she
struck me as being very much like Dylan, with large dark eyes,
a ruddy complexion, candy-brown hair golden on the edges, and
with a bearing that was staunch and self-contained. In the presence of strangers she seemed not so shy as preoccupied and
indifferent. Behind her came Colm, the most beautiful child I
have ever seen. His head might have come winging from some
Tiepolo ceiling on which bodiless cherubs gaze with a vague
sweetness at some sacred event. Silent, attentive only to his
mother, he showed no interest at all in the visitors, and shortly
disappeared with a little hum of self-pleasure back into the
house. As Caitlin worked over her daughter's knotted locks,
Aeron grimaced, screamed, fretted, and otherwise dramatized
her agony; yet she refused to allow her mother to give up until
every hair was smoothly in place. When, finally, the ordeal was
done with, she picked up her books, shot off through the house,
up the garden. In a few minutes, looking overhead to the promenade, we could see her sailing by on her bicycle.

We went to the castle after breakfast, Dylan jauntily leading
Bill and me into the village along the high sea-wall. As we
walked, I noticed a large bird on one of the sand bars exposed by
the receding tide. It was sitting with its black wings stretched
out in what seemed a very painful position to hold for more than
a moment. Dylan said it was a cormorant. I asked him why the

81

bird was holding itself in so awkward and torturous a manner. 'He thinks that's what a cormorant *should* do,' said Dylan. 'Nobody ever told him otherwise.' To enter the castle we had to pass through a turnstile where, at one time, visitors were asked to pay sixpence admission. The turnstile was untended now and we went through and alongside a pink-washed house once owned by Richard Hughes, the author of *A High Wind in Jamaica*. Dylan and Caitlin had also lived in the house at one time, but it was not until more than a year later that I learned how importantly it had figured in their lives.

Little trees and bushes reached out from the castle at all angles. One had the feeling that the whole structure had passed through a kind of transubstantiation, that it was almost one again with the earth on which and out of which it had been constructed. Crumbling everywhere, its life running out like sand in an hour-glass, invaded everywhere by flora and the little fauna of mice and owls, it seemed to be dying into time, quietly and without protest. By climbing wooden ladders placed inside one of the towers we came to a battlement. The roofs of Laugharne lay below and about us, as many-faceted and monochromatic as an early cubist painting. In the continually restless wash of the estuary beyond, snowstorms of white birds lighted on sand-bars, then rose at some invisible signal, wheeled about, and snowed down suddenly somewhere else. The morning had begun to turn damp and grey; we were glad to scramble down from the crenellated heights and follow Dylan to Browns Hotel where, at last, the pub was legally open.

Ivy Williams, of whom Dylan had often spoken, and to whom I knew he was deeply attached, greeted us pleasantly but noncommittally and served us each a glass of pale ale. A motherly, girlish-faced woman with large intelligent eyes, she smoked cigarettes continually in a long black holder as she gossiped with Dylan. At the same time, she kept disappearing into the back of the hotel to watch over pots and pans bubbling on the stove, coming back to tend bar as other villagers came in for a late-morning's pick-me-up. Dylan's greetings to the villagers and theirs to him were made in mumblings and monosyllables—a sort of respectful, familiar, yet at the same time distant exchange. They knew, of course, that he had business in the big world, that he had been to America, and that he was regarded importantly in London, and most of them had probably heard him on the wireless or seen him on television. Yet nothing in their manner toward him suggested that they were particularly impressed, or even that they understood just what Dylan's distinction was. For his part, and without effort, Dylan's manner in his own village seemed to be directed toward looking and acting as much like everyone else as possible.

Leaving Bill and me in the pub to chat with Ivy, Dylan went out to make arrangements for an automobile excursion he wanted us to take in the afternoon, and to call on his father and mother, who lived just across the street from the hotel. The day had become even more grey and cold, with a sea-chill that seemed to get through one's clothing and touch the skin. When we returned to the Boat House for lunch, Caitlin was not at all enthusiastic about Dylan's plans, saying that she would be happy to have the three of us go along without her. But she gave in to our pleadings that she join us, and we all walked back to the village. Dylan had, again, engaged Billy Williams and his old Buick which served as a sort of community taxi. We started out by driving northward to St Clears, then westward, bound for the very tip of south-western Wales. But within half an hour, at Dylan's suggestion, we had stopped at a pub for something to take the chill off the day. As we drove on, slightly warmed by whiskies and the enthusiasm of a buxom barmaid for Americans, Caitlin, seated between me and Bill in the back seat while Dylan chatted with Billy Williams in the front seat, began in a low voice to ask me about Sarah. Where was she now? Was she coming to England? Did she write to Dylan? What sort of woman was she? Surprised, and uncomfortable, I was able to offer only a few vague answers as I tried to find some way of changing the subject. But my evasiveness displeased Caitlin and she did not hesitate to say so. When I could see that she expected me to share with her confidences I had had from Dylan, I was nonplussed, yet hopeful of finding some means to save our being alienated so early in a relationship. I then tried to answer some of her questions but, with Dylan's head barely three feet away from ours, was hard put to say anything that would satisfy her, or to find a way to postpone so inflammatory a discussion.

Because of the Welsh practice of lining roads with high wind-breaking hedges, there was little in the way of landscape to see as we drove along. But eventually we came to an open space just a few hundred yards from the sea and stopped before a barren little pub facing a rather desolate stretch of pebbled beach over which cold waves threw icy-looking dashes of spray. There was not a bather in sight, but Caitlin announced that she, at least, was going in for a swim. While the rest of us adjourned to the pub, she changed into swimming clothes and, as we watched from the doorway, advanced without hesitation toward the black waters and splashed in. Huddling about the bar like orphans of the storm, we tried to warm ourselves with talk and drink until Caitlin returned, shaking water out of her hair and saying she was wonderfully refreshed. Shivery, we had another drink, climbed into the car, and moved on. But now there were further embarrassing questions and further congenial though ineffective attempts to evade or postpone them to the point where I could sense that my lack of co-operation was setting up a tension with which I was quite unprepared to deal. She had finally become silent, and perhaps a little morose, by the time we got to our destination, the village of St David's Head. There we left the car to inspect the ruins of a monastery that once marked the very farthest western point of medieval Christianity in Britain, and to visit the great crude-stone cathedral. We wandered in and out of huge galleries, took photographs on a greensward enclosed by great lichen-covered walls, and for a time almost succeeded in being merry when, as we took photographs, Dylan strutted like Mussolini, and Bill hung upside down from a battlement. The happiest result of our visit was a group portrait of Dylan, Caitlin, Bill, and Billy Williams. In spite of the rather low-keyed enthusiasm with which we had started on the trip, and against the low-voiced conversations and mounting tensions that dogged us, the group in the picture somehow looks beatific, almost biblical. The camera has never lied more gracefully; I still cannot connect the composure of the portrait with the nerve-wracking intimacy of that benighted outing.

Back in the car, Caitlin suggested that we return to Laugharne. Dylan would not hear of this, and appealed to Bill and me. We said we would be happy to do whatever they decided; but we both already knew that no one would be happy no matter what anyone decided. We sat in silence at a cross-roads, the wind singing mournfully about our impasse. Then, with a shrug of resignation, Caitlin gave in, and Dylan directed Billy to drive us to a place where, the pubs now being closed, we might have tea. This turned out to be a stark, white wooden house over-looking marshes on the outskirts of St David's. As we waited, in magnified unhappy silence, for our skimpy servings of toast and tea, Caitlin remained wordless, her mind closed against the company and far away. Everyone was uncomfortable, restive, and no one could find any means of alleviating the worsening situation. Tea warmed our spirits but little, and when we returned to the car I knew that everyone felt as I did: that the trip had already shown itself to be misconceived, ill-assorted, and interminable. Again Caitlin suggested that we go home. I hoped, desperately now, that Dylan would agree, but he did not. He had in mind a place beyond Fishguard where we could have 'a magnificent lobster dinner.'

Heading northward, ever farther away from home, we were now a thoroughly disconsolate party. The pub visits Dylan insisted we make every few miles of the way seemed only to deepen our despair. As we dragged continually out of the car and into dimly lighted rooms full of strangers who stared at us, there were momentary flashes of conviviality due to Dylan's joy in the new pint placed before him, but these were forced and impossible to sustain in the presence of unanswered questions that nothing could cancel. We would straggle back to the car, prisoners of one another, making fizzling little attempts by a word or a gesture to see ourselves in the absurdity of the pre-dicament. But finally, as we rode along in utter silence, we rounded a hill-top to sight Fishguard harbour through a mist so heavy that it seemed permanent, then drove on toward what Dylan described as a famous old cove once used by smugglers and pirates. There, just a few yards from the sea, was a somewhat ramshackle clapboard inn snugly sequestered between cliffs. We were the only patrons. The flustered proprietress, who obviously expected no one on this miserable evening, greeted us with notably more anxiety then pleasure. The promise of a lobster dinner which Dylan had used in goading us onward was, it turned out, rather untenable. The proprietress said she had one lobster—a fairly good-sized one, to be sure—and that she thought she could 'make it do.' The thought of searching for another place to have a meal in which no one was interested led us to accepting her offer without hesitation. We were shortly seated at a well-appointed candle-lit table. Barley soup came first, followed by a sort of salad within the depths of which we might search daintily for infinitesimal fragments of lobster. No one had enough poise to make a joke of this pathetic process, and we picked away in benumbed silence. Then Caitlin ordered our waiter to bring a bottle of white wine. For some reason Dylan vehemently objected to this. A scene ensued, imprecations and sulky threats were exchanged as the wide-eyed waiter brought in the order and scurried back to the kitchen. Caitlin poured herself a glass, and the rest of us, as if we were afraid not to, meekly followed her example. Candles flickered in the appalling quiet as, finally, we sipped tea and picked hungrily at a few gutted lobster shells.

As we were getting into the car to begin the long homeward trip, Caitlin refused to take her place in the back seat. She ordered Dylan to sit between Bill and me while she joined Billy Williams in the front seat. We drove off, more bogged in hopelessness than ever. Dylan willed himself into sleep almost at once. It was dark now and, with Dylan suddenly unconscious, our sense of being encased in a dilemma became even more acute. Caitlin began speaking to Billy and we heard her say loudly that she was anxious to get home where she was expecting a visit from some '*real* friends, not Americanos.' Other remarks, only parts of which I could overhear, carried the resentment.

Bill and I remained silent. Then Caitlin spotted a roadside pub and said she wanted to stop for a drink. I remained with Dylan, now sleeping on my shoulder, as the others went in for half an hour or so. At last, but only after having been lost in fog several times at cross-roads and having been misdirected by Welsh-speaking natives, we came upon the road to Laugharne and got back to the Boat House about eleven o'clock.

Dylan, urged from sleep, went directly and unspeaking to his room. I was waiting for everyone else to retire before going to bed in the sitting-room when Caitlin came up the stairs, brushed by me swiftly, and turned as she reached the entrance to the third floor. 'Now you can see what I mean,' she said angrily. 'America is out!' Without a further word, she left. Bewildered, I conferred with Bill. We would have to leave, I felt, and at once. Consulting a railway time-table we found there was no train from Carmarthen before daylight. With Laugharne already bedded down for the night and 'Bible-black,' we knew there was no exit. We tried to come upon some hidden reason for Caitlin's displeasure, and to arrive, with very little to base judgment upon, at some objective sense of our situation. Unless she regarded my refusal to relate details of Dylan's relations with women in America as a betrayal, we could find nothing overt that might account for her anger or explain her rudeness. We decided, tentatively, that we were but incidental victims of some old grudge, some old unresolved irritation between her and Dylan, or between her and Dylan's friends. Perhaps, we thought, but with no reason or faith, everything would be different in the morning. Perhaps the little storm our presence had brought on had really nothing to do with us. But we knew we were grasping at possibilities and feeding on cold comfort. We went to bed uneasy, unhappy, and wondering what to do.

In the morning Caitlin was as sunny and mild as the weather. She greeted us pleasantly, had big cups of tea sent up while we were dressing, and later sat down with us for breakfast on the terrace. It was as if the dreadful day before had never existed. As we sat in sunny ambience, throwing crusts of bread to expectant swans that floated by under the breakwater, we allowed the bad dream to pass. We would take the new day as it came. Soon Dylan arrived with a shining morning face that showed no sign in the world of the stress which had, just nine or ten hours before, sent him into unconsciousness. When the meal was over, he guided Bill and me into the village to visit his parents in their little grey house, the Pelican, on the main street just a few steps from the post office.

His mother—short, voluble, with frizzy white hair—fussed over us and sat us down to a second breakfast of toast, tea, and a hard-boiled egg in a white china cup. His father, a lean, reserved man, dressed with careful and quiet elegance, sat by the grate fire, an afghan over his shoulders. As Mrs Thomas kept chatting inconsequentials, clucking about the kitchen sitting-room, one had the feeling that Dylan's father was content merely to observe this gathering of his son and his son's friends. Dylan fretted in some embarrassment under his mother's over-attentiveness, yet there was obviously a bond between them that nothing could embarrass. But if he was unquestionably the apple of his mother's eye, in his father's eye he was still an object of a curiously dispassionate interest. There was something respectful yet unmistakably distant and wary between the two men, something that made for a mutual lack of ease. His mother's busy solicitude, one felt, was an old familiar means of denying or ignoring this. When she took Bill into her kitchen-garden to help her dig some vegetables to take home to Caitlin, I had a rambling chat with Dylan and his father about an American's impressions of Wales and then about America and some of Dylan's more respectable adventures there. But no real conversation developed, mainly, I thought, because none of us, and especially Dylan, could break through the formal father-and-son relationship to say freely and unguardedly just what he meant.

David Thomas had been a schoolmaster, I knew, and I had learned from Dylan that much of his own early education had been more the result of his father's tutelage than of formal schooling. Not until after Dylan's death did I learn that his father had had an early unrealized ambition as a poet. This revelation took me back to our visit—the only time when I had seen them together—and explained somewhat my feeling that Dylan's father looked upon him with as much curiosity as with pride. The poet *manqué* had brought forth the poet *réussi*.

When Bill came back into the kitchen with a basket of beets and carrots and tomatoes, we said good-bye and were ushered through the long, dark, middle hallway that conventionally divides Welsh houses. Just as we were about to leave my glance fell on the hand-bag I had sent to Caitlin from New York—the one in which I had cached what was left of Dylan's American earnings—hanging from a nail on the back of a door. I said nothing about this but, later, guessing I may have noticed it, Caitlin explained that since Dylan had neglected to bring his mother a gift from America, she had persuaded him to present the bag to her. The eight hundred dollars in cash had meanwhile been removed. Dylan now wanted to go to the pub at Browns Hotel, but since neither Bill nor I was ready to begin another day's drinking, we all three parted to go separate ways. Bill went off through the village to climb the hedgerowed slopes of Sir John's Hill; I went back to the Boat House and into Dylan's studio to make a first draft of my radio script.

The studio, which Dylan called 'the shack,' was painted green, perched above the house and about a hundred yards from it on the stone-walled path leading into the village. While it was no more than ten feet long and seven feet wide, large windows on two sides brought in sunlight and sealight, saving it from seeming cramped. One window looked upon a watery vista—shallows between long sloping hills—terminating in the Irish Sea; the other looked out across the narrow part of Carmarthen Bay toward Sir John's Hill. The interior, originally whitewashed, was now a grimy, weather-and-insect-speckled grey. On the walls were tacked-up photographs wet weather had curled or faded or mottled with mildew. Topmost in the room over the small wooden table that served Dylan for a desk was a handsome portrait of Walt Whitman. Other photographs showed Mari- anne Moore in a big black hat, a youthful version of Edith Sit- well, a study of a Mexican mother and child by Cartier-Bresson.

As a whole, the studio was a rat's-nest of chewed, rolled, and discarded papers—piles of manuscripts, unanswered (often unopened) letters, empty cigarette packages, small stacks of literary periodicals, tradesmen's bills, and publishers' brochures. Snatches of reworked poetry lay under empty beer bottles. Volumes of poetry mouldered where they had been placed months, years, before. Besides its single table and two straight-backed chairs, the studio contained three or four half-filled cartons of books, and a small black coal-burning stove.

I cleared a small space for myself in the litter of the table-top, opened a window to let out wasps that had suddenly come to life, and sat down to make notes for my broadcast.

A few hours later Dylan and Bill came to take me to the Cross House, where Dylan was to meet friends who had just come over from Oxford. They were a married couple—he a beet-faced, beard-thicketed Englishman who might have stepped out of *Punch;* she a steely-hard patrician with a Marxist, America-hating bias that crept into even the most innocuous moments of conversation. They had come to Laugharne to spend a fortnight's holiday in a little whitewashed cottage. As we drank in rather minimal cordiality in the Cross House, the customary Saturday night song-fest raged about us. We bore it until our eardrums ached, then said good nights and walked by the village route back to the Boat House. Sitting down to dinner some time after ten, we came around to discussing weird murder cases and our various notions of proper punishment for convicted sex fiends. Dylan zestfully told of a man who had disembowelled a young virgin, arranged her entrails in decorative patterns, and written her name in her own blood on a window-pane. Caitlin felt that this was a case where the murderer should receive the same treatment. Dylan felt that all sex-fiends should be shot. There seemed to be no disagreement in their points of view, but, as the gruesome conversation progressed, I became aware of a rising tension between them and of a tendency in Caitlin to ridicule any idea that Dylan might express. Holding an empty match-box in his hand, Dylan suddenly flipped this in Caitlin's direction and it landed on her shoulder. She picked up the match-box and threw it in his face. Dylan said that that was unfair—the match-box had just slipped from his fingers. Before he could finish his sentence, Caitlin, with one fierce grip, reached for his hair and pulled him out of his seat and on to the floor. Before Bill and I knew what was happening, we were in the midst of a *mêlée*. Chairs got knocked over, dishes were pushed from the table as, blow for blow, the combatants wrestled toward the kitchen. Gaping, we sat benumbed over our cooling food and listened helplessly to sounds of skirmish coming from the next room. With a sudden sharp cry, Dylan broke away and we could hear him running up the stairs. In a moment Caitlin came back to the dining-room and, towering over us, her eyes flashing, her face steely, said: '*Thank* you for helping a lady in distress!'

Stunned by the episode, we tried limply to explain that we felt we could not interfere; and otherwise to make some semblance of conversation that might lead us out of nightmare. We were successful in this, oddly enough, and a long discussion of Dylan's and Caitlin's married life ensued. Listening, not without genuine sympathy, to her litany of Dylan's inadequacies as a father, husband, and provider, we had come upon the one means of gaining Caitlin's interest and, temporarily, her acceptance. In our shaken state, Bill and I could contribute little but monosyllables of agreement and, we hoped, understanding. But our small response seemed no discouragement to Caitlin, and she poured out her grievances for more than an hour. During this monologue I found the telling clue to her distrust and dislike of me. 'Dylan always speaks of you as his closest friend in America,' she said, 'but all you do is flatter him and make him feel like some sort of god. When he came back from America his head was bigger than ever. They ought to know what he's really like in America—all those fool women who chase after him while I'm left here to rot in this bloody bog with three screaming children and no money to pay the bills he leaves behind him. He won't go to America again without me—and I shan't go, so that's that.'

She left us to our own devices then. Once more, confounded and dismayed at the unhappiness we had seen so blatantly

91

expressed, we went to bed. The house where lived 'the plagued groom and bride who have brought forth the urchin grief,' the house which Dylan had described as 'a sea-shaken house on a breakneck of rocks' was, we knew, shaken by something more violent and no less threatening than the sea.

While we had now become used to the incredible, we were still incredulous when, once more, the morning revealed everything in order, everyone calm, soft-spoken, and congenially at ease. We played games with Aeron and Colm after breakfast, lazily fingered through the Sunday newspapers from London, and listened vaguely to religious music on the wireless. Dylan turned first, I noticed, not to the literary columns, but to the horse-racing results; he told me that he placed a couple of shillings every other day or so with the local bookmaker. On this Sunday morning the results were all against him.

Late morning I went alone to the studio to make a final draft of my radio script, and came back for lunch on the terrace about one o'clock. Since everyone was curious to know what I was up to in my British radio début, I read what I had written to Dylan, Caitlin, and Bill as we relaxed in the sun after our meal.

'In Cardiff a few days ago I visited the National Museum where the long history of the land of Wales is told in fragments of stone, bronze, pottery and jewellery, in parchment and in pigment—where, by following the guide-book, one can witness from its primordial beginnings the legend of human enterprise on these shores until, descending the steps, point-blank, one faces into the busy daylight of circling cars and buses and emerges, half-blind, into the present. The function of a museum is, of course, to preserve as many evidences of history as is possible in the most compact space, to embalm under glass those traces of time that connect us with preconscious existence.

'One's visit has much the quality of the reading of a scholarly, illustrated volume in which the text provides perspectives for the pictures. As I came away, I felt the museum had provided me with a metaphor I should like to apply to the subject of my talk, the poet Dylan Thomas of Laugharne, Carmarthenshire, and his reputation and influence in America.

'To qualify my metaphor before I go on with it, I must say that among the works of poets writing in English, that of Dylan Thomas is by all odds the least reminiscent of the still air of a museum. And yet I am aware of no other poet whose work carries with it that sense of having encompassed the stratifications of human history, of possessing the past as well as the present, of having sounded again echoes that make the early darkness alive. And it is just this re-creation of the living past in the living present that distinguishes him as a poet, and which contributes largely to the wonder and astonishment with which American readers first encounter him. Although it is not always consciously felt, Americans more than any other people on earth have a basic need for assurances as to their identity. Our history is brief, and our national character, compounded of so many heterogeneous influences, still does not allow of definition. While we have created an American legend recognized by the rest of the world, we ourselves have little real association with it. Most Americans know in their hearts that the American dream is something in which they have but a small part. In spite of the success with which the American myth has been published at home as well as abroad, Americans long for that which other peoples take quite for granted—the simple signs of speech, of place, of character, and tradition that might tell them who they are. As a Welshman rooted deeply in his people and his land, Dylan Thomas speaks to us from sources we have lost, and we are drawn by his native accents with nostalgia and the excitement of vicarious participation.

'Other poets may win our attention when they write as analysts or as philosophical victims of the modern world, and may objectify for us the unexpressed thoughts and emotions that move us, but Dylan Thomas touches us alive, not only to our common dilemma in a violent age, but to our common humanity which in his poems is not merely proffered for contemplation, but recreated. He has made of the history in his bones a speech that we come upon with instantaneous enlightenment, as if the barriers of geography and time had fallen away. We know him and respond to what he says because he speaks to us as an ancient who has somehow survived the impositions of time.

'I do not want to imply that Dylan Thomas is a primitive, or that he is so regarded. We know—even without the evidence turned up by our critics and students of literature—that his poetry is the work of a man immersed not only in his own native history, but that it is the product of a sophisticated craftsman sharply aware of that literary tradition which his contribution both transforms and continues. We find in him not only the lyrical finesse and delicacy of the seventeenth century, but the vigour and breadth of Walt Whitman. For American readers this combination is irresistible. We read Whitman when we are young, and he implants in us a lively vision of democracy that persists as part of our belief. But as we grow older, we find less and less satisfaction in his qualities as an artist, and finally tend to remember him as a prophet rather than as a poet. On the other hand, we find that our youthful acquaintance with Donne and Marvell and Herrick and Crashaw grows into a loving knowledge. While Whitman, the laureate of large ideals, lies forgotten on the shelf, we read these earlier poets with new pleasure and are perhaps puzzled by the change that has come over us. When we read Dylan Thomas, then, we feel again not only the breadth and grandeur that Whitman once evoked, but that finely wrought music of the intellectual eye and ear which charms us back to the seventeenth century lyricists.

'In short, I believe we find a combination of democratic expression and aristocratic artistry which satisfies a dual need which we may not have consciously recognized.

'Beyond Whitman, the other major affinity of Dylan Thomas in American literature would, I think, be Herman Melville; and I believe that the recent rediscovery and revaluation of Melville as an American artist has been based upon quite the same premises as our response to Dylan Thomas. I have not the time to deal with similarities between the two men, but it would appear obvious to me that once the notion had been set before them, few readers would be unaware of the whole range of ideas, images, and historically encrusted metaphors which Dylan Thomas shares with the creator of *Moby Dick*. The liter-

94

ary obsession of both men is the confirmation of a basic human identity transcending the mutations of history—and in pursuit of this, both have written with a consciousness of time not as a sequence of events harking backwards and downwards, but as though history itself were a landscape surrounding the houses in which they lived.

'A further aspect of Dylan Thomas's poetry that appeals to Americans is the exotic unfamiliarity of its imagery. This is perhaps a lesser source of appeal, but an important one. While we think, as a rule, of the exotic as something rarefied and out of reach, and perhaps slightly bogus, the exotic in Dylan Thomas's poems is something that intrigues and charms us because we have every confidence that he is giving us a vision of the world he sees and knows, and that only by the accidents of time and place are we ourselves prevented from confirming the reality of his observations. It has been most revealing to me, for instance, to recognize in Wales something I had known previously only as part of a poem.

'The tangency of literary reality to observed reality is an unimportant consideration in the work of a poet since, after all, in the writing of every poem he is concerned with creating an artifact. But in spite of that critical understanding, we are always delighted when some slight contact with the scene of a poem or a story throws new light on what we felt we had completely known. For years a particular image from one of Dylan Thomas's poems has always pleased me immensely—and that image is, "the heron-priested shore." To me it has always conjured up a druidical series of tall birds standing as if in performance of some ritual along a water's edge. The picture I saw was large and quite pleasantly satisfying as a glimpse of far-away Wales, but since I had never actually seen a heron in its natural state, my experience of this image was, without my ever knowing it, quite vague and limited. But now that I have seen herons along the very shore where Thomas sees them, I am delighted to find that while my first impression has a literary validity, my new impression is based upon the observation that herons *do* stand in sacerdotal attitudes, as if they were perpetually extending bene-

95

dictions, and that, when they are surrounded by kittywakes and oyster-catchers, they do recall priests crowded about by parishioners. One could find hundreds of such instances in which observed reality expanded the literary reality, or transformed it —so that the point I want to make of my own experience is the fact that while so much of Dylan Thomas's world is strange to the American reader, and shut away from observation, he has invested that world with such conviction and presented it so soundly that we accept his most exotic images with absolute confidence that they do not only grace the iconography of his poems but that they are generic to the landscape of his country. As he himself has written:

> 'Who in these labyrinths,
> This tidethread and the lane of scales,
> Twine in a moon-blown shell,
> Escapes to the flat cities' sails
> Furled on the fishes' house and hell,
> Nor falls to His green myths?
> Stretch the salt photographs,
> The landscape grief, love in His oils
> Mirror from man to whale
> That the green child see like a grail
> Through veil and fin and fire and coil
> Time on the canvas paths.

'In speaking of Dylan Thomas's influence on poetry written in America, I believe I can say that it has been profound, but that its real force is somewhat difficult to measure. He has been widely imitated, of course, but almost always with disastrous consequence—and I believe this is so because his methods, which offer many possibilities for approximation in texture and rhythm, simply cannot be seized upon and used to any worthy end. Rather, they must be earned in the same rigid process by which Thomas himself has achieved them—which is to say that his methods develop out of a way of discovering and interpreting areas of feeling in which rhythm and texture are determined by the quality of perception. American imitations, as a rule, have

96

seemed synthetic and manufactured because they have been conceived out of a purely literary experience, whereas Thomas's own poems are conceived out of the living experience of a deeply known time and place.

'It is my own impression that Thomas's real influence is evident in what American poets do not do, or in what they have given up. Since his arrival on the literary scene there has been a great decrease in didacticism in American poetry, a newly recovered awareness of the plasticity of the English language, and, most important, a new realization that the individual psyche can be creatively plumbed. He has shown us that exploration of the inner world of the individual need not result in the pale and rarefied poetry we used to label as "ivory tower," but that the universal lies deep within the individual and invites his resourcefulness.

'Since all American readers of poetry know Thomas, contemporary standards of judgment have of course been affected by his career. Our best American poets are quite unlike him, but none of them writes without having first taken into account his innovations or without studying the masterful way in which he has himself assimilated strong literary influences.

'It will be years before the breadth of his impact on American poetry can be adequately measured, but there is no question of the tremendous response he evokes from American readers. When he came to the States last year, his progress across the continent was marked by the kind of reception which, in the nineteenth century, would have been described as "a triumphal tour." He travelled for three months, reading his poems in colleges and universities and literary societies from Florida to Vancouver and from Los Angeles to Boston, and I do believe that, had he the endurance, he could very well be travelling in America still. As one American poet expressed it, his presence was "a Dionysian experience for the academies." In a time when nearly all our poets are tamed by scholarship and professional respectability as teachers or editors or librarians, when our representative poetry is careful, learned, but quite immovably anchored to acceptable forms and intellectual clichés, his readings and his personality struck us with delight and surprise. We had, for lack of evidence, almost forgotten that, even in our day, poetry and the poet could be possessed of that daemonic character which so disturbed Plato, but which has none the less survived as one of the happier legends of western culture. With Dylan Thomas we have recovered much that we had believed lost, and I know that many Americans share with me the wonder that proceeds from the fact that in our time the voice that speaks to us most clearly comes—not from among skyscrapers or from the great plains or from the wide new cities of the West—but from a little village quite settled in its silence on the far shores of Wales.'

When I had finished reading, Dylan said, as if he were quoting a newspaper headline: 'Randy-dandy Curly-girly Poet Leaps into Sea from Overdose of Praise,' and made as if to throw himself over the sea-wall. 'All there is for me to do now is disappear,' he said. 'I didn't know you thought I was *that* good.' When Caitlin said she liked the piece, lunch ended in the first general good feeling since the beginning of our visit.

As Bill took his camera and was about to set off on a tour of the village, Dylan asked me if I would mind coming to the studio to hear some of his new poems. Taking two bottles of ale with us, we climbed through the brambled garden, walked along the upper wall from which we could see the great esses the tide left in the estuary, the 'scummed, starfish sands/With their fishwife cross/Gulls, pipers, cockles, and sails,' and went into the studio. He first read 'In the White Giant's Thigh,' then 'Poem for His Birthday.' His reading in private, while naturally less loud, was fully as rich and dramatic as in public. His professional attitude toward each poem as a text to be communicated dissolved any feeling of embarrassment that might have touched so intimate a performance. Then he scrawled the inscription, 'To dear John from cheap Dylan, with love,' across the bottom of a typewritten copy of a poem he was going to use as a prologue to the new English and American editions of his *Collected Poems*, and asked me to read it. But first he would have to point out the rhyme scheme, which he did not think anyone would notice without careful study. The first line of the first section rhymed with the last line of the second section—with one hundred other lines between; the second line of the first section with the second last line of the second section, and so on until lines fifty-one and fifty-two formed the only rhymed couplet in the poem. When I expressed amazement at the intricacy of this scheme, Dylan said: 'As a matter of fact, the poem began as a letter to you.' 'What happened to the letter?' I asked. 'I just kept the idea and some of the images and went on with the poem instead.' I told him I was pleased, naturally, that the letter had proved such an inspiration, and suggested, a little caustically, that he write more often, if only as a means of finding his way into new poems.

He had finished another poem, still untitled, which he had written for his father, who, he felt, had but little time to live. It began: 'Do not go gentle into that good night.' I asked him if he had shown the poem to his father. He had not, he said, but hoped he would have the courage to read it to him very soon. What he most wanted me to hear were fragments of a 'kind of play for voices' he was thinking about. This would be called 'Llareggub Hill' (the first word can be read backwards), and was to be a dramatic poem on the life of a Welsh village very much like Laugharne. It would have no conventional dramatic continuity, but would consist of an interweaving of many voices, with the strong central voice of a narrator to supply the unities of time, place, and situation. He then read me the section that revealed Captain Cat speaking the dreams that take him back to a life at sea. This was one of the fragments that was to be expanded into his last work, *Under Milk Wood*.

We began to speak of working methods. I had noticed that on many of his manuscripts Dylan would add a single word or a phrase, or a new punctuation, then recopy the whole poem in longhand. When another addition or revision was made, no matter how minor or major, he would then copy the whole poem again. When I asked him about this laborious repetition, he showed me his drafts of 'Fern Hill.' There were more than two hundred separate and distinct versions of the poem. It was, he explained, his way of 'keeping the poem together,' so that its process of growth was like that of an organism. He began almost every poem merely with some phrase he had carried about in his head. If this phrase was right, which is to say, if it were resonant or pregnant, it would suggest another phrase. In this way a poem would 'accumulate.' Once 'given' a word (sometimes the prime movers of poems were the words of other poems or mere words of the dictionary that called out to be 'set') or a phrase or a line (or whatever it is that is 'given' when there is yet a poem to 'prove') he could often envision it or 'locate' it within a pattern of other words or phrases or lines that, not given, had yet to be discovered: so that sometimes it would be possible to surmise accurately that the 'given' unit would occur near the end of the poem or near the beginning or near the middle or somewhere between.

He had picked up somewhere a notion that he liked: poems are hypothetical and theorematic. In this view the hypothesis of a poem would be the emotional experience, the instant of vision or insight, the source of radiance, the minute focal point of impulse and impression. While these make up what is commonly called inspiration, poetic logic should prove the validity of the ephemeral moments they describe. To look at a new poem, then, is to ask: How successfully does it demonstrate its hypothesis?

About the reading of poetry, he felt that only perusal of the printed page—or perhaps the interior critical monologue, or private discussion—could give to each poem the full concentrated time that any poem is justified in asking for the assessment of its success or failure to demonstrate its own hypothesis. In public only the poem itself can be presented, and there its effect depends upon the immediacy with which the hypothesis, the moment and motive of inspiration, can affect the reader through his ear. In other words, and as he was later fond of saying, the printed page is the place in which to examine the works of a poem, the platform the place in which to give the poem the works.

There was one line in 'Fern Hill,' he said, that embarrassed him. He felt he should not have allowed the poem to be published until the line had been excised in favour of a better one. But months of thinking how to change it had led nowhere. When I asked him what the offending line was, he gave me a copy of the poem and asked me to pick it out. I could not. Then he pointed to the passage,

> And honoured among foxes and pheasants by the gay house
> Under the new made clouds and happy as the heart was long,
>   In the sun born over and over,
>   I ran my heedless ways...

and said with a sneer, *'ran* my *heed*less ways!—that's bloody bad.'

Our talk rambled then, but I remember clearly Dylan saying that now, finally, he was determined to write only 'happy poems.' But that was a great trouble—it was so very much more difficult to write a poem happy in sentiment rather than tragic and still manage to have it come out believable and good. He was absorbed in this notion, I could see, but also troubled. Implicitly, he was saying what many of his poems had already said: that his wisdom was the perception of joy—an insight so comprehensive and instantaneous that the meaning of joy is defined not as a relative state of human emotion but as another name for life itself. Yet there was little joy in his face as he thumbed hesitantly through a clutter of unfinished manuscripts, and little conviction in his voice as he spoke of his writing plans. At last, as if to conclude our visit, he said that his aim now was to produce 'poems in praise of God's world by a man who doesn't believe in God.'

Stepping out of the shack into twilight, we went into the village to the hotel to drink bitter in Ivy Williams's kitchen and play nap with her and two villagers who dropped by. This was a card game; our stakes were big black pennies; a winning hand seldom resulted in a gain of more than sixpence. When we had played for about an hour, Caitlin came in. She had been across the street to visit Dylan's parents who, she reported to the company, were outspoken in praise for 'Dylan's nice American friends.' They had naturally expected that Americans would be coarse and loud, she said, but felt that these two were 'gentle-men.' Still uneasy in the circumstances of the weekend, I was more pleased that Caitlin should want to repeat the sentiment than by the sentiment itself.

Dylan was reluctant to leave the card-table, but after some urging Caitlin got him to leave the game and start for home. It was late evening, calm and starlit, when we reached the Boat House. Dylan said he was too sleepy for supper. Since Bill and I were departing early in the morning, we said good-bye to him with some mention of a possible meeting a few days hence in London or a few weeks hence in Paris. After shaking hands with us in the sad-eyed, apologetic, winning way with which I was now familiar, he went off to bed. Sitting down to our final meal with Caitlin, Bill and I were apprehensive, but we need not have been. We soon talked at ease in the blue glow of the grate fire; Caitlin even spoke of coming to America, as if that was what she most had had in mind all along.

Next morning we were up at five. Caitlin gave us toast and tea, and in a warm farewell that seemed to cancel all our mutual misgivings, we carried our bags up the stony garden path and waved to her from the high gate. A hired car was waiting for us at the end of the sea-wall. We drove through shining morning mist to Carmarthen and boarded a train for London.

I recorded my talk for the B.B.C. at Broadcasting House on the following day, and later spoke with Dylan by phone. He felt quite confident now that Caitlin would agree to come to America in the late winter, and told me to go full speed ahead in making engagements at the Poetry Center and elsewhere. The main idea this time would not be to make money to bring back to Wales, but to earn just enough in reading fees to keep them comfortably in their travels and to allow them one full free month in a place that was sure to be warm, perhaps Florida, perhaps California.

I sent him letters from Italy, where I stayed until early September, and found an answer from him at American Express in Paris just before I sailed for home:

Dear John,

A very brief note of apology and affection. Your letter, waiting for me in John Davenport's, I mislaid, and now don't know where you'll be or when, for a moment, you may come to London. But from your littler letter I see you will call at the American Express, Paris, around Sept. 1-4. I *do* hope this will find you then. And I *am* so sorry that I couldn't get up to London after you left Laugharne, and that I lost your letter, and that I haven't written. I've been in a mess about money, and, in London, about trying to fix a film-job for the winter. Caitlin has mumps, badly, and oh! oh! oh! I'm vague and distressed about me and poems and Laugharne and London—and the States. But, of course, I'll be there for the Columbia date on January 30. I hope, very much, we can meet in London before you return: I want to ask you about these dates, about what sort of poetry you think I should read, what kind of prose I should write for the several occasions. Also, I should very much like to see you again, before next January.

I hope you didn't have too muddled a time down here. Regards to Bill.

Please write soon, if ever you get this, and I'll write back fully. Try to make London.

Caitlin sends you her love. And I send mine.

DYLAN.

As much as it would have pleased me to meet him in London, I had to hold to my sailing reservation from Cherbourg in order to be home in time for the beginning of my classes at the University of Connecticut. Before I sailed I sent him a note, promising to take up at length all the bothersome matters in which I might be helpful just as soon as I was back at my desk. While I subsequently sent him several such letters from Cambridge, where I had taken an apartment after giving up my house in Westport, I heard nothing at all from Dylan until early in December. His letter came from a new address, in Camden Town, a crowded poor district of London. During my visit to Wales, I remembered, there had been some talk of their moving up to London, mainly to spare Caitlin the rigours of another winter in wet, cold Laugharne, but of this I had heard nothing further.

54 Delancey Street
Camden Town
London, N.W.1
3.12.51

DEAR JOHN,

Your letter just forwarded from Laugharne to our new London house of horror on bus and nightlorry route and opposite railway bridge and shunting station. No herons here.

Your letter, just read, has scared the lights out of me. First date in N.Y. January 23rd? I'll have to look lively. I'll also have to look like hell for money (£100) to keep girl and family here while Caitlin and I are junketing abroad.

Questions and answers:

(1) How long do we plan to stay? Between two and three months.

(2) Do we want to confine our movements to east and middle west or do we also want to go to the west coast? We certainly want to go to California, after the other dates you have arranged. Ruth Witt-Diamant, of San Francisco, has recently written asking us the same question, or roughly the same. She says she will, given due warning, be able to arrange some San Francisco readings. I am sure that Hunter Lewis, of B.C. University, Vancouver, would also invite me again. He said so in a letter this year.

(3) I don't think Florida for a month. A California month (or less) for us after New York. And then New York at the end again. I would, incidentally, like to go to Washington. Would that club like me again? The shirtless Biddles have invited Caitlin and me to stay with them there.

(4) Yes, yes, yes. I *do* want you please to be my guide and agent.

On to other things. Oscar Williams, in his last letter to me, said that a group of mid-western universities were getting together to invite me for a jolly week with them at a figure like one thousand dollars. He did mention mid February, but I see that that now conflicts with my prearranged New York commitments. I shall write to him to-day; but do you think you could also get in touch with him and find out if the date—if it is a real date—can be moved to end of February or first of March. Then we could go on to S. Francisco in March sometime. I could leave Caitlin there while I went anywhere else on Pacific Coast where I was invited.

104

The Socialist Party in New York City have written to me to ask for a poetry reading. They say they're a small body (like me) and can't pay much at all, but I would like to do it for them if you can arrange it.

Next things you want to know: (1) Visa. I haven't got one yet. My passport is left in Laugharne, and I will try to go down and get it at the end of this week. Before I get the visa, I am almost certain to need—as before—papers from you explaining the purpose of my visit to the States and instancing some of my more worthy-looking engagements. Perhaps, if easily and quickly obtained by you, a letter from Columbia to you about me, from the Center and from anywhere important else, would considerably help. Anyway, let me have some official papers of confirmation to show the scared baiters in power here.

(2) I have made no ship reservations for Cat and me, not knowing when I was due in New York. I'll try to do this this week early, following your instructions about getting the steamship line to have their New York office contact you at once at Poetry Center for payment.

(3) Caitlin will be coming with me, but *not* the baby.

(4) It's okay to say to the New School I'll do them a second programme of dramatic readings.

Now to *my* questions. What sort of poetry, d'you think, most of my sponsors would like me to read! Modern? Including modern American, or is that presumptuous? Blake, Keats, Donne, Hopkins, Owen? And what about 'dramatic excerpts'? Marlowe, Shakespeare, Webster, Tourneur, Beddoes? Do tell me what, from your previous experience of 'my audience,' they most would like from me. I don't want to read too much of my own, except for a few recent ones. Laughlin, by the way, is bringing out a pamphlet of my new poems for my visit.

What news of Sarah? I hope, God bless her, she's in Mexico.

How are *you?* How goes Sidney G.? He was moaning for weeks about his companions, Raine and Gascoyne. 'Och, there'll be wee orgies with those two sparocks.'

I'll get this off straightaway, without any news or affection; and will see about steamer bookings and visas *very quickly.*

Please you write quickly, too; and do let me know your suggestions as to the contents of my programmes. And do something about West Coast. That's what Caitlin wants most.

Love,

DYLAN.

105

P.S. Mebbe, after all, a bit of Florida would be good, if possible. Miami? Gainesville first, and then Miami?

P .P .S. A very important point I forgot. If we're to spend one whole month in New York *in an hotel*, we'll be desperately broke. Is there anyone who would put us up for, say, a week while we look around for someone else to put us up for the next week, and so on? It's really important. The money I earn we want for the sights, not for board. Can you delicately hint around?

P.P.P.S. I'm writing to-day to Ruth Witt-Diamant, but perhaps you could write as well to see what, if anything, she has done.

D.

Encouraged by this unusually business-like letter, free at last from doubts that he might not come to America at all, I went ahead to line up a long series of engagements that would take him from coast to coast. While correspondence for this took a great amount of time and led me into a maze of paper-work from which, at times, I felt I would never emerge, it was not unrewarding. I was warmed to find that everyone wanted to hear Dylan read, and that I had but to mention that he was coming, to someone in Washington, perhaps, or Missouri, or New Hampshire, in order to put arrangements into motion. Within a month, having meanwhile reported to him on the progress of my activities, I received another letter.

6 January 1952.

Dear John,

Thank you for your two letters, official and not.

Thomas Cook have just written to me to say you've paid for Caitlin's and my passage on the *Queen Mary* on January 15. Thank you. I only hope to the Lord I can make it. The difficulty is over my visa. The American Consulate would not revalidate it until they had 'investigated' me. They're presumably in the process of doing that now. The snag seemed to be a visit I paid to Prague in 1949—the year *before* I came to the States last. I'm hoping to get the visa this week. Do you know anyone important your end who'd say a word to the Embassy, or Consulate, that I'm not a dangerous Red? I'll be seeing a British Foreign Office man myself to-morrow. But perhaps everything will work out okay. It's just that there's such very little time. If the worst comes to the worst, and my visa is withheld *after* the 15th, I'll cable. I'll cable you, anyway, if the *Queen Mary* sails with us. Will you meet us? Please?

Any hope of accommodation yet—or should we stay in a hotel for the first part of our visit? Heard from Ruth Witt-Diamant about possible Californian readings?

I must read Lear again: haven't looked at it for years.

I enclose a letter from McGill University, Montreal. This letter seems, to me, to mean that McGill is prepared to transport me (I suppose at a good fee) all the way from Wales to Montreal. And (I suppose) back. They seem to know nothing about my coming to the States in January. *So*: as my transportation from New York to Montreal will be so much less than from Wales to Montreal, the fee, surely, must be commensurately (or proportionately, I don't know the words) increased. I've written to Storrs McCall saying, 'Yes, delighted,' and that I'd be in New York the end of January. I told him that you would be getting in touch with him as you, and you only, knew what my New York commitments were, and when. Will you write to him, quickly? And as I don't particularly want to go to Montreal, soak McGill for twice (at least) as much as I get in the States—plus, of course, full expenses *by air*.

I'll be cabling you. Keep your fingers crossed for us.

I'm looking forward, a lot, to seeing you. And I hope I can.

Cat got her visa straightaway.

LOVE,

DYLAN.

I sent a quick reply, asking Dylan to be sure to cable me as soon as visa difficulties were overcome and their departure assured. If they *did* manage to get aboard the *Queen Mary* on the scheduled date, I would, I promised, meet them in New York with a red carpet. I heard nothing until 16th January, the day after their scheduled sailing, when the following radiogram from the *Queen Mary* arrived: 'See You Pier 90 Sunday Bring Carpet Love Dylan Caitlin.'

On Sunday, the 20th, I got up at dawn, drove from Boston to New York and arrived at Pier 90 with a small square of royal red carpet and a box of gardenias. The *Queen Mary* was just being edged into her berth. Without a visitor's permit that would have allowed me to join them at baggage examination, I waited in the crowd pressing against wooden barriers outside the waiting-room. David Lougée and Stanley Moss, also on hand to welcome the Thomases, joined me. After two cold hours of waiting, we finally sighted them—Dylan in the great bulky brown parka that gave him the appearance of an errant koala bear, Caitlin looking like a character out of *Anna Karenina* in a black fur hat, carrying a big fur muff, and wearing fur-tipped boots. After general embracing in the noisy daze of the pier, the presentation of a box of Dylan's favourite cigars from David, and my welcoming carpet and gardenias, we arranged to have their bags and trunk taken care of, and put them into a taxi.

It was my plan, readily agreed to by Dylan and Caitlin, to take them into the country for a couple of days—to Millbrook, New York, where we would stay with my friend Rollie Mc-Kenna, the photographer, and where we could at leisure go over details of the new reading tour. But first we had to have a drink to welcome Caitlin to America; we converged on the bar of the Winslow Hotel, on Madison Avenue. Through all of this Caitlin was almost totally silent. When she did speak, she said she felt dizzy, and I sensed that she was a little frightened. Dylan seemed in bright-eyed good health, chuckling and beaming, in spite of his having been seasick for nearly three days. Toward Caitlin he was sensitively deferential and solicitous in a way I had not previously observed. Aware, perhaps, of her lack of ease in being shunted so swiftly into America and into a group of strangers who were Dylan's friends, he showed every sign that his first thoughts were of her. It was the only time I had ever seen them together when the amenities of a husband-and-wife relationship were apparent. While his open concern for her to be happy in what she saw and in whom she met was almost childishly intense, this attitude showed him in a most attractive new light. My experience in Laugharne had led me, at times, to face their coming to America with dread. It was a relief now to see them so transformed, and I hoped for the best.

Caitlin's first question, as we sat in the darkly mirrored light of the Winslow Bar, was: 'Is this a posh bar?' We could only say no, not really, that we had chosen it because it was convenient and uncrowded. For the rest of the hour she was content simply to listen to the conversation which, once the wave of welcome had passed over, became rather spiritless.

Taking leave of the group, we got in my car, headed toward the West Side Highway, and drove out of the city under wintry slate-grey skies. Dylan pointed out the sights of Riverside Drive to Caitlin with an almost proprietary sense of New York. She looked upon them with a bemused air but said little. Halfway to Millbrook we stopped at a rustic tavern decorated indiscriminately with touches of Indian and woodsmen's *décor*. Dylan went directly toward the juke-box with a handful of nickels, ordered super-hamburgers for himself and Caitlin, and made sure that she noticed all of the decorations—the Navajo rugs, the deer's heads, the rough-hewn beams, and the red-spoked wagon-wheels. She was astonished at the size of the hamburgers, charmed by the enveloping music and the stagy *décor* of the place, and said she was at last beginning to feel that she was in America.

As we continued on in early dusk through a rolling landscape that showed patches of a recent snowstorm, Caitlin smoked constantly and played the car radio, a gadget which seemed to delight her. I learned that they had been commissioned to do a book of impressions of America, that they had been advanced a considerable sum of money for this, and that Caitlin, rather than Dylan, was going to do most of the work by keeping a careful day-by-day journal. When I asked about his parents, Dylan said that he was worried about his father who, he felt, was now failing rapidly. I showed them photographs Bill Read and I had taken in Laugharne; Caitlin was especially happy with those of Colm and asked me if she might be able to get a dozen copies. Both of them spoke with dislike of their house in Camden Town, and said they were glad to be out of it for good: on their return they would go directly back to Laugharne. But this was still far off, since they had decided to stay in America until about the middle of May.

Now the landscape through which we drove was completely covered with snow. We arrived in Millbrook about seven-thirty

109

to be greeted by Rollie and a little pack of enthusiastic dogs. She led us into a big room glowing with fire-light on brass and polished leather and set us down to Old Fashioneds. When Caitlin shortly disappeared into her room, Dylan and I talked a bit about plans and possibilities. He was ready to go everywhere and anywhere, and told me to put no limit at all on the number of engagements he might be able to work into his schedule. We had dinner in a room lighted from within by candles and, from without, by the dramatic shine of floodlights on the snow. Afterwards we listened to Bartók and New Orleans jazz for a while, and went early to bed.

We awoke early next morning to unbearably brilliant sunlight reflected on endless fields of snow. As we sat down to breakfast about eight, I noticed that Caitlin again wore the look of expectation and trepidation I had first noticed on Pier 90. While she had gradually joined in conversation the previous evening, she was now silent again in spite of our attempts to draw her into general talk, and soon left us to return to her room and get on with her journal. Dylan and I went out of doors with Rollie, who was hoping for a portrait of him she might include in the gallery of poets the Poetry Center had commissioned her to collect. While the dry, searing cold, and winds that knifed about the house and barns could only be endured for minutes at a time, Dylan was a good subject and a patient one. The finest photograph of that morning shows him wound in the bare branches of a heavy vine that climbed the front of the house. We went yelping back to the fire then, gradually warming up as we drank beer out of cans and talked in a random way of all that was ahead of us.

Since the day was so beautifully bright, we decided to drive out into the snowy landscape for lunch somewhere. Dylan wanted to know if there were a Howard Johnson restaurant near by. He felt Caitlin should be introduced to that particular aspect of America. Since there was one on the outskirts of Poughkeepsie, only fifteen miles away, we drove there at once to eat frankforts, hamburgers, and several of the twenty-six chromatic varieties of ice-cream. The restaurant was only half a mile from the Vassar

110

College campus. Since Rollie was an alumna, and I, as a former teacher there, had my own associations with the place, we felt we should take the opportunity of introducing Caitlin to her first American college. We drove like spies through the winding roads of the campus, almost hoping to be spotted and hailed by one of the more alert English majors. If my memory of Vassar enthusiasm for Dylan was true, his presence there, if discovered, would have provoked a riot. But we edged through the chilled, blue-jeaned multitudes without being recognized. Caitlin was outraged by the costumes of the Vassar girls and could not accept our explanations about the collegiate fad of the casual. 'Ridiculous!' she said, 'they look like intellectual witches.'

We drove on to Hyde Park for a distant sight of the Roosevelt estate and a visit to the Vanderbilt Mansion. But when the latter was 'Closed on Monday,' as we learned from a sign, we retreated to Rhinebeck, to a 'coach-house tavern' full of horse brasses, decorative harness, and hitching posts serving as coat-hangers. Caitlin played the juke-box and Dylan the pin-ball machine between drinks, and we drove in good spirits back to Millbrook, where Caitlin disappeared until mid evening, presumably to work on her journal, the demands of which at this mere threshold of her visit seemed curiously absorbing.

Rollie had invited to dinner old friends of hers and mine, a husband and wife who were both professors. When they arrived in the early evening, Caitlin remained in her room while we had cocktails. Dylan was affable, outgoing, easily monopolizing conversation with a flow of sometimes hilarious self-deprecatory remarks and stories. When Caitlin finally descended some time after eight o'clock, she acknowledged her introduction to the guests, then took a chair in a corner of the room and sat silently drawing caricatures of the company. Now and then she would take Dylan aside to whisper something to him, but otherwise seemed to want to remain withdrawn. To break the little spell of ill ease, brought on by her refusal to join us, I put some records on the turn-table and asked her if she would care to dance. She accepted without hesitation and put down her drawings. We pushed the bearskin rug away from the fire-place and danced on

111

the waxed-brick flooring. The others, including Dylan, followed suit, and we were more or less of one spirit when, after half an hour of assorted fox-trots, rhumbas, and waltzes, we sat down to dinner. Dylan was full of stories during the meal, but could relate few of them without interruptions from Caitlin who now, it seemed to me, was fully self-possessed in a situation she relished. She offered corrected versions of his narratives, stoutly denied the truth of some of them altogether, and otherwise managed in nearly every case to have the final say. When Dylan asked a serious question about some aspect of teaching at the college where our friend was chairman of the history department, he was being answered seriously when Caitlin intruded with: 'And are they all stuffed shirts like yourself?' Everyone pretended not to have heard this and Dylan took off on another story as we went back to the fire-place for coffee. During the rest of the evening Caitlin again stayed in her retreat in a corner of the room, drawing new caricatures, then fingering, preoccupied, through a stack of fashion magazines. After our friends left about midnight, I said good-bye to her and Dylan, promising to meet them in New York two days later.

They drove into Manhattan with Rollie the next day and took a room at the Hotel Earle. When I joined them there, our first item of business was to find a suitable apartment for their stay in the city. But we made little progress in looking into this problem because both Dylan and Caitlin were wan and shaky from a disastrous evening before. They had, I learned with something not far from stupefaction, been to dinner with Dylan's old *inamorata*, Doris, and things had gone badly—so badly that when the meal was over Doris lay in a state of collapse in her boudoir. They had made a round of Village bars until well on into the morning. As we were lackadaisically discussing ways and means, Loren McIver and Lloyd Frankenberg came by. We all went out together then, bought half a dozen newspapers in which to peruse classified advertisements, and stopped in at a bar on Sixth Avenue. Taking turns phoning to inquire about advertised possibilities, we turned up discouragingly few. Finally someone remembered that the Hotel Chelsea had one-room kitchenette apartments. Loren went along with Caitlin to inspect one of them, and they returned shortly to say that it looked like just the thing. Dylan said they could move in that very evening.

I felt they were well launched into their American adventure now, and I hoped that they had some real sense of the plans I had outlined to them. In any case, I resolved to see them only when practical matters of money and schedule made meeting necessary—at least until opportunities arose when I could again see them on terms more propitious to friendship. I enjoyed being with them, in spite of my feeling that a long time would elapse before Caitlin and I could meet in mutual confidence. But on the days when Dylan had no schedule to follow, our time was apt to pass in a maundering series of bar-room visits. Dylan seemed to enjoy gregariousness for its own sake. While I could not be sure of Caitlin's reaction to a constant circle of strangers, she seldom refused to accompany Dylan on the daily junkets in which he criss-crossed the Village. But long days of this tended to wear me out, caused me to neglect appointments and to fall behind in my work. During the next week or so I dropped in at the Chelsea a couple of times, but only to fill in some new page of Dylan's travel diary, or to supply them with money which, inevitably, but rather too soon for the resources of my pocket-book, had again become a primary problem. Since they had arrived penniless, their publishers' advance having been spent to take care of matters at home, I had supplied the few hundred dollars they felt would be needed to see them through the period when Dylan would be earning nothing. This sum vanished within two or three days. Caught short of cash, I was able to give them only seventy-five dollars one evening, promising to turn up at lunch the next day with more. By that time the seventy-five dollars had vanished too. Curious as to how that amount could have been spent between late afternoon of one day and lunch of the next, especially when they knew that I was now as penniless as they, I asked Dylan what had happened to it. He said he was puzzled himself. They had gone out to dinner with a small group, but he could not remember if he or someone else had paid the bill. In any case, the money was gone and they were again flat broke. Since I had paid the Chelsea hotel bill for a month in advance, I was able to cash my own university salary cheque with the management and to leave them newly supplied. But this little episode had made me fearful. Dylan was due to make a substantial sum of money on the coming tour, but if their living was to cost, as it already had, one hundred dollars per day, even several engagements a week would not bring in enough to see them through.

On the night before his first reading, I came by at Dylan's somewhat nervous insistence to discuss the choice of poems he would read. Caitlin, in negligee, worked on her journal which, I noted, was already voluminous. Still not having recovered from a day-long hang-over, Dylan was in bed. We spread out a sheaf of poems on the bed-covers and, one by one, made a selection and fixed them in reading order. When I called for him the next night, I found him blue, sober, petrified anew at the thought of having to face an audience. We taxied uptown, Caitlin silent, Dylan writhing, wishing it were all over with, asking for my assurance that we had chosen the right poems, wishing we could stop for one final drink. The Poetry Center auditorium was packed, with a crowd milling about the box office hoping for last-minute cancellations. Just before programme time Dylan asked for beer, and a bottle was brought in by one of the ushers. I was standing beside him and Caitlin in the darkened wings, and was about to step on to the stage to introduce him, when I heard Caitlin say: 'Just remember, they're all dirt!' While she probably meant this as a kind of encouragement, Dylan took exception to the remark and countered with something I could not hear. A whispered, high-pitched argument ensued, but the next minute Dylan was on stage. A roar of applause that seemed as if it would never die down kept him standing, beaming, nodding humbly for nearly two minutes. Besides a group of his own new poems, his programme that night included selections from Louis MacNeice, William Plomer, D. H. Lawrence, Edith Sitwell, W. H. Auden, W. B. Yeats, and his own hilarious imitation of T. S. Eliot's voice in a reading of Henry Reed's parody of

114

'Four Quartets,' a poem entitled 'Chard Whitlow.'

Somewhere in this series of brief, harried visits, I had at Caitlin's request promised to spend a day with her and Dylan when we could forget all about schedules and engagements and simply look at some of the sights of New York. Her own movements, she said, had been almost wholly confined to 23rd Street, except when she and Dylan went out to a Village bar or were escorted to a party somewhere. Finally a likely day arrived, and I joined them at the Chelsea on a bright, cold morning, ready to follow their inclinations. After a stroll into the Village that left our hands and ears nipped with cold, we went on Dylan's suggestion to the White Horse Tavern on Hudson Street for lunch. This place, to which English friends had introduced him, had become his favourite rendezvous, much to the pleasure of its proprietor, who found his business doubled by the many people—friends and mere 'ardents'—who would assemble there at all hours in the chance that Dylan might turn up. This wave of prosperity at 'the Horse,' as it came to be called, was to continue until Dylan's death.

We stayed drinking at the White Horse which, in *décor* and atmosphere, is very likely as close an approximation to a London pub as any other bar in New York, until mid afternoon. By this time, whatever appetite for mere sightseeing either Dylan or Caitlin might have set out with had become quite dissipated. We decided, rather wanly, to go to the Radio City Music Hall. After sitting through an interminable movie about the circus, our spirits picked up with the appearance of the robot-like Rockettes. Dylan marvelled, like any small-town tourist, at the inhuman precision of their movements, and even seemed to enjoy the rest of a gigantically florid presentation, including a scene in which scores of madly enthusiastic male singers descended from a ring of covered wagons to sing cowboy ballads around a camp-fire.

Then Caitlin said she would like to see the Rainbow Room; we went there to watch the lights of the skyscrapers in the early dark. But it had already been apparent for hours that there was no gaiety in our freedom of the city. Caitlin, only mildly participating in the outing she had herself suggested, seemed preoccupied, or shy, or in any case unwilling to give herself to our entertainments, or to this rare chance to be comfortably by ourselves. Dylan, continuously solicitous of her, nevertheless seemed not committed to this sort of tourist activity. A cocktail lounge was not his element and, even for Caitlin's sake, he could not disguise his restlessness to be somewhere else. When we stared down upon the fantastic lighted canyons, I realized sadly, almost hopelessly, that I was the only one who was interested, and that the lack of pleasure either Dylan or Caitlin showed was only to be expected. I felt like a museum guide who, enraptured by the painting he has been discussing, turns to find his audience gone.

As we were on our way toward the elevators, Dylan's name was called out, and we turned to find Arthur Koestler motioning us to a table where he was entertaining two friends. Caitlin was now outspokenly impatient to get on; we joined them only briefly. Dylan and Koestler exchanged gossip of mutual friends abroad, spoke with a professional toleration of the rigours of lecture-tour life, and then of the unique vertical beauty of New York at this hour. As we were getting up to leave, Koestler asked us all to come to his house in New Jersey for the following week-end. Dylan readily accepted the invitation and we said good-bye. In the crowded elevator, Caitlin said angrily that she had no intention of going to Arthur Koestler's for the week-end. Dylan said he hadn't either, but what else could he do but accept? Above the Rockefeller Plaza skating-rink I parted from them as we took separate cabs to separate appointments. I wondered again if we three would ever be able to spend more than an hour's time together without being overtaken by the disharmony we felt, the causes of which we could not or would not name.

Next afternoon, I again helped Dylan to make a selection and arrangement of poems for the night's reading at the Poetry Center. Caitlin had gone out shopping with a new friend, Rose Slivka, but had assured Dylan that she would be in the audience. Dinner was out of the question for Dylan, in spite of his not having had a morsel all day. Instead, and as usual, we settled for

116

a few glasses of beer in a 23rd Street bar. Our taxi ride uptown was again an anxious and unhappy progress as Dylan huddled into himself one minute and over-dramatized his distress the next. But his reading was superb, evoking a crescendo of applause and a chorus of bravos, and he had to return to the stage for two encores.

When he had politely pushed his way through a horde of autograph seekers in the reception lounge, we were joined by Caitlin and Rose, and an acquaintance who, having had Dylan's promise to join him after the reading, piloted us all to a little Greek night-club in mid town. There, in a twanging din of exotic instruments that made the slightest conversation impossible, we watched Attic folk-dancers from a long table made up of whoever had followed us from the Poetry Center. After a quick, probably pointless conference with Dylan in the cloakroom—the only part of the establishment where we could hear one another—I left to take a train for Boston.

With many people interested in entertaining them, and still greater numbers seeking to be entertained by them, Dylan and Caitlin were now guests of honour at one or more parties almost every night of the week. Caitlin spent a good part of every day wandering between 23rd and 34th Streets, shopping for clothing and presents for the children as Dylan, quite on his own, drifted back into his old day-long routine of Village bars. While money was not being spent at the rate of one hundred dollars per day, the amount I turned over to them at their request was frequently very little less. In spite of her long hours moseying about in the shops, Caitlin's purchases were comparatively few. On one occasion, as we were waiting for Dylan somewhere, she said she wanted to buy a portable radio for Llewelyn. The one she had in mind cost thirty-five dollars, she said, but Dylan felt this was extravagant and that they could not afford it. She wondered if I would give her the money without telling Dylan about it. I agreed, and this was to be our secret—along with any other amounts I might give her, especially in those periods when Dylan's absence from New York left her without funds to buy clothing or gifts.

117

With engagements in Washington, Baltimore, Montreal, and upper New York State, Dylan was continually in and out of the city now. Money had begun to come in fairly large sums, much to the relief of my own hard-pressed bank account, which, more than once, had to be supplemented with personal loans I would make and then turn over to Dylan.

One morning when I dropped by to deliver some railroad tickets, written travel directions, and a big new roll of ten-and twenty-dollar bills, I found Dylan in a state of almost immobile wretchedness. Supine on his bed, he was able to speak only in grunts and whines, punctuated by profane sighs and anguished moanings about the condition of his head. Caitlin worked on her journal as I made ineffectual attempts to get his mind on something besides his hang-over. As we sat there in a sort of sick-bed trance, the phone rang. Pulling himself up on one elbow, Dylan took the phone Caitlin handed to him. All at once his manner was comparatively bright and, I could see, deferential and co-operative. Then he put down the phone and slumped back on to the bed. 'It's a girl from *Time*. She wants an interview and I told her to come round. O God, I can't do it! I don't want to do it!' Caitlin looked up from her writing. 'Let Brinnin meet her downstairs and tell her you're too sick.' 'No,' he said, 'I'll go through with the bloody business. It's *Time*, after all.' I suggested I might arrange another date for him, but Dylan turned this down. In a few minutes she would be at the bar on the corner. 'Cat,' he said plaintively, 'you'll come with me? She'll take us to lunch. John? You'll come?' 'If you want me to.' 'You both come —she'll give us a posh lunch on *Time* magazine.' I helped him into his clothes and he went off to meet the interviewer, a Miss Berlin—who, I learned later, was the daughter of Irving Berlin —at the appointed bar. Caitlin and I joined them there shortly. Darkly pretty, with uneasily observant eyes, Miss Berlin asked few questions during our first minutes together but simply joined us in having Tom Collinses Dylan brought from the bar to the booth in which we sat. She asked us where we would like to have lunch. Since, beforehand, we had agreed that Cavanagh's, only a block away, would be the happiest choice, we

118

set off, Dylan stopping on the sidewalk to cough himself out of a paroxysm once or twice. We were elegantly ushered to the bar of the restaurant and, after a short wait, to a table.

There Miss Berlin became earnest: one question followed another. In a curiously giddy mood, Dylan began replying to those with a series of parodies of himself. No one who did not know him intimately would possibly have been able to separate fact from outrageous fiction. Nonplussed, Miss Berlin turned to me for corroboration or denials of some of his fancier flights. I felt I could only assent to the truth of everything he said, in the assumption that it was safer and more amusing to let him blow his little bubbles of nonsense than to intervene with the few sober facts I might supply. But I soon sensed that something in the situation had wakened in Dylan the old determination to reduce to absurdity everything on which the conversation touched. Some of his statements, utterly untrue, were of such a nature as to provide very spicy copy for the pages of any magazine. Thinking of possible consequences, and of the frankness which is sometimes one of the pleasures of *Time*, I began to be alarmed. I was not alone in this. Caitlin had begun openly to scold Dylan and not, this time, I realized, only because he was being cavalier and skittish in an essentially serious situation. At least one of the details of his life that he had already stated as truth intimately concerned her, and its implications were far more scandalous than possibly amusing. Since Miss Berlin now seemed to be accepting almost everything at face value, with but momentary and wordless appeals to me, I attempted to bring some balance into the situation. 'Dylan's in his naughty mood,' I said. 'If you'd like to talk with me later perhaps I can help you to separate some of the fact from the fiction.' I felt this was not enough to allay Miss Berlin's bewilderment, but soon, apparently realizing that conventional techniques would not do in this case, she gave up her professional approach and we settled down to our expensive lunch. While I wondered in some apprehension just what part of this fanciful autobiography would find its way into *Time*, my fears were groundless. No word of it ever appeared there.

My meetings with Dylan and Caitlin now occurred just once a week, when I went to New York for Poetry Center duties. We would go out to lunch, usually, but these occasions were never happy because I was always witness to some new chagrin I could not understand, and because I was always forced into being partisan toward some contention of Dylan's or Caitlin's in regard to which I was either genuinely indifferent or unwilling to commit myself. More than once I had to leave the luncheon table with attacks of migraine, the first signs of which Caitlin had learned to detect almost as soon as I could. Dylan was invariably harassed and depressed, always trying to outlive just one more hang-over, always caught in details of some appointment he did not want to keep, or had all but forgotten. But the unhappiest development of their visit had come about through loud and stormy scenes at parties where their private marital war had been needlessly opened to public view. I had witnessed one of these myself—an evening party, given in their honour. After watching their skirmishes, incredulous guests had abruptly departed from rooms littered with smashed glasses, overturned tables, and broken *objets d'art*, leaving their hostess in a state of hysteria as she contemplated her loss, part of which was a plaster section of the wall of her bedroom. When it became apparent that, for the Thomases, the scene of a party was but a likely new arena for mayhem, many potential hosts and hostesses quietly dropped their plans for entertaining the distinguished visitors.

As far as I could see, their only comparatively happy time in America so far were those few expectant hours following their disembarkation from the *Queen Mary*. Certainly they had not found here release from pressure and responsibility, or whatever it was between them that made their friends feel they held one another in a death-grip. Instead, their freedom to enjoy new experiences, new people, and perhaps a new sense of one another seemed only to have aggravated their old dilemma. Statements they had made to me or, for that matter, to anyone within earshot, proved their marriage was essentially a state of rivalry. Yet they must have known themselves what was apparent to others: that victory for either party could only lead to defeat for both. Nevertheless, the lengths to which each would go to find, or to press, an advantage was sometimes puerile, sometimes absurd, often intolerable to contemplate. To begin to understand Caitlin's resentful unhappiness, one would have to acknowledge her feeling that Dylan's great success in America had become just one more weight on the cross she had to bear.

Perhaps, I thought rather groundlessly, we would be more congenially together when they came to stay with me in Cambridge, where we could meet at leisure, and possibly find our way back to the comparative good feeling and intimacy of our first days. At the same time, having seen with my own wide eyes the physical and emotional damage in the aftermath of some of their already famous New York battles, I could not entirely put aside a touch of apprehension when I thought of them as house guests.

On 7th March, two days after he had read at Princeton where, I learned, a cavalcade of motor-cycled policemen had sirened Dylan to the lecture hall from his late train, I came home to Cambridge to find him and Caitlin moved into my apartment for a five-or six-day visit. I had but a few moments in which to greet them before they went off, accompanied by Bill Read, who escorted them to an auditorium at the Massachusetts Institute of Technology, on the campus of which my apartment is situated. My mother, who had welcomed them in my absence—and to whom I had carefully reported nothing of their extraordinary behaviour in New York—already found them both delightful. When they returned after Dylan's reading, we all sat down to dinner in a relaxed mood and Dylan ate probably the first full meal since his arrival more than a month previously. I had warned my mother that she should not be disappointed when Dylan would refuse to touch a morsel of the meal she had been at great pains to prepare. As Dylan praised one dish after another, consumed everything, and asked for second helpings, she glanced at me as if I were mad.

The evening's engagement was at the DeCordova Museum, in Lincoln, some twenty miles north and west of Boston. Caitlin

121

and I delivered Dylan into the care of the director of the Museum, and then, because she did not care to sit through another reading, drove about the snowy suburban countryside in darkness. Inevitably, she spoke of Dylan, of money troubles and now of a new dismay, the adulation of Americans which, since it was something she could not cope with or begin to understand—and would not accept for the simple homage it was— had loomed up as her inescapable and hateful Nemesis. She had come to feel like a camp-follower in America. For this she blamed both Dylan and his admirers. Because he merely doled out money to her, she said, she never had enough to buy much-needed clothing for their children, or to act independently of him in enjoying friends and entertainments of her own in New York. As a consequence she found herself in the same abhorrent position in which she lived at home—made worse now that she had nothing to do with her time but follow Dylan about and be swallowed up and silenced in the crowd surrounding him. She spoke calmly, almost winsomely, and, if not in confidence— since she had little gift for that—in an obvious trust that even my brief experience of her life with Dylan had shown me these feelings were justified. As we drove through back roads—waiting upon Dylan, as it were—at the same time that he was spotlighted before new hundreds of applauding listeners—it was impossible not to feel a sympathetic sense of the loneliness out of which she spoke, or not to read in her present distress the anguished story of many long years. Yet I knew that to go beyond sympathy in trying to understand the causes that predestined this unhappiness was but to be drawn into an abyss in which extravagance, poverty, infidelity, and a thousand evidences of incompatibility were but the surface signs of a fathomless dilemma.

We returned to the Museum in an hour or so and, guided by Richard Wilbur, the poet, and his wife, Charlee, drove on winding roads over wooded hills to a large house where a reception was about to be held. Warmed by whiskies, the late gathering soon became a full-fledged party as Dylan, talkative and bouncing, became its natural centre. My newly acute awareness of

Caitlin's pent-up feelings and suspicions as she watched Dylan magnetize every group kept me from participating. While I remained with her a good part of the time, trying without success to have her overcome her resistance to people whom I thought she might enjoy, our talk was listless because her attention was always centred on the group about Dylan. As he, and a young married woman he had just met for the first time, lingered on the edges of the company in a conversation which, obviously, they were both enjoying, Caitlin turned to me to ask: 'Who is that bitch with him now?' I began to tell her exactly who the young woman in question was, only to have her interrupt with: 'Does Dylan sleep with her?' Under a suspicion so unreal I knew then that nothing I could say would put her at ease, and so gave up trying to placate her. With the small zest I could muster, I made an attempt to join the party and the gaiety Dylan's presence had generated. But Caitlin soon decided it was time for us to leave. A suddenly gloomy little trio, we said good night. Driving back to Cambridge I was silent, listening to the bickering that now seemed to be the only epilogue to evenings like this.

The next day, a Saturday, we had planned—in a mood of naive expectation of which we were still curiously capable—as another rare 'day to ourselves.' The morning passed pleasantly and lazily over a long breakfast, and I hoped for the best as, a little after noon, we set out for a leisurely exploration of the North Shore and a sight of the sea. Impeded all the way by long lines of traffic, we soon succumbed to the greyness of the day and the dreariness of the dirty March landscape. All that we had had in mind to see became too much effort. After nearly three hours of frustrated milling about we went to a restaurant in Salem for lobster, found the place overheated and the service bad, and hurried back to Boston. There a happier prospect, at least in Dylan's mind, was the early show at the Old Howard. He had told Caitlin at length of our previous visits and, as we entered the theatre, I had foolishly mounting hopes that the day, in its physical discomfort and spiritual edginess, so much like the fiasco we had endured on our trip to St David's Head in Wales, would somehow be salvaged. But at the first appearance of one of the featured strip-teasers, Caitlin announced, for our ears and those of the patrons in several rows about us, that she thought the whole thing ridiculous and that she was bored. We escorted her out into Scollay Square, Dylan angry and mumbling, I disappointed to the edge of desperation by still another misguided and useless effort to please her. Drinks at two or three of the district's show-bars did nothing to relieve the situation, as Caitlin, stonier than ever, simply withdrew from conversation and stared into space. On the way home to the apartment, she said she wanted to stop for another drink. I suggested a quiet bar in one of the Cambridge hotels, but Caitlin wanted nothing elegant— just some place where there were people and music on the jukebox. I drove them to a beer parlour within walking distance of home and left them there.

On Sunday morning in the apartment we were lazy over newspapers and coffee and conversation that went pleasantly nowhere. Caitlin had already struck up a friendship with my mother which, along with those she had made with Rose Slivka and Rollie McKenna, was as warm as any she was to make during her months in America, and which was to continue long after. She and my mother talked endlessly, often carefully lowering their voices when Dylan and I were within earshot. While laughter was the last thing anyone would associate with Caitlin, suddenly now she laughed freely and often, and seemed to have lost altogether her ambiguous air of withdrawal and aggression. Instinctively, it seemed to me, she had found in my mother one who would listen with sympathy to her side of the long, sad story of her life with Dylan. While this was true, also true was the fact that my mother's feeling for Dylan approached adoration. This allowed her to forgive by fiat whatever failings of Dylan's that might be recounted to her. Caitlin must have sensed this—and it may be that her knowledge of my mother's affection for Dylan allowed her to speak freely of the most intimate aspects of their lives together. In any case, their conversation went on unceasingly for days in the cosy atmosphere of a perpetual tea-time, punctuated by long redolent baths, discussions of cosmetics and experiments with them, analytical discussions of the particular problems of blondes and, eventually, shopping trips and cocktail hours in the smarter places of Boston.

The Wilburs had asked me to bring Dylan and Caitlin to their house in Lincoln that afternoon. Dylan was pleased to go, but Caitlin, tête-à-tête with my mother across the tea-table, said she would prefer to stay at home. When we could not prevail upon her to change her mind, we left without her, spent an entertaining few hours with the Wilburs, and returned to find Caitlin and my mother who, seen from a short distance, looked so much alike they might have been taken for twins, exactly where they had been when we left. Our return, we could see by their suddenly muted remarks to one another, was in the nature of an interruption.

The staff of the Harvard *Advocate*, the University's literary magazine, was giving a party for the Thomases that evening at their headquarters on Bow Street. Again Caitlin said she preferred to stay at home. But when Dylan would not hear of this she finally consented to come. As soon as we arrived they were both immediately swallowed up in a crowd composed of Harvard and Radcliffe undergraduates and a few faculty members. I stayed on the margins of the gathering to chat with a number of acquaintances. After an hour or so in the jam-packed room, I turned to find Caitlin moving away from the group surrounding her and edging toward me. Amused to think that she would seek me out when so much other attention had been lavished upon her, I was about to ask if she were enjoying the party when, airily surveying the room as if it were crawling with vermin, she said: 'Is there no man in America worthy of me?' As I fumbled for an answer to her rhetorical question she was taken in by another eager clutch of Harvard boys. She allowed this new group to detain her for a few minutes, then went over to Dylan to make some *sotto voce* remark. Whatever it was, he was annoyed, and snapped back at her. It was obviously time to go. Without any prompting from me, Dylan suggested we leave. As we started for the cloak-room a group of undergraduates bound for Scollay Square asked him and Caitlin if they would care to come along. He said he would like to go, but Caitlin demurred. Dylan went ahead of us, and was being helped into his overcoat when Caitlin and I caught up with him. He made no attempt to disguise his anger toward his wife from the crew-cutted boys escorting him. As we went downstairs, Caitlin asked: 'Do you want me to come?' Dylan answered loudly: 'Only if you stop being so awful!' Much to my dismay, Caitlin said with decision: 'I'm going home with Brinnin.' Dylan got into a car with his group of attendants, and I put Caitlin into my car. No word broke our silence as we drove to the apartment; I bid her good night at the entrance and went off to the house of the friends with whom I was staying.

Since I had classes to teach the next morning, I dropped by at the apartment to pick up some books just before seven o'clock. The first thing that caught my eye was a note on the reception table. It read simply: 'Stay out, you scum.' While I had a frightful moment of doubt, I learned shortly that the note was meant not for me but for Dylan. When he had come trundling in very late and very tipsy, he had found the door to his and Caitlin's room locked against him. My mother, having listened to Caitlin's railings against Dylan and against me, had realized that Dylan would be shut out for the night and had given up her room to sleep on the living-room couch. When Dylan saw the situation, he refused to let my mother sleep outside of her room and tried to force Caitlin to let him in. He pounded, made threats and entreaties, but nothing would budge her. Under my mother's persuasion, he had finally to accept her bedroom.

When I went in to see him, I found him nude, curled up in a foetus-like position, all the lights in the room blazing about him. I took bedclothes that had slipped to the floor, covered him, put out the lights, and left without attempting to wake him.

Dylan was uneasy about his reading at the Brattle Theatre in Cambridge that night. For the first time in America, he was going to perform dramatic excerpts from such exacting works as *King Lear, Faustus,* and perhaps *Hamlet*. No rehearsal was planned; and he was plagued by embarrassing memories of a time when, reading on the B.B.C. from similar works, he had

126

made several interpretative gaffes which caused letters from irate scholars to descend upon him. But his apprehension on this score was less deep than his concern over a new development: a letter had just come from England informing him that Llewelyn's tuition fees remained unpaid. If the money were not forthcoming very shortly, the boy would be dismissed from school. I offered to supplement Dylan's present funds in order to cable an immediate payment, but he refused this, saying that there was a good chance that he would shortly be in possession of a gift of one thousand dollars from a woman whom he had been invited to meet in Cambridge.

This meeting came about at the home of Richard and Betty Eberhart. But through the course of a long drawn-out afternoon party, Caitlin had taken a dislike to the potential donor and had addressed insulting remarks to her. Dylan had apparently continued to remain in her good grace, however, and before the party was over had made a date to meet her for lunch on the following day.

With one of his most important readings scheduled for that evening, Dylan and Caitlin came back to the apartment to change clothes and have a light supper with my mother. At one point just before the meal, Dylan fingered through a selection of texts, wondering aloud just what passages he should read. Finally he announced that he would read from *Hamlet*. Caitlin, seated across the room, spoke up. '*You*—read *Hamlet*,' she said derisively. '*You* can't read *Hamlet*.' Picking up one of his books, Dylan threw it across the room, missing his wife but knocking over a table-lamp. 'I'm going to read *Hamlet*,' he said, as if he were challenging the ghost of Edwin Booth, 'as *Hamlet* has never been read before.' My mother then managed to step in and calm them both, and the *contretemps* went no further. But Caitlin's doubts had apparently registered. Dylan did not read from *Hamlet* that night. His readings from other works allowed him to make full range of his great voice, but, at least in the report of a number of actors who were present, his performance was not as successful as they had expected. It lacked finesse, they felt, and the flexibility without which much of the natural beau-

127

ty of his voice was muted. Nevertheless, a review in the Boston *Herald* echoed the feelings of most of Dylan's auditors: 'Mr Thomas has the rare gift for a literary man, of verbal facility. In fact, he lives up to an introduction that placed him in the rather awkward position as "one of the finest readers of poetry in the world to-day." He sets forth his program with a true sense of its worth; he is not an actor and there is no sense of affectation; Marlowe's mighty line speaks through him simply and radiantly, aided only by a voice capable of infinite shading and inflection...In his own understated words, his program consisted of "a few purple patches from Webster and Beddoes, one drop of Marlowe, some of my own—God help me—poems." The Webster consisted of the moving "Mad Scene," from *The Duchess of Malfi*...there were selections from Beddoes's *Death's Jest Book* ...the death scene from Marlowe's *Faustus*, selections from *King Lear*, and, finally, Mr Thomas's own *Poem on His Birthday* and *Do Not Go Gentle Into That Good Night*, which, despite his own assertion, are the products of a genuine poet, marked by the mastery of form, lyric impulse, and feeling that informs only the finest works...Of all the solo dramas, monodramas, Chautauqua "readings," selections from the classics, or whatever such an event is called, this was the most stirring of the season. Here was one of the leading talents of our day (exhibiting a warm personality as well) combined with the most soaring words ever written, communicating not as figure in grease-paint, but in the best sense of Wordsworth's conception of a poet—a man speaking to other men.'

Dylan and his would-be benefactor met for lunch at one o'clock at the Ritz on the next afternoon. Caitlin and my mother, ostensibly in town on a shopping tour, arranged their itinerary so that they just happened to be passing by the hotel at that hour. Under Caitlin's urging, they peered like spies at Dylan and his potential patroness, but managed to keep them from becoming aware of this surveillance. Unknown to Dylan, the thousand dollars was already lost to him. While he later reported to me that the lunch had been pleasant, two or three days afterwards the rich young woman phoned me to say that, while she at first had every intention of giving Dylan money for his son's tuition, Caitlin had been so intolerably rude to her that she had been forced to change her mind. I tried to get her to see the matter in a different light, to explain that Caitlin's jealousy of attentions to Dylan was not entirely unnatural, and to point out that, after all, this had really nothing to do with the urgent need for money for the boy's tuition. But my efforts were unavailing. When, a few days later, I overheard Dylan berating Caitlin for having spoiled his chances, she answered: 'I don't care, I'd do it again.'

After a reading at Boston University that evening and a large reception afterwards, where Caitlin frightened nearly everyone who spoke to her, retorting to kindly inquiries as to how she liked America with: 'I can't get out of the bloody country soon enough'—the Thomases returned to New York. When I went to see them on the following Thursday, a literary young man who had just turned up unannounced at the Chelsea took us to lunch. But this was a listless affair because of generally sodden morning-after spirits and because Dylan was suffering from a new and specific pain. While brushing his teeth two days before he had smashed a drinking-glass by knocking it into the wash-basin. Somehow, he believed, one of its splinters had then got on to his toothbrush and into his gums, where now it was apparently festering. This struck me as too potentially dangerous to disregard, so we excused ourselves and went to a physician with whose office I had become familiar when migraine attacks had driven me from previous lunches. There we learned that Dylan had not picked up a piece of broken glass but only a nylon bristle from his toothbrush. This was easily extricated and within an hour we had returned to the hotel to pack his bags and then to taxi uptown to the Airlines Terminal. Dylan was off to Albany for an evening's engagement at Skidmore College, in Saratoga Springs. I would not see him again for nearly six weeks; after Skidmore he would return to New York and then set off with Caitlin on the transcontinental part of their visit.

In preparation for this I had bought railroad tickets, making arrangements for him and Caitlin to stop off first at Pennsylvania State College and later in Arizona, where they were to visit the painters, Max Ernst and Dorothea Tanning. With all travel costs paid through to San Francisco, all New York expenses taken care of, I handed them four hundred dollars as travel money for the five or six days they would spend in reaching the coast. To my consternation, they had been gone only four days when I received a telegram: 'PLEASE URGENTLY WIRE ONE HUNDRED DOLLARS CARE OF ERNST CAPRICORN HILL SEDONA.' By mischance this telegram did not come into my hands until four days after Dylan had dispatched it. By the time I could wire money they were already in San Francisco. A letter from there, not without a note of chastisement for my failing to have kept them at least financially secure arrived some three weeks later.

> Dear John,
> Three letters lie—I don't, of course, mean that—before me; dated March 20, March 26, and April 1st. Here's a brief, but none the less stupid, reply to them all.
> I'm awfully sorry, *re* March 20, that you've been sick. And not of us? A *mysterious* illness; probably test-tubing out from M.I.T.—to whose English students I owe a forever unwritten apology for never turning up. But I'm very glad you're better (April 1st) now, and on such a good day.
> Thank you for the damnably urgent and answerable letter from Higham. I'm supposed, as perhaps you read, to write an introduction to the English forthcoming edition of my *Collected Poems* which, I suppose, entails my reading them all. Daft I may be...
> Now, *re* March 26th. Those 'mishaps' that caused you to miss my wire from Sedona proved agonising to us. Caitlin was frightfully ill all the way from New York to Pennsylvania State College and on the night-train to Chicago. During the Chicago journey, my bottled up bottle illness also grew severe; indeed, we were both so near to undignified death that, on reaching Chicago, we just *could* not go straight across the city to catch our next unrocking bed. So we went to a cosy little hovel of an hotel and wept and sweated there until next day. The hotel was fabulously expensive; the Pullman reservation for Tuesday, the 18th, fell out of date. I had to buy a new one, and so we arrived at Flagstaff with less than a dollar. The Ernsts were lovely, charming, and hospitable, but had no ready money and none to lend. We stayed there, absolutely penniless, for

8 days, being unable to buy our own cigarettes, to post a letter, or stand with a beer at Sedona's cowboy bar, or even wire you again. We stayed there, saying, 'Beastly John Brinnin,' until help came from San Francisco. Arriving at San Francisco, we found your two letters, and two cheques, and also a letter from the headmaster of Llewelyn's school saying he would be thrown out unless a hundred pounds were paid by April 5. I then wired you again. You sent a cheque for 200 dollars. And so, I had 400 dollars altogether. 300 dollars I wired to Llewelyn's school. The other 100 I spent on a Vancouver ticket. So (again) HELP. On top of this, Caitlin had carefully arranged for some laundry to be sent on from New York to San Francisco. This cost 40 dollars.

I can just manage to get to Vancouver; and I'll leave Caitlin the fee for my San Francisco State College reading which is tonight and which will be only 50 dollars.

About other engagements: Is the date, on April 26, at the University of Chicago the same as that, on April 24, at North-western University, Chicago? Or can't I read?

It's summer here, not spring. Over 80. At Easter we go to Carmel and on to see Miller at Big Sur. We are both well. *Please* write very soon, with any news, some love, and a bit of money. Caitlin sends her love. And, as always, so do I.

Yours,
DYLAN.

While rumour, travelling faster than air mail, brought me amusing, shocking, or mischievous items of news about Dylan and Caitlin every few days or so, this was the only direct word I had from them for a period of nearly six weeks. I wrote two or three letters every week, and sometimes Dylan acknowledged these by telegrams. While this seemed to be a most tenuous exchange by which to conduct so rigorous a programme of appearances, experience of a previous tour allowed me to feel confident that Dylan was following the substance if not always the letter of the itinerary he had asked me to prepare. Only at the penultimate stage of his sweep across the country and back was my confidence shaken.

On Thursday, 24th April, he was in Chicago where, according to schedule, he would at some point over the week-end take leave of the hospitality of Ellen Barden Stevenson and board a plane for New Orleans, where he was to give a reading at Tulane on the following Monday. He phoned me in New York—a rare gesture in itself—and reached me in the late afternoon. He was worn out by his travels, he said, and wanted to come back to the Chelsea just as soon as he could. The reason for his call was simply to tell me that he was going to give up his reading date at Tulane. This upset me more than I allowed myself to show. While I could easily comprehend his weariness and his wish to be home, I was also greatly disturbed to think of repercussions that would follow should he cancel at the last minute an engagement made long before in good faith. That he should choose to omit, of all places, New Orleans was also a little puzzling. From the first day in America, he had urged me to get a date there, saying that, next to San Francisco, it was the one place he wanted to be certain of visiting. The reading in New Orleans had taken more effort and had involved a more protracted exchange of letters and telegrams than any other I had ever managed to secure. I reminded Dylan of all of this and asked him, with perhaps a note of entreaty, to reconsider his decision and make one final effort, if only to maintain his record of dependability. But he was doggedly weary and adamant, saying that he just could not face the idea of another day's travel that would not be in the direction of New York.

When I could see that his mind was set and that his exhaustion, whether it was something new and serious or merely the old familiar drain and dredge of a hang-over, could not be discounted, I asked him to phone James Feibleman, who was in charge of his visit to Tulane, and explain that he was too ill to come to New Orleans at this time. Having repeatedly given Feibleman assurance that, in spite of his reputation for irresponsibility, he had always been faithful to reading commitments, I felt that only the word of Dylan himself would carry final authority. Dylan agreed with this, and seemed relieved to have come upon a means by which he could compensate for his failing me by making his own personal excuses to Feibleman. Before the conversation ended, our original positions were reversed: Dylan was now trying to importune me, not to do something, but to accept his decision with more cheerfulness. I realized, but with no lessening of dismay in this instance, that his responsibility towards me seemed to weigh upon him more heavily than his responsibility toward the institutions to which I had assigned his services. We concluded with promises: Dylan's, to phone Feibleman immediately; mine, to meet him and Caitlin in New York just as soon as they had stepped from their train.

Between classes at the University of Connecticut on the following Monday, I was summoned to the phone. It was James Feibleman, calling from New Orleans. When he said that he was alarmed at having had no word of Dylan's arrival for the reading that evening for which more than eight hundred tickets had been sold, I knew, in one collapsing moment, that Dylan had finally made the misstep everyone had waited for. I tried to explain what had happened, but, in the realization that nothing now could be done, our conversation ended in understandable bad feeling on Feibleman's part and, on my part, in the fatally delayed recognition that I should never have counted upon Dylan's promise to make the phone call that would explain his defection. This single instance of default—the only one of nearly one hundred and fifty engagements in America for which he eventually was contracted—was to plague Dylan and me for more than a year. His failure to turn up in New Orleans was published the length and breadth of the academic world, with the consequence that, whenever anybody later contracted for his services, I had personally almost to guarantee his appearance in letter after reassuring letter, up until the moment when he would walk out upon the platform. Dylan himself eventually came to recognize the seriousness of his broken engagement but, like every other such failing, this knowledge was simply packed into the indiscriminate bag of guilt that grew more heavy every day of his life.

Eager to see him and Caitlin and to hear of their experiences first-hand, I went to see them at the Chelsea on the morning of May Day. But again I walked into crisis: a terse cable from England had just arrived, containing the information that Llewelyn had been dismissed from school because his tuition fees had not

133

been paid. While Dylan had written me on 1st April that the necessary amount had already been forwarded, he admitted now that it had not been sent for weeks afterward, too late to save their son the humiliation to which he must have been subject. In a spell of anguish that drove him to pace the floor and to avert his eyes, Dylan said that Llewelyn would surely hold this failure against him for the rest of his life. Caitlin, so angry that she refused even to speak to Dylan, announced that she was leaving America at once; Dylan could make his own plans for his future life since for good and all she was leaving him. She asked me for money so that she might buy a return passage, adding that if I would not give her the necessary funds she would get them somewhere else. In any case, she declared, there was no possibility of her remaining in New York for one more day. Weighed down with new guilt, wincing under Caitlin's verbal assault, Dylan asked me to come out with him to a bar. There he sat silent, his head in his hands, unable to speak, indifferent to the drink before him. While we sat together in a trance of despair, Caitlin came by briskly to say that she was going out to make her travel arrangements. Nothing would help Dylan now, neither liquor nor my words of comfort that attempted to convince him that Caitlin was but justifiably upset, and that I at least did not take seriously her threat of leaving him. 'She knows just how to hurt me most,' was all he said.

After a sad silent hour or so, I took him back to the hotel and put him to bed. He begged me not to leave and I said I would not. He slept deeply for a few hours while I tried to read one then another of the collection of Mickey Spillanes and other luridly illustrated thrillers with which the hotel room was strewn. When he awoke he was quite a different man; as if, somewhere in his sleep, he had struck bottom and then risen to the surface. There was to be a late afternoon reception for him at the Gotham Book Mart. While he had said earlier that he was going to phone Frances Steloff to say that he was too ill to come to her party, now he was quite ready to set out. We taxied uptown to the bookstore and walked into a swarm of poets. There Dylan autographed various editions of his books, signed the first copies of some new recordings, and mingled freely and in apparently good humour with the assembled literati. When I was about to leave for dinner with some friends, I took him aside to ask him if he were going to be all right. He felt fine, he said, thanked me for having pulled him through the day's despair, and told me not to worry about him.

Like every other crisis, this one passed as quickly as it had loomed. Caitlin did not persist in her plans for leaving either America or Dylan. Llewelyn was soon reinstated, and the air was cleared and the way opened for the next still nameless but inevitable crisis.

One week later, in the company of Leonard Dean, the head of the English Department at the University of Connecticut, I awaited Dylan's plane at the Hartford airport. We had driven over from Storrs in order to escort him to the campus for an evening reading. Dylan was presumably *en route* from Washington, having changed planes at LaGuardia for the short hop to Hartford. As we waited about, I realized that in spite of my easy show of confidence to Leonard Dean, I was acutely uncertain about Dylan's punctual descent. For once I was in precisely the same situation as those hundreds of other sponsors who had awaited Dylan at airports and depots with no confidence that he would show up, and with only the vaguest notion of what they might say to their disappointed audiences. I spent a good part of the time allaying Dean's doubts and in so doing was perhaps able to disguise my own. The scheduled flight landed on time and we went out of doors to meet it; Dylan was not among the deplaning passengers. A voice over the loudspeaker paged me. Dylan was on the phone from New York. His plane had missed its connections; he would be aboard the next one. Three hours later, just half an hour before he was scheduled to begin his reading some fifty miles away, we anxiously watched passengers stepping down from the next plane. One by one they emerged and, finally, the 24th passenger in a 24-seat plane, came Dylan. We hurried him into the car, shot through the night toward Storrs, and got him on to the platform only forty minutes late. As if he had prepared for it the whole length of the day, his reading was rich, vigorous, and professionally serene.

Responding to an impressive popular demand for still another reading, the Poetry Center scheduled a farewell performance for Dylan on 15th May, the day before he was to sail for home on the *Nieuw Amsterdam*. Equipped with a meticulous and, to my eyes at least, gleaming statement accounting for all of his earnings and expenditures from the moment he had set foot in America four months before, I went in the early afternoon to see him at the Chelsea. There I found only Caitlin, looking wan and helpless, surrounded by gaping suit-cases in a room draped with more clothes, presents, books, and random papers than could possibly be fitted into them. We set about organizing things, packed bag by bag, and were wearily strapping them up and putting labels on them when Dylan arrived. I sat down with him to go over the pages of figures on which I had spent long hours, only to find him listening half-heartedly. When I could see that he was not only indifferent to the financial details of his visit, but bored with my determination to have him grasp the reality of income and expenditure, I gave up, turned the accounts over to him, and implored him to take good care of them.

That evening, as I awaited him at the Poetry Center, Sarah came backstage unannounced, and said she hoped that she might be able to see Dylan. She had just returned from Mexico where she had gone to live with the journalist to whom she had been married for nearly a year, but whom now she had left with the intention of seeking a divorce. When Dylan arrived I directed him to her in the Green Room and left them alone there for about twenty minutes before performance time. I was never to know the nature of this meeting. Dylan said nothing of it, and neither did Sarah. But whatever this present encounter might mean, I had long been aware that the love for Sarah that had once brought Dylan to despair had either faded away through neglect or had been buried.

The farewell reading turned out to be a gala event, the auditorium being filled with enthusiastic friends and acquaintances of his, and other people who, having heard him read before, came back with whole parties. He was carried off by a group of strangers afterwards, but not before he and I had made a private sentimental appointment to meet at 'the Horse' for a *bon voyage* drink. With a girl who had come down from Boston for the reading, I went to the Tavern about midnight, finding it packed with other people alerted for Dylan's appearance. Two hours of waiting in the expectant din of the place brought no sign or word of Dylan. Since I had to leave New York very early in the morning, I had to admit that this farewell, for my part, at least, was already another irretrievable fiasco. Upset by this, and by the vast accumulation of errors and crises and unhappinesses of which it reminded me, I put my companion in a taxi and went to a Western Union office to send a wire to Dylan's ship. Sad about the turn of the night's events, forced to recognize that Dylan had little care for the farewell gesture that meant much to me, I sent a wire that I hoped would transcend all our trials and express my biting disappointment in having been able to protect for him but a paltry few hundred dollars out of the thousands he had earned.

A week or so later I received a letter written at sea from Caitlin in which she thanked and excoriated me with equal fervour, and to which Dylan had appended a postscript:

My dear John,

I'll be writing very soon, from the Boat House, Laugharne, where we hope to be by the end of the week. This is just to thank you for everything; I wish we could have been more together. And thank you for cabling love.

Ever,
DYLAN.

V

1952: June—September

There was no way in which Dylan could have known that the ensuing months were among the unhappiest in my friendship with him. Like many other people whose affection had given them insight, I had come to feel that he was in a state of devouring unhappiness and in need of help. The causes of his wretchedness were easy to determine, but their sources lay beneath the purview of everyone. His inability to settle down to creative work—for which his American trips had become partial excuse and explanation—was, in Dylan's mind, a consequence of financial pressures and the domestic strife they made inevitable. Yet when his financial difficulties were analysed they seemed less pertinent to his distress than they first appeared. One of the great surprises in my knowledge of Dylan came when I learned that, in spite of his enforced preoccupation with money and with the anxieties attending existence on the edge of poverty, actually his income had for a number of years been twice or three times the size of mine. On far less than this amount, families larger than his lived in Wales or England not merely with security but in luxury. I could only conclude that Dylan's propensity to squander money was a compulsion related to his obsessive drinking which, in turn, fed his passion to participate fully, thoughtlessly, and to excess in every human activity—as if his enormous mental and physical energy, denied its creative channel, had perforce to spend itself otherwise. When he found himself unable to write because he was financially harried, it was nearly always himself who had made such harassment unavoidable. From this recognition, it was only a step to the realization that, should Dylan have somehow been relieved of every financial care, he would most likely continue to be driven, restless, wracked with guilt and remorse, and no less obsessively drawn to the forms of self-exacerbation that had become his way of life.

The little help I could give Dylan, it seemed to me, was two-fold: by doing all that I could to help him earn money in America, and by showing an undemanding affection for him as a person and faith in him as a poet. When my efforts to increase his financial security were confounded by his extravagance, I tried to show him that I regarded this as no important failing, and to emphasize the deep bond of acceptance and trust we had come to share. But I knew as well as he that his unhappiness lay in the conviction that his creative powers were failing, that his great work was finished. He had moved from 'darkness into some measure of light,' a progress attended by the acclaim of the literate part of the English-speaking world; but now that he had arrived, he was without the creative resources to maintain and expand his position. As a consequence, he saw his success as fraudulent and himself as an impostor. While he expressed such thoughts largely as self-deprecating jokes, he could not disguise their gnawing reality or force.

He was, of course, not an impostor, and his work was worthy of all of its public rewards. But his growth now depended not only on inherent genius and the skills of master craftsmanship, but upon the additional faculties of intellect and moral compulsion that mark nearly every major poet. While Dylan's intellect was great, his indifference to ideas limited its exercise; while his moral discipline was amply demonstrated in his craftsmanship—a point never to be underestimated—it was apparent almost nowhere else. To foresee Dylan in middle and later life was to pose two questions, each of which answered itself: Would he continue, year by year, to be the roaring boy, the daemonic poet endlessly celebrating the miracle of man under the eyes of God? Would he, by some reversal of spirit, some redirection of his genius, become the wise, grey, and intellectually disciplined poet moving toward an epical summation of his lyrical gifts? It was my sense then, as it is now, that the term of the roaring boy was over, and that the means by which Dylan might continue to grow were no longer in his possession. I was convinced that Dylan knew this and, whether or not he comprehended the meaning of his actions, that the violence of his life was a way of forgetting or avoiding the self-judgment that spelled his doom. Poetry itself had become, as he said, 'statements made on the way to the grave.'

The resolution he made to overcome the terror of this knowledge came from desperation, and yet he pursued it not without valour: since his genius had come to jeopardy, he would employ his talent. He turned to prose, to the drama, and to the opera. While he did not live to write the opera he had conceived, his achievements in the other two forms are of an order high enough to have satisfied any but the expectations of genius. Yet the fact remains that when Dylan Thomas came to the attention of Americans as a major poet, he was creatively already past his prime. The record of his days in America is one of which it might be said: 'Thou knowest this man's fall; but thou knowest not his wrastling.'

While I was unhappy in not having found some means with which to break through the turmoil of spirit in which Dylan and Caitlin had concluded their American visit, I was resigned to the hiatus of silence that followed. When the two or three letters I sent to Wales went unanswered, I assumed, correctly as it turned out, that Dylan was quietly in Laugharne except for roistering periods in London when he would go up for perhaps a single appointment with the B.B.C. or with the editor of a magazine, and remain for days or weeks out of touch with everyone, including his wife. Since I planned to be in London on two occasions in the summer, I did not press for his answers. For one thing, I had a fairly definite feeling that Dylan's American tours were a matter of past history. He had himself said to an American interviewer that his recent trip was 'my last visit for some time. I will have had the universities and they will have had me.' He had seen more than enough of the United States to satisfy his mild curiosity about places, and while he enjoyed Americans and American life enormously, the cost he continually paid to learn this was disproportionate to its rewards. Another reading tour was too exhausting now to contemplate, not only for Dylan, who had to do the travelling and survive the attendant social life, but for me, who but stood and waited for the descents of new crises. Within the limits of his fame and the hospitality of colleges and universities, he had already done as much as he could ever do. Months away from his desk would only increase his inner, barely spoken fear that he had already written all the poems he was going to write.

In spite of this, I knew that if I saw Dylan I would bring up the subject of his returning to America, if only to dispose of it as a factor in our relationship. While we had both felt that another tour would be an intolerable assignment, Dylan had repeatedly expressed the belief that a happy solution to domestic difficulties might be reached if he and Caitlin were to come to America with the two younger children and settle in any one place where he might have the assurance of a livable salary. A university in California had made him a tentative offer of a year's appointment, and this had struck him as ideal, especially since the position would be a sinecure in which his duties would be secondary to his mere presence. When this possibility fell through, I had offered him my own teaching job at the Poetry Center, with the promise of a salary considerably larger than mine, and had been otherwise able to assure him basic livelihood through contacts I had made on his behalf with people connected with academic life. But his failure to answer letters in which I outlined these possibilities had led me to believe that, even if he were still interested, circumstances in Laugharne were such as to leave him unable to make any decision about them.

When, later in the summer, I was travelling between Ireland and Italy, I phoned Laugharne from London; Dylan said he would come down to see me the next day. When he did not arrive at the agreed-upon time and place, I again phoned Laugharne. Dylan said he had wired that he could not make the trip; the telegram must have gone astray. The real reason, he said, was that he simply did not have the train fare. Since I was leaving for the Continent that night, he suggested we plan to meet in London, or that I come to Laugharne, when I would return to England in September.

A month later, on my last day in London, and after a two-day confusion of missed notes and phone calls, I reached Caitlin in Wales. She told me that Dylan was in London, staying with friends whose address she gave me. I phoned him, and through the familiar groans and sighs of his hang-over we arranged a meeting. The place he chose was a pub, the Mother Red Cap, in Camden Town, where he had lived so unhappily for part of the previous winter. When I found him there about noon, our greetings were warm, overly dramatized by accusations and expostulations, and rather giddy. I could see that, in spite of his chipper bearing, Dylan had reassumed his 'London look'—bloodshot and yellowed eyes, blotched complexion, inextricably tangled locks, an air of having slept in his bulky clothes for nights on end. He said he felt awful, but our conversation was intimate, easy, and buoyant—a welcome change from those lugubrious interviews I had come to expect when last he was in America. We toasted American friends and enemies, framing nice or nasty epithets for each of them, then took our pints to another part of the pub where, by inserting sixpence in a slot, we could play a mechanical soccer game involving quick coordination of both hands. Dylan played wildly, urging on his little lead footballers with shrieks and gulps and profane encouragements, and beat me every time. When we tired of this, we settled down for another drink at a table surrounded by a noonday crowd of workers.

As we lingered on I learned, with sharply conflicting emotions, that Dylan very much wanted to come back to America, and that he was already counting upon me to make another visit possible. When, merely by way of report, and in review of previous conversations, I began to tell him of plans and schemes that had from time to time passed through my mind, and of sources of income—none of which would involve another tour —that I felt I could guarantee, he was clearly not interested in details. All that was apparent was his wish to come and his trust that, without drawing him into responsibility and commitment, I would arrange a visit by one means or another. Again I realized I would have to give up my attempt to win his participation, even in those plans that would most acutely concern him.

143

When we had put aside this onerous, brief, and, to me, frustrating consideration of means of livelihood, Dylan became determinedly playful again and at one point composed a little obscene verse, wrote it down on a ragged scrap of paper, read it aloud, and gave it to me. The poem—three quatrains in length, two beats to a line, and tidily rhymed—shows him in his fey bar-room humour, but his unabashed use of the vulgar tongue prevents its publication here.

Shooed out of the Mother Red Cap at the afternoon closing time, we queued up for a bus and climbed to the upper deck. As we inched through depressing Camden Town in stops and starts, Dylan seemed suddenly gloomy and sober. 'How I hate London,' he said. 'Look...' and motioned toward the blaring commercial ugliness of the street through which we crawled. Then, as if he had brushed away whatever doubts of mine that may have registered upon him, he began very seriously to speak of returning to America. What might he offer in the way of new programmes? Was his stuff as stale to American audiences as it was to him? Where could he read where he had not already read? I assured him that there were thousands of people who would come to hear him read for a second and third time, and that there were still hundreds of colleges and universities that would be happy to invite him. About new material, he felt that by the spring he might have four or five new poems. Still, that would not be enough, he felt. Perhaps he should concentrate on dramatic readings—from *Hamlet*, say, or *Faustus*, or from Djuna Barnes's *Nightwood*, especially some of the monologues of 'Dr Matthew-Mighty-grain-of-salt-Dante-O'Connor.' I felt that all of these might be worked into his programme for the sake of variety, but insisted that his reading of his own work was still the major point of audience interest.

When I asked him about the progress of *Llareggub Hill*, the 'play for voices' he had been writing on commission for the B.B.C., he said it was coming along well enough and that he hoped to have a final draft within two or three months. This led me to suggest that his own play might furnish him with a complete new programme—he could read it himself or, better, I could round up a cast of actors and arrange a reading production for one or two nights within the Poetry Center season. In that it would supply a new programme for him Dylan felt this idea was a good one. But he was dubious about thinking in terms of a production, even a minimal reading production, mainly because authentic Welsh accents would be essential. He doubted that these would be available in New York. I told him that I could draw upon a great number of skilled but unemployed actors, and urged him to let me go ahead with the goal of a reading production in mind. If such a programme should work out, he might in the future be able to travel with it and so be relieved of the continuous strain of having to carry the whole show himself. He agreed to have a completed script in my hands by March, two months before the first performance, which we would schedule for some time in May.

When our bus had made its snail's way into Soho, we climbed down on to Shaftesbury Avenue and walked to the Mandrake. The little club was sultry and silent in the late afternoon, none of the few members who sat about playing chess or poring over newspapers even bothering to nod to Dylan as we came in. We had a drink in the hushed dimness of the bar before I left to accomplish some last-minute errands. Dylan supplied me with directions for rejoining him at a pub called El Vino, in Fleet Street. When I got there just before six o'clock I found him surrounded by young members of Parliament in pin-striped suits and bowlers. He had a glass of red wine in his hand, was smoking a cigar, and being hearty, manly, anecdotal, and altogether one of the boys. His well-kempt circle of admirers kept him the centre of attention, but I felt that he was not quite comfortable and, for all his jovial participation, that his talk was not quite in character. A few minutes after I had come into the group, having been introduced around as his American mentor and guide, Dylan began to make unflattering whispered remarks to me about this or that individual at our elbows, and I began to understand how consciously he was playing the role of man of the world among his peers.

My boat train was due to leave at seven-thirty. We piled into a taxi with an intense, obsessively talkative girl of about twenty who had somehow insinuated herself into the group at El Vino and who was now clinging to Dylan as though she had not been out of his sight for days. *En route* to Waterloo Station, I recapitulated to Dylan my sense of the plans we had touched upon during our bus ride, but he simply asked me to go ahead with whatever I thought best. When I suggested that perhaps he might find a better title than *Llareggub Hill* for his 'play for voices,' he agreed at once. The joke in the present title was a small and childish one, he felt; beyond that, the word 'Llareggub' would be too thick and forbidding to attract American audiences. 'What about *Under Milk Wood?*' he said, and I said 'Fine,' and the new work was christened on the spot.

In the loud and smoky din of boat-train departure, we said our good-byes with embraces and handshakes. As late passengers for the *Île de France* hurried through the gates, Dylan began, as always, to make his half-spoken apologies for his bad behaviour, his inadequacies, his trouble-making ways, and a prediction that, God help us, we'd be together and sick again in New York through another whole roundabout of a tour. Then out of nowhere came Dylan's high, wild, wonderful laughter, interrupting his apologies and dismissing them.

VI

September 1952—June 1953

Under Milk Wood, but partially completed in the sanctuary of Dylan's little studio, was nevertheless set to come out into the world. In October the Poetry Center issued its annual brochure of the coming season's events, including a reading performance of the new work scheduled for early in May. But the distance between October and May was almost incalculable to Dylan, who suffered through another troubled winter in Laugharne and London with little thought of the commitments I had proceeded to make for his next visit. I sent him several letters, naming dates and places, asking him just how far I should go in assigning his services, but he made no reply. Since I had become used to not hearing from him, sometimes even in the most urgent of circumstances, my confidence in his intentions to keep our London agreement was shaken somewhat, yet not really jeopardized. But by the middle of March, when we had selected a cast of young actors ready to begin rehearsals of *Under Milk Wood*, and had already sold hundreds of tickets for the *première* performance, I felt we could proceed no further without an immediate and definite word of assurance from him. On 17th March I phoned Wales from Cambridge and by good chance found Dylan at home. With what sounded like the full wash of the North Atlantic between, we had a brief conversation. Every nuance was lost, but over the crackle and splash of the transatlantic connection, I did hear with reasonable clarity that he was ready to come, and that he wanted me to go ahead with all of the plans which I had broached in correspondence.

Four days later I received this letter:

> Dear John,
> After all sorts of upheavals, evasions, promises, procrastinations, I write, very fondly, and fawning slightly, a short inaccurate

147

summary of those events which caused my never writing a word before this. In the beginning, as Treece said in one of his apocalapses, was the bird; and this came from Caitlin, who said, and repeated it only last night after our Boston-Laugharne babble: 'You want to go to the States again only for flattery, idleness, and infidelity.' This hurt me terribly. The right words were: appreciation, dramatic work, and friends. Therefore I didn't write until I knew for certain that I could come to the States for a visit and then return to a body and hearth not irremediably split from navel to firedog. Of course I'm far from certain now, but I'm coming. This unfair charge—flattery, idleness, etcetera—kept me seething quiet for quite a bit. Then my father died, and my mother relied on me to look after her and to stay, writing like fury, pen in claw, a literary mole, at home. Then a woman—you never met her—who promised me a real lot of money for oh so little in return died of an overdose of sleeping-drug and left no will, and her son, the heir, could hardly be expected to fulfil that kind of unwritten agreement. Then a publisher's firm, which had advanced me money for an American-Impressions book of which I never wrote a word, turned, justly, nasty, and said I had to do the book by June 1953 or they would set the law on me...Then...Margaret Taylor said that she was going to sell the rickety house we wrestled in, over our heads and live bodies. So this was the position I was in, so far as my American visit was concerned: Caitlin was completely against it; my mother was against it, because I should be near her and working hard to keep the lot of us; and I was reluctantly against it, because I was without money, owing to an unexpected suicide, and I could not, naturally, leave a mother and wife and three children penniless at home while I leered and rib-thumped in Liberty Land; and the publishers were legally against it, because I had to write a book for them quickly; and on top of all that, the final reason for my knowing I could not come out this spring was the prospect of the rapid unhousing of dame, dam and the well-loved rest. (I write like a cad. I should whip myself to death on the steps of my club for all this.) Well, anyway; I won a prize, for the book of the year, of £250 (pounds), and a brother-in-law in Bombay said he would look, from a distance, after my mother's welfare. And Margaret Taylor has, temporarily, relented. And I think I can give the demanding publishers the script of *Under Milk Wood* (when finished) instead of, for instance, *A Bard's-Eye View of the U.S.A.* And Caitlin's hatred of my projected visit can be calmed only by this: that after no more than 6 weeks' larricking around I return from New York with enough money to take Colm, her and me for three winter months to Portugal where all, I hear, is cheap and sunny. Or, alternately, that I find, in a month, a house for us, in your country, and can send for Caitlin to join me in the early summer and keep us going, through summer and autumn, by work which is not cross-continental reading and raving. Of the alternatives, she would far prefer the first. So do you think it possible? Do you think I can earn a lot in six weeks: enough, that is, for a Portuguese winter? I do not care, in those six weeks, how much I read, or how many times, or where. I think, for economy, it would be best for me to stay in a New York hotel—the Chelsea, I trust—for only a little time and then to move in, manias and all, on to friends. I am hoping that perhaps my old friend Len Lye, who lives in Greenwich Village, near Ruthven Todd, will put me up: I am only small, after all, and alone, though loud. I haven't his address, but will get in touch with him once Chelsea'd in New York.

I have put down, in more or less true detail, all the above little hells to show why I have been unable, till now, to write and say: 'It is fine. Go ahead.'

About *Under Milk Wood*. I shall not have the complete manuscript ready until the week of my sailing. I have, anyway, some doubts as to the performance of it by myself and a professional cast. Some kind of an approximation to a Welsh accent is required throughout, and I think I could make an hour's entertainment out of this myself. Shall we discuss it later? I shall have the MS with me, embarking, from the liner, and if you still think, after reading it, it needs other and professional voices, then I don't believe it would need all that 'careful preparation' you mention. I should be *very* glad, by the way, to hear from you, as soon as possible, about any ideas you might have as to what I should read aloud in my general verse-reading programmes. What poets, and of what centuries? I'd like a wide repertoire. Caitlin sends her love to your mother. Yours always, dear John, Dylan.

At the top of the page there was this postscript: 'I shall be applying for a visa this week: in Cardiff, this time. I do not think they are quite so screening-strict there as in London. URGENT, and just remembered: let me have, at once, a formal and official Poetry Center letter Dear Mr Thomas-ing me and saying what cultural, and important, engagements you have fixed up for me.

On the morning of 21st April 1953 Dylan arrived in New

York aboard the S.S. *United States*. As I waited on the pier, I expected I would be joined by others of his friends and acquaintances, but no one came. He disembarked hatless and coatless, and I was happy to find him clear-eyed, hale, sober in that characteristically sturdy sense of himself that always meant that he was at ease. We took a cab to the Chelsea, which was home to him now, and he told me of his intolerably dull five days at sea. The only person he had spoken with on the voyage was a Texan named Herb Money who, according to Dylan, was a back-slapping caricature of everything one knew or imagined about the state of Texas. Except for moderate drinking sessions with Money in the ship's bar, he had done nothing except read book after book, mostly detective stuff, until he felt he was losing his eyesight. His boredom ultimately became so overpowering that the only thing he could think of doing was to stand like a scarecrow in the wardrobe of his stateroom, just for a change of perspective. Definitely, he said, he would return to England by air.

Glad to see him back, the staff of the Chelsea—from the manager to the coloured bell-boys—received him with smiles, spoken greetings, and an attitude that was both deferential and familiar. When he had been ushered into a large, exceptionally well-appointed room on the fifth floor, we put down his bags and proceeded directly out of the hotel and on to Seventh Avenue, where the big cut-rate bars were now as familiar to him as the little pubs of Laugharne. *Under Milk Wood* was still far from finished, he admitted, in confirmation of my unhappiest suspicion. But he felt it would be no trouble at all to have the script in final shape for the announced date of its first performance. Unwilling to cast a shadow over his self-confidence, I pressed him no further on the progress of the play. We spent the whole day in a series of bars, working our way from 34th Street down to the Village. At the White Horse Tavern, which we reached by mid afternoon, everyone along the bar turned to greet him. Ernie, the rotund proprietor, sent Scotch to our table and sat down with us to reminisce about memorable evenings of the year before. Dylan seemed happy, more than a little excited,

150

and, most of all, at home. His only genuine ease, I had long before observed, was among friendly faces, known or unknown, in places where the only propriety was to be oneself. In the spell of this protracted good feeling, I put aside the list of urgent appointments and lecture-tour matters I seemed never now to be without, and simply basked in Dylan's open and infectious delight in having come back to America.

Around six o'clock we left the deeper part of the Village and went uptown to the Algonquin to have a drink with Howard Moss, whom Dylan had specifically wanted to see on this first day of his return, and Mildred Wood, a friend of mine who, like Howard, was also on the staff of the *New Yorker*. People at adjoining tables and people passing through the lobby were quick to recognize Dylan. Wherever we looked we would spot whispered conversations and heads nodding in our direction. When one of us remarked upon this surrounding buzz of attention, Dylan dismissed it with a joke. Yet in his beaming acknowledgment of the situation it was apparent that he was enjoying the stir his presence had caused. We were joined shortly by Liz, a close friend of mine since our meeting fourteen years before, when she had been a student at Bennington, who, just within the past year, had become my assistant in direction of the activities of the Poetry Center. In this position it had fallen upon her to round up a suitable cast for *Under Milk Wood*, and to undertake the many preliminary arrangements for its production. Dylan's long failure to answer letters, or to send the script in advance of his coming, and the consequent sense of working in a vacuum that marked the whole project to date, had been a particular trial to her. While I knew that she was anxious to meet him, her interest was largely in terms of her job. A long season at the Poetry Center had dispelled whatever illusions she may have originally entertained as to the charm or glamour of poets, domestic or foreign. Their few remarks to each other after they were introduced were rather markedly restrained—Liz's because she was at the moment interested only in getting the script of *Under Milk Wood*. Dylan's because this tall, beautiful, and obviously efficient young woman was already a figure of

151

authority with whom he would have to deal. I learned later that they had taken an instant dislike to one another.

Our cocktail hour was not a bright one. Dylan, feeling the effects of a long day of random drinking, reminded of his default by Liz's presence, losing his sense of ease in the carefully decaying elegance of the Algonquin, soon became almost wordless. He spilled his martini, tried clumsily to retrieve it, and sat up to meet the admonishing eye of a waiter. This put him off altogether. When we had quickly decided to move on, he said that on this first night in New York he wanted to do something brashly American—something like a visit to the Statue of Liberty—and asked for our suggestions. Harlem? It was too early for that. The Village? No, he would run into too many people he wasn't quite ready to see. After a number of other choices had been named, we finally decided upon the loudest and brassiest musical comedy we might find. *Guys and Dolls*, then in its third Broadway year, was still on the boards. We would have to go without dinner to make the curtain, but, for Dylan, this was always the most inconsequential of decisions. Taking leave of our friends, we hurried toward Times Square, bought expensive tickets at an agency, and got to our seats just in time for the opening curtain. Within fifteen minutes we were ready to leave. Years of success had removed all lustre from the show, apparently, and mesmerized its cast into a band of performing robots. Merely to watch the first scenes demanded painful effort and concentration; one wanted to take every actor by the shoulders and wake him up. After we had exchanged several disbelieving glances, I suggested we leave, and Dylan agreed on the instant. We shot out of the theatre and into the Astor Bar. But the impetus that had carried us through a long day and into the evening was dissipated, and neither of us had any heart for drumming up new entertainment. Half an hour later I left him at the Astor and went to Grand Central to catch a train for Connecticut.

It seemed to me that Dylan was quite capable of taking care of himself in America now. At least, this was the excuse I gave myself for my newly relaxed attitude toward him and his affairs. Actually, I knew that he could never take care of himself, just as well as I knew that no one on earth could take care of him. In tempering my solicitude for his success in meeting reading or social engagements, or in dealings with publishers, and by maintaining a wide gap between our professional association and our friendship, I was really taking care of myself. Arrangements for his public appearances had become systematized by this time, and I found them comparatively easy to carry out. But Dylan's personal progress was still chaotic, whimsical, and, in its daily drink-induced miseries and guilt-ridden despair, saddening to watch. Wary of useless involvement, I had come to pay little attention to his habits or his movements. As far as I could see, my previous intimate attendance, with all the affection it implied and the sometimes dredging effort that it demanded, had done nothing to help him or to make him happy; it had only reduced me to a kind of nervous despair. While my new attitude was self-protective, it was also dictated by a recognition I had never expected to make and never believed I could accept—the fact that Dylan's way of life was not merely wearisome and tiring but that, ultimately, it was just plainly boring. Having long ago registered the first impact of his great personality, having come to know and to participate in all of his moods, having shared confidences in every phase of his life, I found it only tedious to sit through half the day with him as he groaned and fretted about one hang-over and, at the same time, set about guaranteeing the next.

With his new tour already begun, I had still not been able to allay doubts about his dependability in the wake of his last tour. The endless recriminations resulting from his failure to keep his engagement at Tulane had been directed not toward him but toward me. I had been shocked, perhaps naïvely, to learn that many people looked upon my efforts on behalf of Dylan not as the gestures of a friend but as the actions of a business man for whom he was working. Since I could not, without unbecoming and special pleading, point out what my association with Dylan was costing me in time and peace of mind, I had to accept, with a sullen frustration that soon became a shrugging resignation, the role that was continually assigned to me. This, among many other evidences that in the minds of a great part of his public Dylan was an ineluctable and blameless entity, warned me to take care. Yet for all my tongue-tied distress over the Tulane episode and the troubles it caused, I could not blame him either. There was a seam of primal innocence at the core of him that caused judgment to be obliterated, accusation to dissolve in mid air. And yet I knew that absolution from the judgments and accusations of others only left Dylan to wrestle with his guilt alone.

I did not see him again until he came to Boston, for his first engagement outside of New York—at Boston University, where an arts conference of a number of New England colleges was assembled. Since I was myself occupied with a speaking part in this conclave, I asked Bill Read to meet his plane. When they arrived together to pick me up after my lecture, we went to Charles Street for a few beers in a vaguely Bohemian estab-lishment before going on, at Dylan's enthusiastic suggestion, to the Union Oyster House for broiled lobster.

Mindful of his reading that night in Boston's famous Jordan Hall, he was by mid afternoon settled in my apartment in Cam-bridge, and we spent an hour making a choice of poems. There he pre-empted a spot in which I find it easy to remember him— a chair beside a table from which he could look through a wall-sized window over the Charles River, toward the gold-domed top of Beacon Hill, and from which he could watch sea-gulls gliding and pivoting against the Boston sky-line. By the time *Under Milk Wood* was ready for performance, the table showed permanent marks of forgotten or mislaid cigarettes and, branded into the light wood, the ghostly circles of beer cans.

He stayed in the apartment while I went to New York on Poetry Center duties over the week-end. When I got back on Monday morning I found him, over a breakfast of beer and cig-arettes, at work in his favourite place, the table already littered with titbits of paper on which were scribbled disconnected scenes and experimental phrases from *Under Milk Wood*. He might have been a man working on his income tax report rather than a playwright attempting to sustain a lyric mood. As we

154

talked through the morning, I became aware that he was at last feeling the press of time, and that the unfinished part of his play was no longer merely a matter of scenes to be filled in and lines to be brushed up but a problem that would demand all of his creative resourcefulness. The making of *Milk Wood* had assumed the first proportions of a marathon that was to continue up to, and, as it developed, beyond curtain time, now two weeks hence.

He was due in Bennington in the late afternoon. I drove him to North station and waved him off on a brief circuit of readings that was also to include Syracuse and Williams.

Five days later, as I met his returning train, he trundled from a day coach, smiling, weary, and stone sober. There was no club car, he explained; all he could do was read a copy of the *New Yorker* until it was a rag in his hands. We went to the apartment for cocktails with a young Harvard professor of psychology and an Englishwoman who had come for tea and remained to catch a glimpse of the poet. Dylan chose beer over the martinis he was offered; nothing else could assuage his afternoon-long thirst. After dinner, almost now in a sense of pilgrimage, we went to the Old Howard. Dylan laughed at the droopy-trousered comedians and loudly applauded the strip-teasers, even the plump and awkward ones who did apprentice turns before the stars came on. But the sad, sleazy vaudeville acts by professionally nervous acrobats and mangy little high-keyed dogs depressed him and forced him to hide his face in his hands. Nevertheless, we stayed through the long repetitive show and then went on into Scollay Square and a series of slam-bang bars until closing time. It was one of those occasions when Dylan's capacity for being entertained showed as strongly as his gift for being entertaining. The honky-tonk floor shows we watched were, by almost any standard, unrelievedly sad spec-tacles. Yet Dylan looked on with none of the sophisticated indifference one might expect, but with active delight and an odd feeling of concern. His sense of discrimination was professional and keen, and while he could only have been appalled by much that he saw, some unjudging witness within him allowed him to be identified with the meanest and most vulgar of entertainers, so that he was happy when they succeeded and sad when they failed.

Since Boston night life closes down early, he got a normal night of sleep after we returned about one, and the next day worked until late afternoon on *Under Milk Wood*, drinking beer out of cans, smoking incessantly, and stopping now and then to stare at the changing spring-time light on Beacon Hill. Then, very carefully, we went over his selection of poems for the evening, when he was to read at the Fogg Museum at Harvard under the auspices of the Poet's Theatre. He was uncommonly apprehensive about this evening, perhaps because he now had many friends and acquaintances in the Harvard community. In any case, he chose a large group of his best reading pieces and put new touches to the little speech he was now in the custom of giving as an introduction. The large lecture hall of the Fogg was jammed to the doors. After he was presented to the audience by Howard Mumford Jones, he launched into one of his greatest reading performances and was rewarded with storms of applause between each poem.

After the reading, we were to go to the home of a lively young clergyman who had invited a number of people to a reception at his house just off Cambridge Common. As we drove there, Dylan sat silent, in dejection or deflation—I could not tell which—as I tried to cheer him by reporting my own enthusiasm for his superb performance. His sobriety continued throughout the reception. The effort of the reading—and who knows what nameless other stresses or grimacing demons—had put him into one of those states where his mind and body seemed impervious to the effects of liquor, so that he became unrecognizably passive, polite, and preoccupied. Among the people he conversed with at some length was I. A. Richards, whom he had met only that evening and for whom he had long had great respect. Dr Richards could not have known it, but in Dylan's mind he represented another world, another sphere of experience, another level of judgment. Just as Dylan harboured a conviction that certain persons, by circumstances of birth or fortune or both, were hermetically sealed away from him in the category of 'the grand,' he regarded eminent scholars and men of letters as something apart from his own concerns, and perhaps inimical to them. In the company of such men he gave the appearance of being amiable and intellectually at ease; actually be was never quite himself. It was as though he had to prepare a face and to find a language that would be acceptable, to prove that Dylan Thomas was not only the confounding poet of dubious personal reputation but, as well, a scholar among scholars and a critic among critics. On such occasions I was reminded of his attitude toward his father which, it struck me, was of quite the same nature—a combination of dutiful respect and jejune play-acting by which he disguised his buoyancy and presented only a touchingly bookish version of himself.

When the reception broke up, Dylan came to life on his own terms. Seven or eight younger members of the party followed us to Cronin's, the Harvard undergraduate hang-out. We had been there only a few minutes when we were joined by an astonishing girl, unknown to anyone present, whose cheeks were painted geranium red and who wore substantial twigs of apple blossoms in her dishevelled hair. She came at us out of nowhere, squeezed into our overcrowded booth, fixed her shining eyes on Dylan's face, and started to ask him questions about some of the poems he had read that evening. While her speech was vague and disconnected, Dylan attempted seriously to answer some of her questions, only to have her correct his statements. Unnerved, he shortly made indications to me that it was time to go and we quickly fled the nymph, whose drilling eyes followed Dylan to the door. We hastened to another bar where, having recovered equilibrium, our party showed signs of lasting out the night. I left some time after one o'clock, certain that no power on earth could send Dylan to bed before daybreak.

When I returned to the apartment about nine the next morning, I found that the all-night party had just ended, not only for Dylan, who sprawled in bed quite naked, a night-lamp blazing into his sleeping face, but for others, who had slept in chairs and on the living-room couch. Just a few minutes before my return they had picked themselves up and departed shakily

157

back toward Harvard.

Dylan slept late that morning. As soon as he was awake he wanted a drink, not at home, but in a bar. We went to Harvard Square to talk and, intermittently, to watch television until mid afternoon. By now the unfinished *Under Milk Wood* had become a burden and a goad. Dylan tried valiantly to relax in the broad confidence that, somehow, it was going to be brought to conclusion; at the same time, certain ideas he wanted to incorporate into the work proved more troublesome and evasive than he had anticipated. Part of the difficulty lay in getting back into the rhythm in which the play was originally conceived and written. It was as if he had the words but could not find the melody. The process of working in fits and starts between drinking bouts was one in which it was almost impossible to retain sight of the work as a whole. The constant telephoned urgings of Liz, who was already rehearsing the cast in New York, reminded him how much was still to be done, and kept him in a state of anxiety from which the only escape seemed to be another drink. While he reiterated through the length of many days that it was time for him to go to work, he was always ready, at his own or anyone else's suggestion, to leave his work-table for the pleasures of the grimier side of down-town Boston.

At one point in the afternoon I left him for twenty minutes or so when I went out to buy him a few shirts. When I returned, he was a man of new resolution. Putting down his glass, he said simply: 'Time for work.' We drove directly to the apartment, where he settled down at his window-side for four uninterrupted hours. Afraid that even my presence in another room might be a distraction to him, I left him alone through the afternoon, but when I came back about seven he was eager to put down his fountain-pen and go out again. We drove to an apartment off Harvard Square and were welcomed with acclaim into the sodden remains of what had earlier been a lively cocktail party. Here Dylan had to submit to the maudlin attentions of a tipsy schoolmistress and to be otherwise mauled and questioned by people too saturated with gin to know quite what they were doing or saying. I had seldom seen Dylan annoyed by drinking-party behaviour—and not once by the drunkenness of anyone—but on this occasion his distaste was clear-cut and we left within half an hour.

We drove into Boston, where our first stop was a rowdy sailor bar which Dylan had discovered for himself on an evening around Scollay Square. There we listened to ballads sung fervently and badly by a buxom Italian girl whose acquaintance Dylan had made several nights before. At the time of their first meeting, she had come to his table between stints at the microphone, and they had arranged to meet at closing time. But when closing time came Dylan had found himself without money, and had left the bar without explanation. He had been brooding over this defection for days, and was hopeful now that some *rapprochement* would be possible. But as he sent pleading, hopeful looks in her direction only to find his songstress ignoring him, he could only agree with her apparent decision to write him off as a bad bet. We listened to her stentorian renditions and applauded them, but there was no joy in the occasion now that Dylan knew she was going to have nothing to do with him. It was another curious instance of the way in which Dylan could be sent into almost unshakable depression—a state in which his easily tapped feelings of guilt were magnified and burdensome, another occasion when he had to take the consequences of his default. It had apparently never occurred to him to explain to the girl just what had happened. With no will to redeem himself, he sat in glum silence, his sense of *mea culpa* spoiling any last chance of the evening's success. What weighed most upon him was not having lost favour with the girl, whose attractions beyond her Sicilian milkmaid proportions were minimal, but his simple realization that he had insulted a human being who was most likely quite used to the insults of others. This hurt and humbled him, and opened up a reservoir of remorse out of all proportion to the incident which caused it.

When he had wholly retreated into gloomy somnolence, glancing, dog-like, now and then, at the girl as she whooped it up for the sailors standing around the circular bar, I wondered what could be done to cheer him. I took him to the Casino, just a block away, where the featured comedian was Irving Harmon, one of the few comic geniuses still on the burlesque circuit. This did the trick. Never had I seen Dylan more delighted as we watched the performance of Harmon, whose gimlet-eyed, small-town slicker expression and rocking-chair gait show off a technique that combines the sophistication of a literate revue with straight vaudeville corn. This was Dylan's favourite kind of comedy and he was glowing when we left the late show. But all the bars were shut down now and unless we were to take advantage of the 'after hours' drinking places—the existence of which I had concealed from Dylan—there was nothing to do but head homeward. For once, at least, he was in bed and asleep shortly after one o'clock.

Under Milk Wood's first public hearing was scheduled for the next evening, Sunday, 3rd May, with the Poet's Theatre again serving as sponsor. Dylan was to read the still unfinished play in a solo performance. He worked on revisions and additions from late morning until late afternoon, but when six o'clock came around he was ready for a party that had been arranged in his honour at the home of a Cambridge portrait-painter. There he drank moderately, chatted politely with a score of Cantabrigians, and was obviously mindful of the challenge of the evening still to come. He refused my suggestion of supper between the party and the reading, and we were at the Fogg Museum lecture hall well before the scheduled hour. His reading that night was again one of his memorable performances. As a solo piece, *Under Milk Wood* afforded him every opportunity to demonstrate his skill as a reader and, to the surprise of a great part of his audience, his ingenuity as an actor. He was continually interrupted by extended bursts of laughter, and the play proceeded in an atmosphere of crackling excitement from its first solemn moments to its later passages of zany comedy and its final mellow embrace of a whole village of the living and the dead. As soon as he had left the platform, he said he needed a drink. We hurried to a bar before going on to a late evening party. He had exhausted himself again, but I could tell that, unlike his reactions to his first reading at Fogg, this time he was enormously pleased, and somewhat surprised by the electric response to his lines, and in particular by the long laughter evoked by the funny ones. From that time on his concern for the success of *Under Milk Wood* was deep and constant. He had, at last, heard in public performance the response he had but dimly anticipated and hoped for in private. As a consequence, he seemed to have come upon a whole new regard for himself as a dramatic writer.

He left Cambridge the following morning for engagements in Washington and Lynchburg, Virginia, and I did not see him next until the following Thursday. Victor Weybright, publisher of the New American Library, had invited scores of people to a party for Dylan at his New York apartment. Through an embarrassing mix-up, the P.E.N. Club's New York chapter had announced that Dylan would be the guest of honour at a reception they were giving at precisely the same time. I had accepted this latter date for Dylan weeks in advance of his coming to America. While I had told him of it and learned of his intention to accept it, and had later noted it in his diary, he had carelessly forgotten the engagement and agreed to Weybright's invitation. Then he had further complicated a tangled situation by accepting, unknown to me, reading engagements in the south. By a series of explanations and manoeuvres we had managed to change the dates of his readings. But when I got to Weybright's party I was still apprehensive as to whether its guest of honour would show or not.

As it turned out, Dylan's train was hours late and, while he had to forgo the gathering of the P.E.N. Club, he had not forgotten his commitment to Weybright and rang the door-bell just as the first departing guests were on their way out. His arrival gave new life to a party that had begun to grow a little dim with anticipation. His host, gruffly delighted, and perhaps vindicated, showed his pleasure as Dylan chatted in quiet animation over cocktails and made himself congenial to anyone who cared to address him. After he had made conversation with a number of people, including Michael Arlen, Jarmila Novotna of the Metropolitan Opera, the novelists Charles Jackson, Gore

Vidal, and Elizabeth Janeway, and with his publisher, James Laughlin, he relaxed on the floor with the few of us who had stayed until the end of the party. Around nine o'clock we left, together with Arabel Porter, an editor of the New American Library, Howard Moss, and Joseph Everingham, a friend of mine and Dylan's from Cambridge, to go downtown for hamburgers at Julius's. This was again the onset of a long night of bar-hopping. We next went to the crowded San Remo, where, notably, Dylan's presence was no longer a notable event, and then to the White Horse, where the usual crowd awaited his entrance. But since none of us either could or cared to keep up with him as the night went into its roaring phase, we had to leave him finally to his own more than adequate resources.

He was in a bar near the Chelsea Hotel when Joe Everingham and I found him late the next morning. Oscar Williams, with a paper bag full of new anthologies, joined us there and we drank with him until one o'clock. Then I went to the Poetry Center to help put things in order for the first group reading of *Under Milk Wood*, the *première* performance of which was to be given only one week later. When Dylan joined me in the late afternoon, he had forgotten to bring not only the books and manuscripts from which he planned to read a programme of poetry that evening, but even the suit he was going to wear. Leaving him to get on with the rehearsal of his play, I taxied downtown to the Chelsea, gathered up his forgotten books and papers, canvassed the neighbourhood to find the dry-cleaning establishment that had his suit (he had forgotten where he sent it), then returned to the Poetry Center. There I found him ruddy with pleasure in his co-actors, full of admiration for the skill they had brought to roles he felt could only have been played by Welshmen, and bristling with new notions as to just how the play should be staged. His unexpected delight in his acting company prevented him from falling into the customary pre-reading slump. With Liz, we went to Rollie McKenna's apartment for a drink and a steak before returning for the evening's performance. Again the house was sold out, with many standees, and he read a long programme in full command of his best gifts.

A reading in Philadelphia came next; then four days later I was to meet his train at Back Bay station in Boston on my way home from Connecticut. When I got to the depot I encountered Sarah in the waiting-room. She had also come to meet Dylan. They had met again in New York and arranged to be together for the one day Dylan would be in Boston. I was naturally happy to see her, but also puzzled by the meaning of her appearance after so long a lapse of relations between them. Dylan's train pulled in as we strained for sight of him, but he was not among the scores of passengers who disembarked. I phoned my apartment in the hope of some message and learned that a telegram had just arrived from Dylan saying that he was coming by plane. Sarah and I drove to the airport and got there just in time to see Dylan come swinging briskly down the ramp, brief-case in hand. He was wearing dark glasses, a new and ominous note, yet seemed to be quite steady on his feet. We drove to my apartment long enough for him to have a glass of beer and to put on a clean shirt, then were off to a cocktail party in a penthouse flat over-looking Boston Common. While this was just another party among a series of parties, the reappearance of Sarah provided an undercurrent of new interest to most people present and, to me, a new source of apprehensiveness I was reluctant to acknow-ledge. As far as I knew, Dylan had accepted Sarah's new life with finality and something of a sense of relief. Not since our day in London on the river-bus excursion had he shown any sign of his feelings for her. I had not myself seen Sarah at any length since her return from Mexico. While I knew of her decision to end her marriage of hardly a year's duration, I had no real notion of her present feelings for Dylan or of the impulse that had led her once more to seek him out. In any case, I decided to follow my instincts and to remain apart from any second involvement that might be in the offing.

I drove Dylan and Sarah to the Massachusetts Institute of Technology for his reading at eight o'clock, then went off to din-ner, planning to meet them later at another party in Cambridge. Though I merely looked in on this later gathering of some thirty or forty Boston literati, Harvard instructors, and Poet's

Theatre personnel, I still had time to observe that Dylan and Sarah moved about as an intimate twosome and that a good part of conversation at the party was inquisitive gossip about them. When in the morning I drove him to the airport to catch a ten-o'clock plane, he said he had stayed with Sarah in the apartment of a Cambridge acquaintance, offering no other comment except that he supposed she had already returned to New York on an earlier plane. He flew off to North Carolina, where he was to give a reading that night on the Duke University campus at Durham.

By early afternoon of the next day he was back in Boston. Visibly wearied by the quick round-trip flight, he explained that he had been to bed for only two hours after staying up all night exchanging stories with a Welsh clergyman who was a member of the Duke faculty. Now we were about to start off directly for the University of Connecticut, ninety miles away, and another reading scheduled for eight o'clock. As we drove along, I broached to Dylan some notions and conjectures I had been harbouring uneasily for a long time, and of which I had been meaning to tell him at the first appropriate moment. These had simply to do with my conviction that this constant series of readings was an undertaking insufficiently rewarding financially and seriously debilitating physically, quite apart from the fact that it kept him from creative connection with his poetry and threatened to turn him into a public entertainer. To correct this state of affairs, I suggested that we agree between us not to think of another such tour for years to come. I was certain that there were other ways in which he could make as much money as his readings brought him, and offered my services in any way that might assist him in money-making projects other than a series of readings. Whether these sentiments impressed him or whether he merely read a new note of conviction in the tone in which I addressed them, Dylan responded with quiet serious-ness and agreed with everything I said. Yet I remained wary of his true feelings, partly because I had long ago learned how easy it was to direct him and partly because I knew that his mind could be changed in a moment. While his agreement came readily, I felt this might be due to his having received only a few days before a fifteen-hundred-dollar advance on some unpublished fiction, or perhaps that it came out of the physical weariness of the previous few days which had brought him to a condition where nothing seemed more arduous than the thought of further travel. Nevertheless, I was glad that the matter had been brought up, and that there was at last opportunity to tell Dylan that I, at least, would do nothing to initiate another reading tour.

We broke our trip to Connecticut by a stop in Sturbridge, to drink ale before the wood-burning fire-place of an old inn, and arrived at the University just in time to spend an informal hour with the fourteen students of my graduate seminar in modern poetry. Here, as usual, he was charming and outgoing in his warmest manner and, as usual, tending to turn the more earnest questions of the students into jokes against himself and his work. But, just as often, he took great care to make literary distinctions and to answer worthy questions in full measure. This little interview provided another demonstration of his mercurial attitude when he had to face people as a personality rather than as a performer. If he sensed that his interviewers wanted him to be amusing, iconoclastic, or whimsical, he had ways of satisfying each expectation. When he was addressed intelligently and knowledgeably, his answers were in kind. While these quick shifts of emphasis always made the interview lively, they were sometimes disconcerting, since cherubic playfulness one minute and critical sobriety the next tended to qualify any strict sense of him.

We left the classroom with Leonard Dean, who took us to his house on Faculty Row where, in the warm spring evening, his wife, Dorothy, served us a light supper on the veranda. Our leisurely meal—for Dylan the only period of respite in many days—was interrupted by a phone call from New York. It was Liz, suggesting that she come to the University in order to assist him in working through the night on additions to *Under Milk Wood*. Dylan conveyed this rather alarming notion to me and asked me what I thought. Liz's suggestion, prompted by a necessity of which Dylan himself was well aware, did not strike me as feasible—especially in view of his exhausting past few days—but I asked him to make his own decision. He returned to the phone and, by promising faithfully to work until dawn, was able to convince Liz of his assiduous concern for the punctual completion of his manuscript.

He gave a fine, full-voiced reading later that evening, and afterwards there was a brief reception. In spite of his good intentions, and the careful preparations his hosts had made to see that his bedroom was an adequate work-room, Dylan was asleep at a comparatively early hour. But when I came to call for him at seven the next morning, I found that he had been awake since dawn, scribbling on the little pieces of scratch-paper that made up a good part of the script of the play. We drove to Hartford, where we boarded a train for New York. A bottle of beer comfortably before him, Dylan worked on his snippets of manuscript in the club car *en route*. By the time we got to the Poetry Center he had completed a whole new series of scenes on which the nervously waiting actors could begin. He rehearsed with his company—Nancy Wickwire, Sada Stewart, Roy Poole, Al Collins, and Dion Allen—until late afternoon, then gave them a dinner-time rest. With a final run-through scheduled for seven-thirty, the first performance of *Under Milk Wood* was to begin at eight-forty. Liz and Dylan went to Rollie McKenna's apartment close by, where I later joined them. With two typists in attendance, they worked from five until after seven. When new pieces of manuscript were finished, Dylan handed them to Liz, who looked them over, made the illegible parts legible, then handed them on to the typists. But in the middle of this frantic piecing and pruning, Dylan suddenly gave up. He was ill and weary, he said, he simply could not go on. Since the final third of the play was still unorganized and but partially written, Liz felt that the evening's performance would have to be called off, that she or I would have to go before the audience and make an announcement to that effect. When she expressed this to Dylan, he said it was unthinkable, absolutely unthinkable. He buckled down then, and in sober determination finished up one scene after another. In spite of every last-gap effort, he had finally to

166

give up the thought of completing the work in time for its *pre-mière*. But in those last minutes he devised a tentative conclusion that would serve. Twenty minutes before curtain time, fragments of *Under Milk Wood* were still being handed to the actors as they applied make-up, read their telegrams, and tested their new accents on one another. Some lines of dialogue did not actually come into the hands of the readers until they were already taking their places on stage.

After I had made a short curtain speech to the packed auditorium, I went around to the back of the house to stand beside a very tense Liz as the curtains opened. The stage was dim until a soft breath of a light showed Dylan's face: 'To begin at the beginning...' One by one the faces of the other actors came into view as the morning light of Milk Wood broadened and Dylan's voice, removed and god-like in tone yet pathetically human in the details upon which it dwelt, made a story, a mosaic, and an aubade of the beginning movements of a village day. Expectant, hushed, and not at all prepared to laugh, the audience seemed as deep in concentration as the actors on stage until, finally, unable not to recognize the obvious bawdy meaning of some of the play's early lines, two or three people laughed outright. But still there was a general uneasiness, an incomprehension, as if these outbursts had been mistaken laughter. Then, as soon as it became evident that this story of a village was as funny as it was loving and solemn, a chain of laughter began and continued until the last line. When the lights slowly faded and the night had swallowed up the last face and muffled the last voice in the village, there was an unexpected silence both on stage and off. The thousand spectators sat as if stunned, as if the slightest handclap might violate a spell. But within a few moments the lights went up and applause crescendoed and bravos were shouted by half the standing audience while the cast came back for curtain call after curtain call until, at the fifteenth of these, squat and boyish in his happily flustered modesty, Dylan stepped out alone.

Six days later, on 20th May, I drove to Amherst College in

Massachusetts to meet Dylan after he had given a reading there and attended a beer party as the guest of a large crowd of under-graduates. When I registered at the Lord Jeffrey Inn in the late evening, I found a note at the reception desk asking me to come to the house of a member of the English department. Dylan was having a talk over a highball with a young professor and his wife when I joined them, and seemed unusually quiescent for that time of the evening. We stayed only a little while longer and went back to the Lord Jeffrey together. When I said good night and went to my room, Dylan had chosen a paper-backed detective story from a news-stand rack and was hungrily studying a large assortment of nickel candy bars.

When I rapped on his door about nine the next morning Dylan was not there: he had already found a bar and was in it. When (I could do it now almost by instinct) I had located him, he said that one beer was all he wanted—just one beer and no breakfast. It was an enchanted New England morning, with acid-sharp sunlight filtering through old trees around the village green and through masses of lilacs knocking against white clap-board houses. We got into my car, put the top down, drove slow-ly past Emily Dickinson's house, at which Dylan stared with no particular show of interest, and out into the rolling tentative early green of the countryside. Thus began an unhurried day of casual sightseeing and random talk which, later, on a number of occasions, Dylan remembered as his happiest in America. Except when he was rushing from one engagement to another, and tense in the prospect of having to meet still other people and to face still another audience, he had never before seen the whiteness of New England, and it was a revelation.

I avoided main highways as, with the whole day before us to spend at leisure, we began to drive eastward. While automobile trips I had made with Dylan earlier had always turned into a tipsy progress from one drinking place to another, on this day we stopped but once, to have a beer in a ramshackle tavern on the edge of a shining little lake. Following wherever the winding back roads would take us, we slowly circled the greens of many villages, looked long at bone-white churches with gold-leafed steeples, and at old colonial houses freshly painted. It was a wonderful rare feeling to be suspended at leisure from the harassments of the schedule that seldom allowed us opportunity to be together except in its own relentless terms, and we basked in its unfamiliar freedom. Dylan seemed more relaxed and happy than at any time I could remember—and perhaps no better proof of this was his showing only the mildest inclination for a drink. On a typical day he would have by this time consumed at least half a dozen bottles of beer. No small factor in his obvious contentment was the great success of *Under Milk Wood* in its first crucial test performance. He could not disguise the satisfaction he took in its reception, and was looking forward to its next performance without anxiety. Already he had begun to think about another 'play for voices'—a work that would be designed for reading performance by himself and Nancy Wickwire, whose brilliant work had contributed so much to the unveiling of *Under Milk Wood*. This new play would begin not with words, but with screams—the screams of women in labour, and of new-born babies; it would be concerned with the lives of two very ordinary people, a man and a woman who grew up in a Welsh industrial town. They live uneventful lives waiting for some fulfilment of their great capacity for life; and while, in the routine of their days and years, they pass close to one another hundreds of times, they never meet. But then, perhaps, Dylan added, perhaps they *should* meet, but just at the very end of the play, when it is all too late. It would be the love story of two people who were never to be lovers.

We stopped to buy a basket of spring flowers at a roadside stand and, as we drove on, Dylan became reminiscent. He told me of his first meeting with Caitlin, and of the early days of their marriage. They first saw one another at a party in London—a large loud party where they had talked for hours and promised to meet again. But when the party was over, Dylan found he had either neglected to record Caitlin's address, or had lost it. He went back to Swansea, where he had been doing newspaper work, counting only on chance to bring them together again. Some weeks later he received a note from Richard Hughes,

169

the novelist, who was then living in the village of Laugharne. Hughes, who had read and admired a group of Dylan's first published poems, asked him to come for an afternoon visit. Flattered by the attention of so famous a writer, Dylan one day asked a friend to drive him to Laugharne, about thirty miles away. While they were visiting with Hughes, Augustus John drove up to the house in his Rolls-Royce. With him, as usual, according to Dylan, was a beautiful young woman; this time his companion was Caitlin, a daughter of John's lifelong friend, Francis Macnamara.

Dylan's friend drove back to Swansea without Dylan. Augustus John, after a tea-time conversation with his host, also left without his companion. Dylan had found Caitlin again, and was not going to let her move out of his sight. They stayed on as Hughes's guests for days and did not leave until they had decided to be married. After they had taken their honeymoon on the south coast of England, they had to think of where they would establish their home. Since chance had reunited them in Laugharne, and since, for a decisively practical reason, Hughes, who was about to go abroad, offered them his house, they came back to Laugharne. There they found the Boat House, and learned that it was To Let. Not long after they had moved into the Boat House, Dylan's parents came from Swansea to occupy the Pelican.

Our progress toward Boston became even slower as the day grew softly warm, and we seemed always to be getting lost on roads that wound back upon themselves through flowering orchards and shining newly ploughed fields. Between long easy silences our talk rumbled too. I was particularly curious to know how he and Liz had managed to work so well together during the hectic weeks of the staging of *Under Milk Wood*. While they had both made a point of reporting to me the instant antipathy they had felt at their first meeting, for weeks now I had sensed that their mutual distaste had either been tempered or forgotten. In answer to my question as to how they had finally got on, Dylan assured me that everything was changed. Liz was the most wonderful woman he had met in America. I might have convinced him of this from the beginning, he said, instead of having forced him to find out for himself. I reminded him that I *had* spoken to him of Liz, but that his first impression of her had put him in no frame of mind to credit my praise. He admitted this was true, and told me that now she had not only taken charge of *Under Milk Wood*, but had also taken charge of him. She was his producer, his secretary, and his girl. He did not elaborate, but I could tell by his secretly smiling reticence that he was happy about the change of circumstance, and that it was the telling clue to his curiously quiet state of mind.

In Concord we stopped at an old inn for a lunch of sea-food and white wine. We were now within forty minutes of Boston, but the suddenly increased traffic made us reluctant to go farther. I suggested we pay a call on my friend Norman Lindau, a man of sixty odd years and a semi-invalid, at his sprawling old estate in nearby Bedford. We turned off the main road and drove up to the big, low, vine-covered clapboard house. Norman, an avid reader and long-standing admirer of Dylan's, was totally unprepared for the visit and received us with pleasurable astonishment. He and Dylan took to one another instantly, and were shortly deep in conversation about the novels of Caradoc Evans and the works of other Welsh writers completely unknown to me. When Norman's wife, Margaret, came in from her flower garden, she brought us highballs and sat down with us as Dylan, in his most mellow and beguiling manner, led the conversation for an hour or so. I could not help thinking how rare it was for anyone to see him in this light: polite, genial, witty, showing none of the thirsty restlessness that seemed now to be the whole of his social reputation, he spoke modestly and entertainingly, sustained discourse without seeming to dominate it, and accepted the role of the distinguished visitor without insisting upon it. Dylan's first talent for simple human relations, and his natural ability to give himself to those who sought nothing from him, or from whom he could gain no advantage, was never more evident.

When we got to Cambridge about five o'clock, Bill Read came to the apartment with huge T-bone steaks for Dylan, who received the gift with zest. Continuing in his strange outbreak of comparatively normal behaviour, he consumed a full meal. He wanted to go out on a Scollay Square pub-crawl that evening—just a very quiet one, he said, and without a lot of people in tow. Since I had tickets for a play, Dylan phoned Joe Everingham, his favourite Cambridge drinking companion, and they arranged to meet at a bar they knew and to carry on from there.

I drove to my classes in Connecticut the next morning; when I returned in the late afternoon, I found Dylan pacing the floor in an entirely new and unexpected excitement, the reason for which I learned in one happy outburst. Igor Stravinsky had come to Boston to conduct performances of *The Rake's Progress*. Through the music department of Boston University, which sponsored the local production of the opera, he had reached Dylan at my apartment to arrange an interview. Dylan had just now returned from the composer's bedside in his suite at the Copley-Plaza. Stravinsky had not yet recovered from a psycho-somatic upset induced by a performance of the opera during which, by his standards at least, everything had gone awry. While the cheering audience was calling for him after the final curtain, Stravinsky was alone in an alley behind the theatre being violently ill. Now, five days later, he was still recovering from the attack and the complications that had followed it.

Aldous Huxley, who had initiated Stravinsky's collaboration with W. H. Auden on *The Rake's Progress*, had suggested that Dylan might well serve as librettist for a new operatic work. Dylan was immensely pleased and, I could see, not a little flat-tered to have been considered for this assignment. I had seldom observed him in so buoyant a state of creative agitation. In his talk with Stravinsky, they had outlined the idea on which they planned to proceed. They would do a 're-creation of the world' —an opera about the only man and woman alive on earth. These creatures might be visitors from outer space who, by some cos-mic mischance, find themselves on an earth recently devastated and silenced by global warfare; or they might be earthlings who somehow have survived an atomic miscalculation. In either case, they would re-experience the whole awakening life of aboriginal man. They would make a new cosmogony. Confronted with a

172

tree pushing its way upward out of radio-active dust, they would have to name it, and learn its uses, and then proceed to find names and a definition for everything on earth. The landscape would be fantastic—everything shaped and coloured by the dreams of primitive man—and even the rocks and trees would sing. The music would be utterly different from the formal sophistication of *The Rake's Progress*—a reversion, in operatic form, to the earlier Stravinsky of *Le Sacre du printemps* and *L'Oiseau du feu*. Smoking one cigarette after another, circling the room as if it were a cage, Dylan seemed imagination afire.

Practically speaking, this collaboration would be commissioned by Boston University, and Dylan would be given an advance big enough to relieve him of financial worry for many months. He would return to Wales, come back with Caitlin in July, and proceed directly to California. There he would stay and work with Stravinsky at his home in Hollywood; Caitlin would spend that time in San Francisco with their friend, Ruth Witt-Diamant.

All this news was exhilarating, all the plans were wonderful— just what Dylan needed to lift spirits that had become heavy under the press of too many engagements and under the prospect of a return to Wales where all the old financial problems would move in as inevitably as the tides in the estuary. We must make a gala of the evening, Dylan decided, and how better could we begin than by opening the bottle of *vin rosé* Stravinsky had presented to him? Through dinner, Dylan made up one absurd opera plot after another and we toasted Stravinsky anew after each one as Dylan extolled the breathtaking movement of the composer's imagination and the childlike turns of his thought as he groped for English words in his thick Russian accent.

Dinner over, we could do nothing but allow excitement to carry us out on the town. Johnnie Ray, then at the height of his career as a sobbing, floor-pounding minstrel, was the big attraction at an enormous night-club in South Boston. By all means, we must go to hear him, said Dylan—if only for Caitlin's sake: she had a crush on Johnnie Ray and listened to his recordings

173

endlessly. It was apparent that Dylan was somehow fascinated by the singer himself. We drove to the jam-packed establishment, got a front row table among some fifteen hundred other devotees, and drank double Scotches awaiting the entrance of the juke-box idol. At the carefully prepared moment, catapulted on to the stage in an ear-splitting fanfare of songs he had himself made famous, he came at us roaring, moaning, beating his hands on the floor and clubbing the piano, holding a portable microphone in his hands as if it were a bride about to be ravished. As the cavernous room echoed the din of shrill screams and orgiastic sighs, Dylan shouted in my ear: 'He's terrific! Fantastic!' And, in a strange and evangelical way, he was. As Johnnie Ray tore, shredded, and annihilated one song after another, Dylan applauded and cheered with the devastated shop-girls and, with the most insatiable of them, called for half a dozen encores. But finally the lights were dimmed and the show was over. Exhausted, we drove to Scollay Square for a night-cap in the comparative quiet of a neon-red honky-tonk, and got home to bed about two.

Next morning Dylan sang snatches of *Madame Butterfly* and *Aida* all the way to the airport and flew off to New York in the happiest of moods.

Friends of hers and mine had invited Liz and Dylan and me to dinner before his Poetry Center reading the next evening. When I joined them in an apartment high above Central Park West, I could see that Dylan was still buoyant and remarkably untroubled. For the only time I could remember, he showed no qualms about his reading, and instead of his usual beers, even allowed himself several pre-performance highballs. When Liz and I taxied with him across Central Park, he had a moment or two of apprehension as he invoked his evil destiny and damned its eyes, but this time it was all more of a joke than the real thing, and we arrived singing. When he walked on to the stage of the Kaufmann Auditorium, he did so with a staunch confidence and a ramrod bearing that made him a happy caricature of himself.

William Faulkner was in the audience that night. When Dylan had finished a long reading, I brought Faulkner backstage

174

and introduced them. But the hubbub of visitors and auto-graph-seekers allowed them no opportunity to talk. I suggested we retire to a bar near by and, with seven or eight others in ret-inue, led them to a neighbourhood Irish hang-out. I did not sit at the table with Dylan and Faulkner, and cannot report what actually passed between them, but when I spoke to Dylan later he said that he found the man self-effacing and charming, quiet almost to a fault in manner, and that they had come upon no sus-tained conversation because others were always breaking in upon topics Faulkner himself had no zest to continue. After we had said good night to Faulkner, we finished the evening back at the apartment on Central Park West. Dylan got drunk very quickly, boomed and ranted in a happy excess of spirits, and was eventually escorted homeward in the competent hands of Liz.

Three days later I went to see him at the Chelsea for what I believed would be my last visit with him before his scheduled flight back to England. I found him in bed with a broken arm and an attack of gout. Two nights before, he explained, while leaving a dinner party to attend a performance of Arthur Miller's *The Crucible*, he had fallen down a flight of stairs. Liz had been his efficient nurse ever since then, and she was with him now, determined that he stay in bed to rest and eat before his reading of *Under Milk Wood* that evening. Even though his goutish foot made him feel 'as if I were walking on my eyeballs,' he was cheerful and restless and wanted to go out. But Liz, who could apparently now make decisions he would accept, refused to hear of this. A group of people whose acquaintance Dylan had made when he lectured in Vermont came by to see him, but Liz pointedly allowed them only one drink and saw to it that they did not stay for long. It was a pleasure to me to find Dylan so well cared for and, in spite of his restlessness and his inveterate need to break the rules of health and deportment, I could see that it was a pleasure to him. While my own experience had put me in a position to understand that love for Dylan could only lead to a devastating denial of oneself, what this role would even-tually cost Liz was not yet apparent to me, and perhaps not to her. Only when a close mutual friend of hers and mine made

175

the situation clear to me did I realize that her care for Dylan and his utter dependence on her had led her into the same state of distraction I had known in my first few months with him. After our friend had twice suffered through the same experience, and had found both times that he could not impose on our actions his sounder judgment, he wryly pointed out the identical ways in which each of us had been drawn out of our usual orbit of sanity into a maelstrom of doubts and anxieties in the calm centre of which, blowing his bubbles, floated our beloved poet.

On 28th May *Under Milk Wood*, now enlarged beyond its first version, was given a resonantly beautiful performance, in spite of Dylan's having to nurse his broken arm which, for the duration of the reading, he carried in a black sling. But the strain of public performance was more intense than anyone in the audience might have guessed. His face went chalk-white and he became ill immediately afterwards. Liz and I quickly got him through a crowd of admirers, took him back to the Chelsea, and put him to bed. Since he would be flying to London in a few days, again it was time for me to say good-bye. While we had learned to make little of either hail or farewell over the years, I was acutely sad to be going away from him, especially now when he was so ill that even the briefest exchange of words was impossible. As he lay on his bed, I mumbled something about hoping to find him 'loud and vertical' when next we would meet, probably in London or in Wales, and he mumbled back something apologetic, and smiled thinly, but with a sweetness that told me all was well between us.

On the next day, in the course of treating him for his broken arm, Dr Milton Feltenstein, who also succeeded in bringing Dylan absolute deliverance from the pain of recurrent gout, found occasion to talk seriously with him about the general state of his health. In the compounded misery of his several ailments, which now included a siege of alcoholic gastritis, Dylan responded soberly to the doctor's warnings, said he would act upon his advice to find a physician in London with whom he could work toward general physical rehabilitation. To demonstrate his new resolution, Dylan gave up liquor for whole days at

176

a time. While this abstention tended to leave him restive and bored, he was constantly active during the final days of his visit. With Liz he made a quick flight to Washington to confer with the income tax office; spent all of one night making recordings of his poems for commercial distribution; went to lunch with Samuel Barber, the composer; said good-bye to friends, including Sarah, on visits to the White Horse Tavern; and shopped uptown and down to find a bracelet of Navajo silver to take to Caitlin as a present from America. Since his plane was due to take off on the morning of 3rd June, the day after the coronation of Elizabeth II, I phoned him late in the evening to say farewell. He sounded dismally depressed again, and while he tried valiantly to put some cheerfulness into the few syllables he was capable of uttering, I sensed that he was once more in that state of despairing loneliness in which all of his responses were dimmed to the point of atrophy. Putting down the phone, I felt a sudden flood of old feelings of helplessness I had almost believed had retreated for good.

VII

1953: June—September

In the middle of June I received the following letter:

My Dear John,

    Just arrived back here, fractured and barmy, to torpor and rain and Ivy's dungeon, and I've nothing to tell you except a thousand thankyous and how much I miss you. In spite of milk fever, bone-break, some nausea, Carolina, old Captain Oscar Cohen, I enjoyed myself a lot, especially in Cambridge and Boston. And thank your mother too for every kindness.

    I haven't heard yet about the opera, and wrote to Stravinsky only to-day, so I don't know yet any autumn plans. But there's an International Literary Spender-less Conference at Pittsburgh in October, to which I've been invited, and, though to hell with con-ferences, I shall quite likely go there on the way (I hope) to Cali-fornia via (somehow) Cambridge; and with Caitlin, too.

    I'm going to start work to-morrow and shall revise *Milk Wood* for publication and broadcasting here. I'll also be seeing David Higham soon, and will get *Milk Wood* copyrighted as a play for pub-lic performance. Could you, then, d'you think, do something about getting it done across the States? And then, after finishing *In the Skin Trade*, I want to begin on a new, and in one sense, proper-er play. About this I'll tell in—is it?—August. Do write me, however briefly, though please not shortly.

Ever,
DYLAN.

    In subsequent letters to him I inquired into the progress of these plans, but no answer came. Late in July I sailed directly for Italy, having written Dylan that I looked forward to seeing him in Wales early in September. This plan had come about through Cyrilly Abels, managing editor of *Mademoiselle*. Having seen the *première* performance of *Under Milk Wood* she had enthusiasti-cally bought first serial rights for publication in an early issue of her magazine, had asked me to do an accompanying article on Dylan's daily life in Laugharne, and had commissioned Rollie McKenna to take a series of photographs of the village and its countryside.

On 5th September I joined Rollie in London. We set out late morning in a hired Hillman-Minx, drove leisurely across the western midlands, and arrived in Laugharne in the long marine twilight. After parking the car at the end of the path by the sea-wall, we loaded ourselves with photographic equipment, walked to the Boat House, and picked our way carefully down the stony steps of the ragged garden. We could hear scratchy music on the wireless as we approached and the sounds of children's voices with which the house was always humming. Surrounded by her brood, Caitlin opened the door to welcome us with the charac-teristic momentary shyness that always made her expression beautiful. Dylan was not at home, she informed us, but was awaiting our arrival at Browns Hotel; we would all go there for a drink before returning to dinner at the Boat House.

Dylan was in the midst of a card game when we got to the smoky, dimly lighted little pub. A Woodbine hung tremulously from his lips, and his brow, marked with a livid gash in the flesh above his right temple, was furrowed as he sat absorbed in his grimy handful of cards. He left his game to greet us and we sat down at a table under a naked light bulb. Ivy Williams chatted with us and served us Scotch; the other villagers gave us shy looks and furtive, inscrutable smiles, and went on with their games of cards. Dylan wanted to know just where I had been in Europe and whom I had seen, chided me for keeping posh com-pany, and asked me how I could possibly bear the contrast between life on the Italian Riviera and life with him in the gloom of god-forsaken Laugharne. This was an old game between us and we played our familiar parts. While he had long ago seen every evidence that I would choose to be with him over every other acquaintance I had made in the course of my travels, he still found satisfaction in teasing me into an explicit statement of preference for which I could never find the words.

He and Caitlin had recently been up to London for a holiday. Tales of their visit set us off on gossip about people whom we knew there and in New York, and we all got merry and outrageously unkind. When in the course of things I had to ask him about the ugly gash over his eye, Dylan explained that it was the result of another fall, at night, when he had lost his footing somewhere along the dark passage from the pub to his doorstep. But the scar was healing rapidly now, and he seemed unconcerned about it. Two or three drinks later, having lightheartedly tried, condemned, and dragged to the guillotine a number of inflated literary reputations, we were on our way through the dark sea-heavy evening toward the Boat House.

Someone had made Caitlin the gift of a brace of wild duck. To insure its proper preparation she had consulted a French cook-book. There she had been warned that the one offence against wild duck was over-cooking; it was a delicacy best eaten as close to its natural state as possible. As we took our places at table in the close-quartered little dining-room, where coals hissed in the grate against the chill evening, we were all prepared for a festive meal. Since Dylan was inefficient in the art of carving, Caitlin asked me to serve the duck. When the platter was set down before me, I merely touched one of the ducks with a carving knife when dark wine-coloured blood spurted out. This did not seem right to me, but since everyone's eyes were expectantly fixed on the platter, I thought I could only try again. When I had made a second, very tentative, incision, another spurt of blood flowed out over what I could see now was nothing but gristle. The prospect of putting any of this into my mouth turned me pale. 'What a bloody mess you've got there,' Dylan said to Caitlin. 'I cooked it just the way the bloody book said,' she answered. Llewelyn, the only one of the children privileged to dine with adults, began to make faces from his corner of the table. Dylan told him to stop or he would be sent upstairs to bed. Attempting somehow to anesthetize myself against what I was doing, I persisted in my dissection of the little cadaver. When everyone had been served a clammy slice or a dripping leg, we all began to nibble courageously. 'It's delicious,' Caitlin announced through the laborious silence, 'nothing wrong with this duck at all.' 'I can only eat it if I keep my eyes closed,' said Llewelyn, and made a series of disgusting noises. 'For God's sweet sake,' said Dylan, 'take that bloody thing off the table.' Caitlin removed the offensive carcass and we filled up, finally, on vegetable greens and milk and gooseberry tart.

There had been a murder in the neighbourhood of the Boat House a few months previously, and the terror of it was still on the village. An old woman had been knifed in the darkness by an unknown assailant. Circumstantial evidence had caused a deaf-mute to be apprehended, but no one felt at all sure that he was the real culprit. When I was about to escort Rollie to Dylan's mother's house, where she was to stay, both Dylan and Caitlin announced that we could by no means go there alone. I protested, but Dylan insisted that he accompany us, particularly since I would be returning alone. Rollie and Dylan and I walked hand in hand through the Stygian lanes, brushing against overhanging brambles that switched our eyes, tripping over stones, and scaring ourselves further with fearsomely detailed horror stories as we went. On our walk back—the first time we had been alone for many months—Dylan asked about Liz and said that Caitlin was continually suspicious that he was receiving letters from her. Then he spoke of his unhappy restlessness through the long summer in Laugharne, and of his desperate attempts to remain anchored to his writing-table long enough to complete new poems. There was one new work that he thought might 'go.' This was a companion-piece to 'Do not go gentle into that good night.' While it started off in the same tone, it then changed abruptly toward a more syncopated use of metre and a looser stanzaic organization. As we inched our way, step by step, down through the roots and brambles, he recited the first lines:

> Too proud to die, broken and blind he died
> The darkest way, and did not turn away,
> A cold, kind man brave in his buried pride
> On that darkest day.   Oh, forever may
> He live lightly, at last, on the last, crossed

Hill, under the grass, in love, and there grow
Young among the long flocks, and never lie lost
Or still all the slow days of his death...

When we had come through the dangerous darkness unscathed,
I said good night and went to bed in Llewelyn's room, to read
for a little while in a boy's book of adventure, and to wonder, as
my thoughts went back to my previous visit to the Boat House,
what storms were brewing, what crises to prepare for.

After a long, deep sleep I was woken up in the reflected dazzle of the estuary. At the side of my bed stood silent little Colm
with his agate-blue eyes and golden curls, staring at me as if I
were Gulliver asleep. To my perhaps overly-cheerful 'good
morning' I got no reply but a large-eyed slow examination of my
face. As I continued to make one-sided conversation while I
dressed, Colm studied me with distant judicial interest, then
suddenly went babbling away with the dog, Mably, who had just
come in with his lazy tail wagging expectantly. I went down to
breakfast on the terrace with Dylan and Caitlin, ate kippers and
toast with strong tea, and watched the skitterish movements of
hundreds of sea birds wheeling through the sea-rinsed morning.

For months now nothing had been said about coming to
America again, and I had speculated why the enthusiasms of
May and the projects outlined in Dylan's letter of June had been
so quickly dismissed. As we lingered over the sunny breakfast
table, I asked Dylan what his plans were. He said he was unde-
cided. There were so many perplexing matters to take into
account. The offer to come to the 'Spender-less' conference in
Pittsburgh had apparently been ill-timed or mistaken, since he
had heard nothing further from the sponsoring organization
whose plans, he recalled, had struck him as nebulous, even on
paper. But the most disheartening news of all had come from
Stravinsky; he had written that dealings with Boston University
for the commission of a new opera had fallen through and that,
for the present at least, no sponsorship would be forthcoming
from that quarter. Meanwhile, Stravinsky was looking for other
sources of financial support. He wanted very much to go on with

the ideas he had discussed with Dylan in Boston, and hoped he was still planning to come to Hollywood in the fall. Dylan's pleasure in the opportunity of working with Stravinsky was as strong as it had been on the day they met. But the prospect of having to bring this about by his own finances made the possibility remote. One other strong temptation from America was a letter sent by a lecture bureau, offering Dylan a transcontinental tour at fees astronomically far above those I had been able to get for him on the purely academic circuit. If he accepted this offer his audiences would be of quite another stripe—mostly women's clubs and 'culture series' appearances. While this aspect of the offer was little inducement, the fat fees he might command as a 'personality' were a genuine allure. At home there was still another good possibility—any day, he said, he might be given a high-salaried contract to work on the script of a new movie in London, a movie about the voyages of Ulysses. Against these developments there was his determination to get on with his novel, *Adventures in the Skin Trade*, sections of which had already been purchased in America by *New World Writing*. He was anxious, too, to begin on that 'proper-er' play he had mentioned in his last letter, and of which he had told me on our springtime drive across Massachusetts.

Listening to Dylan's somewhat anguished account of so many uncertainties, I had one strong and simple reaction; he should stay in Laugharne and get on with his work. When he asked me what I thought he should do, I first of all tried to have him put aside the notion of another American reading tour of the sort he had completed only three months before. This, I felt, would be something to do again, certainly, but at least not for four or five years hence. I had expressed this conviction when we were together in April and, while I felt then that he had for the most part agreed with me, I sensed, now that he was back in Wales, beleaguered by financial worries and creative aridity, that almost any means of escape seemed attractive. I told him I felt he should try to stay in Laugharne, by whatever devices, and find his way back toward a working routine, adding that I was certain *he* knew that this would be best for him. And of course

Dylan did know in his heart that his energies would be more properly directed toward remaining where he was than toward all the distractions that would come should he set about planning another busy adventure abroad. But he was in the same sort of mood of which he had written not long before:

Oh no work of words now for three lean months in the bloody
Belly of the rich year and the big purse of my body
I bitterly take to task my poverty and craft:

To take to give is all, return what is hungrily given
Puffing the pounds of manna up through the dew to heaven,
The lovely gift of the gab bangs back on a blind shaft.

While he could easily admit the truth of his better instincts and could acknowledge that the rigorous patience they demanded was essential, he had no confidence that he could force himself to remain at home to work, and no assurance of livelihood that would make such a decision tenable. To earn money he would have to spend a great deal of time in London. There he would have to work even harder and with less certainty of income than in America. When I could see that, in Dylan's mind, the idea of another tour was a real one, I spoke again my decision not to be involved in its arrangements. In giving substance to this decision I made little of my reluctance to commit myself to another six months of onerous correspondence, schedule-making, and vicarious financial anxiety, emphasizing only the harm I knew Dylan would be doing to himself. I had still never made clear to Dylan, except as a sort of conspiratorial joke between us, the devastation such responsibilities had brought to my general peace of mind and my attempts to get on with my own creative work.

While we discussed these matters under high white clouds, in the soft warmth of late morning, a distant hiss and rumble resounded through the sea wind, and the whole house suddenly went into a little fit of trembling. Dylan cursed. 'I *can't* stay in this place!' He explained that Her Majesty's Government had recently established a testing range for guided missiles within earshot of Laugharne. As I soon learned, these whooshings and grumblings, and the sort of minor earthquake that shook the house after them, were apt to punctuate any time of the day. Dylan said he could never get used to them. 'I know I won't do a bloody thing between now and Christmas. We've got to find another place to live, away from here—away from London, too, somewhere on the sea, perhaps on the east coast.'

Through these outbursts, I was aware of a self-deceptive ambiguity in Dylan I had frequently encountered before. It was not dishonesty, but a confusion of reasons overlying a simplicity of sentiment. One thing was clear. He did not want to condemn himself to months at home, even though staying at home would be the only way in which he could ever meet and begin to overcome the challenge that now, beyond all other known or unknown forces, dominated his existence. While he perhaps did not know the way toward his creative salvation, he did know ways in which creative exercise could be postponed or superseded. It was sadly apparent that Dylan's energies were directed not toward fighting through to freedom but toward escape from drudgery and the inadmissible thought of failure. The draining forces of guilt, indolence, and onerous little commercial assignments had brought him into a state of mortal anxiety. Desperation had so muddied his sense that even his most intimate relations werc affected. He could not admit to himself, much less to Caitlin or to me, that he wanted above all to come back to America, and that he *would* come back to America. Attempting to give himself the certificate of reason, he seized on anything—financial worries, guided missiles, or invitations from Hollywood—that might support his assertion that he could no longer exist productively in Laugharne. I did not want to give in to his attempts to make his reasoning seem logical, even though I could see that his heart was set on getting away. But at last I did give in—and so abetted his final effort to escape from himself.

When it became obvious that he was waiting for my direction, I became practical, point by point. If America were what he wanted most, these would be the justifying reasons: first, collaboration with Stravinsky on an opera might very well lead to the bettering of his yearly income for a long time; second, signing for a tour under the auspices of a high-powered lecture agency would mean that in ensuing seasons he could come to America and, in very short periods of time, earn enough money to support him through the whole year. If, as he thought, lack of money was the main factor that kept him from working, the thing to do was to get money. Nothing else, to my mind, could justify another trip to America. Dylan agreed. But, he asked, how was he to get to America and support himself there, and his family in Wales, while he was working with Stravinsky? I answered that, while I would not again undertake to plan a full-scale tour, I could, of course, offer him readings at the Poetry Center, not only of his poems, but further productions of *Under Milk Wood*. If the fees involved were not sufficient to underwrite his whole visit, I would reach out to get him engagements involving a moderate amount of travel along the eastern seaboard.

Caitlin remained with us most of the time through this discussion. When, every now and then, she left to attend to household duties, Dylan would call her back—to listen to some new idea of his, or to have me repeat some notion of mine. I had the feeling that Dylan wanted to convince her that we were not engaged in any sort of complicity that might exclude or displease her. From the beginning of our discussions she had been outspoken in her reluctance to be left alone in Laugharne, no matter how brief Dylan's contemplated absence might be. When America entered the picture as a real possibility, they discussed the feasibility of her living in London with Colm while Dylan would be in California. Since both Llewelyn and Aeron would be off to school in late September, their welfare would not bring new problems. But Caitlin was not happy in this prospect and gave Dylan no encouragement to entertain it further. I offered the suggestion that, if they would not mind travelling inexpensively across the Atlantic, they might be able to stretch things so that there would be just enough money to take care of them

187

both. Dylan seemed pleased by this, and immediately tried to have Caitlin agree. But, wary, disbelieving, she held back. It struck me that she knew Dylan's real feelings were not his spoken feelings.

It was a disheartening conference. I knew that no matter how deeply implicated I seemed to be in the issues we discussed, no matter how assiduously Dylan asked for encouragement in every turn of the knotty problem, I was actually but super-ficially involved. Unable, as always, to resist Dylan's appeal for help, I had become party to an action I had determined not to support. But at least I had made my feelings plain: against my better judgment I would act for him within the limited resources at my disposal. The dominant problem—the endless, old, and insoluble problem—was money and how to get it. The problem of how to keep it seemed never to have entered anyone's head. None the less, if an American trip could be viewed by both Dylan and Caitlin as an investment in future security, and if Dylan were determined that he could and would not write in Laugharne, I could only go along with him and offer my help. Should he finally decide to come over, I suggested that he plan to stay no longer than eight weeks—about half of that time to be spent with Stravinsky, the rest to be given over to a few readings at the highest fees he might command.

Just before noon we strolled into the village, where the high sun made the little pink-washed and white-washed houses look like candy houses, and went to visit Dylan's mother in the Pelican. She moved about the house on two canes and, in spite of her long convalescence from a broken leg some months before, was as chipper and sweetly hospitable as I had remem-bered. Rollie had already been out with her cameras for hours. After a chat with Mrs Thomas, Dylan and I retired into her small, air-tight parlour, which had the atmosphere of a room embalmed for generations. All of Dylan's books were kept here in a neat state of preservation, not only his own published works in plain and fancy British and American editions, but also his school books and those he had read as a child. Our business there was an accounting of Dylan's American finances which the

188

income tax inspector had demanded. When he had left New York in May, I had given him a complete record of earnings and expenditures from the hour of his arrival, but this had been lost. Fortunately I had kept carbon copies, and had been led by some intuition to bring one of them to Wales. The only thing to do was to make a new copy. I settled myself in the little coffin of a parlour while Dylan went across the street to have a pint of bitter and pass a morning's gossip with Ivy Williams. Rollie returned from her reconnaissance of the village just as I was tediously completing long lists of figures. We called for Dylan at the hotel and went back to the Boat House to have lunch in high sun on the terrace. Over our meal we again discussed the plans and possibilities which had occupied us all morning. Both Dylan and Caitlin were still in a state of distressed uncertainty, and our talk was rambling and without the resolution that might have brought relief to us all. Rollie made photographs of our conference: the results show us independently absorbed, thoughtful, and not very happy.

Our project for the afternoon was a drive into the countryside of Dylan's childhood—to the places he visited in the summers when his Aunt Annie Jones was still alive, the landscape of 'Fern Hill.' Caitlin said she preferred not to join our excursion. We called for Dylan's mother and set out toward St Clears. There we gained the road leading into Carmarthen and drove a few miles before turning off at Banc-y-felin. The day was blue, the country still in its midsummer green. Mrs Thomas entertained us with a flow of anecdotes of gentry and yeomanry, called Dylan's attention to a hundred houses or woodlands or chapels, and seemed altogether delighted in her role of cicerone. In Llanybri we stopped for ices we got in a shop and brought to the car. Villagers passing by recognized Mrs Thomas and stopped to chat. 'These are Dylan's friends,' she would tell them, 'they've come all the way from America to see my boy.'

Outside the village we stopped by the hill-top church one can see from the Boat House—the one which Dylan had in mind when he wrote: 'Pale rain over the dwindling harbour/ And over the sea wet church the size of a snail/With its horns through

189

mist'—and walked in pastures around it to look back on Laugharne and to pick out through the distance landmarks we had
come to know. From Llanybri we soon came to Fern Hill, the
highland farm where Dylan spent long childhood holidays with
his now deceased aunt and uncle. A yellow-washed wall glowing
in the afternoon light hid nearly all of the house from the road.
As we drew up, the new owner and his dog came out, as if by
appointment. When Mrs Thomas had introduced us, he led us
through a little fine-gravelled courtyard and into the house by
way of a tiny conservatory roseate with giant geraniums. Great
sides of cured bacon hung in neat rows from the rafters of the
dining-room above heavy dark tables and chairs and a glinting
exhibition of blue and white china. When our host suggested we
wander through the house at our own pleasure, Dylan led Rollie
and me through a series of curiously antiseptic and lifeless
rooms. In the parlour, that memorable room of 'a stuffed fox and
a stale fern' where, once, Dylan was 'a desolate boy who slits his
throat/In the dark of the coffin and sheds dry leaves,' there
stood now only a few overstuffed pieces of mail-order furniture.
It all seemed much smaller and emptier than he remembered,
Dylan said, and I could see that he was becoming nostalgic and
unhappily thoughtful in this pilgrimage to a house memory and
imagination had furnished so differently. We went then through
the front door out on to a greensward hedged by boxwoods,
walked half way around the house, and into a sprawling old
orchard where rotting apples lay by the hundreds under gnarled
trees, and out on to the spongy turf of surrounding pastures.
Seen from a little distance, the house assumed a simple beauty,
black shutters against yellow-wash giving it the appearance of a
child's drawing of a house. The high-domed barn was still as it
used to be, and the long sloping view through heavy air resonant
with far-off chapel bells and the lowings of cattle. We picked red
and yellow apples from boughs that almost touched the ground,
munched on them as we walked, and Dylan told us stories about
people who had lived at Fern Hill—about a hangman who, overcome with remorse for his long career as master of the gallows,
had hanged himself; and about his roistering uncle whose

fabulous drunkenness had made him the terror of the district. But the experience of Fern Hill so many years after his last visit had saddened Dylan, and he remarked many times how shrivelled and colourless everything now seemed. These were, after all, the same fields where

> the blue altered sky
> Streamed again a wonder of summer
> With apples
> Pears and red currants
> And I saw in the turning so clearly a child's
> Forgotten mornings when he walked with his mother
> Through the parables
> Of sun light
> And the legends of the green chapels
>
> And the twice told fields of infancy
> That his tears burned my cheeks and his heart moved in mine.
> These were the woods the river and sea
> Where a boy
> In the listening
> Summertime of the dead whispered the truth of his joy
> To the trees and the stones and the fish in the tide.

When we came back to the car after our rambling tour of the farm, Rollie took shots of Mrs Thomas and Dylan as they chatted with the congenial new owner, and then we drove to the village of Llanstephan and on to Lords Park. Mrs Thomas seemed as happy as a baby in a pram when we left her in the car to saunter a while through tall groves of druidical trees, to stare at the moss-grown ruins of a castle, and to watch from a distance the movements of a few solitary bathers on the long strand at the point where the River Towy flows into Carmarthen Bay. But there was nothing to linger over, and we soon went on to pay a call to distant relatives of Dylan's in their ancient homestead.

To get there we had to turn off the macadam road and follow a wagon track uphill. At the top of the rise we turned into a

191

mud-filled farmyard surrounded by big and small buildings stark with new whitewash. A cluster of people, from infants to withered crones, suddenly popped out of half a dozen doors to look at us with curiosity, and then to welcome us. Since Rollie was anxious to get some pictures, we left Mrs Thomas to the women, who led her into the main house, and went with Dylan and an old man to wander the surrounding pastures. We could not understand a word of our guide's English, but Dylan seemed to, so we left all conversation to them. Sinking in the soaked fields up to our ankles, we followed the old man as he limped along on his staff, found little of special interest to photograph, and returned through mounds of 'house-high hay' around which white chickens pecked and scratched. Inside the bare, scrubbed kitchen, with its fire-place big enough for five men to stand abreast in, its hanging sides of bacon, great black iron pots and witches' brooms, we were given large cups of warm milk out of a pail brought in by a red-faced milkmaid. We drank it, bravely, and were surprised to find we liked it. Four women, gathered in a semicircle, chatted with Mrs Thomas. While we could make out but snatches of their Welsh-accented English, we could tell by their kindly but curious glances toward us that we were at least part of their conversation. The fifth woman of the farm, the matriarch of the family, remained in an adjoining room. When she was ready to receive us, we were led by Mrs Thomas, proceeding slowly and almost ritualistically on her two canes, into her presence. We were told that she was ninety-six years old, quite deaf, and unable to speak a word of English. As she sat in the reflected glint of long shelves of heir-loom china, her shrivelled little body entirely covered in a Spanish profusion of rich black silks, she addressed us with an interest and pleasure that made a kind of benediction. Deeply moved by the dignity of the woman and the power of matriarchy that sustained her bearing, we could only bow and smile and somehow try to convey our respects. Through Mrs Thomas, who acted as interpreter, she extended an invitation to stay for tea. Mrs Thomas felt we could not refuse, and we could see that she herself wanted us to accept. But Dylan demurred, partly on his own account and partly, we supposed, because he knew we wanted to take advantage of the early evening light for more photographs in the region.

Everyone attended our departure, and we waved to figures in all the doorways as we drove out of the yard and down the wagon-rutted hill. Not far along the bramble-lined road we came to a little grey house. A smiling old man in an unblocked felt hat that made him seem taller than he was by a whole foot was standing by his gate. Mrs Thomas said: 'There's old Tom, my brother. We'll have to stop.' As we drew up alongside the sagging wooden fence, she spoke to him through the open window of the car. Looking puzzled, he merely smiled. Then Dylan realized that, since Mrs Thomas was wearing sunglasses, her brother did not recognize her. When she took the glasses off, he grinned broadly but still did not seem disposed to speak. Mrs Thomas asked him a number of questions in quick succession, but his answers were mumbled and inaudible. Undaunted, she went on, promising to come over soon to help him out, reporting the names of some of the people we had encountered on our drive, and asking about the health of relatives. Then she waved him a blessing and we drove off. Tom, she explained, had lived alone ever since the death of his wife forty years ago. Once a year she came over to his house to help him put things in order.

Near Llanybri again we stopped close by a grey chapel surrounded by a graveyard in which stone crosses and wind-smoothed grey slabs stood in little huddles. The sun was low in the sea now, and the music of hymns from the evening service floated over the windless hilltop. This was the burial place of all of Dylan's maternal ancestors. When we left the car and walked toward the crowded gravestones, Dylan and his mother went ahead. Proceeding slowly on her canes, she paid respects to one grave after another, pointing out to Dylan names he had probably forgotten. The newest inscription, outlined in shining gold that seemed inordinately bright among the uniformly weathered greyness, was the name of Anne Jones. Dylan followed after his mother silently, listening to her little stories of the dead. Mrs Thomas moved staunchly yet laboriously, her eyes wet as she now and then looked away from a grave and into the yellowing distance, her words to Dylan merely informative, betraying little of what we could tell she was feeling. In the cool evening sun, each with his own thoughts, we stood in a glassy silence. The only sounds coming into our meditations were a rumour of vespers from the chapel, a low chorus of voices answering one voice, and the sweet whistling cries of swallows as they wheeled and dipped over the churchyard.

The drive homeward, over the Coomb, into St Clears and across a little stone bridge over the River Taf, was lighted operatically by a long gaudy afterglow that coloured our faces as we caught glimpses of the sea from the many hilltops we climbed and descended. Mrs Thomas, sprightly again, laughed with Dylan as they recounted old stories the day's visits had recalled, and waved greetings to friends who, in their Sunday best, stood by gate-posts or fished from bridges. We came back to Laugharne at dusk. Except for a single glass of beer at Browns Hotel in the late morning, Dylan had had nothing to drink all day. This fact seemed memorable—reminding me of the long day in the Massachusetts countryside we had spent together when he showed neither the desire nor, apparently, the need for alcohol. My understanding of just what it was that led Dylan to over-indulgence at almost all other times was again confused.

When we had seen Mrs Thomas to the doorstep of the Pelican, we dropped by at Ivy Williams's. She took us into the kitchen that was always comfortable with gurglings and rumblings, and served us a pint before the card players arrived, settling themselves by habit around the oilcloth-covered table. Leaving Dylan to sit in on a game of nap, Rollie and I went to join two fishermen who had that morning offered to take us out on to the tidal flats. These were villagers whom, once, Dylan had described: 'Out there, crow black, man tackled with clouds, who kneel to the sunset nets.' When they mounted a motor-cycle, we sped after them on a road running through darkening sand dunes, then walked with them in our bare feet through the cold sand scabrous with cockles for nearly a mile into the sea. There they picked up the silvery wriggling fish, mostly plaice, that had

194

become ensnared in the little fence-like nets, and plopped them into burlap bags slung over their shoulders. When we got back to the Boat House, Dylan had returned from the pub and was listening to the news on the wireless. We warmed our benumbed feet at the grate fire in the dining-room and Caitlin served us heavy soup and bread. Then she brought in an enormous tin pail of cockles which we cracked open and ate by the hundreds.

Dylan was still asleep when I went into the village early the next morning. At the Pelican I found Mrs Thomas and Aeron in bed together, propped up on huge downy pillows, having a morning's chat with Rollie. While Aeron made drawings with her crayon set, among which was a picture of a princess who looked for all the world just like her grandmother, Rollie and I had breakfast on trays, talked with Mrs Thomas of Dylan and America, and showed her a number of photographs of Dylan that had been taken in New York. Since the morning sun was good, we then set out to make an attempt at documentary coverage of Laugharne. We climbed brambled walls, peeked into gardens, moseyed through narrow lanes, and otherwise insinuated ourselves into every nook and cranny, from the muddy edge of the estuary to the top of the hill from which the shining roofs and gables made patterns that sometimes looked medieval and sometimes cubist. We got many suspicious glances as we went and, at times, found that whole streets would suddenly be shut up against us. Trying to look harmless and genial, we patted the heads of dogs and spoke to those children who had not been snatched inside by wary mothers. But the evil eye of the camera could not be concealed or the threat of its spell overcome. For half of the time we went like pariahs.

Lunch at the Boat House was occasion for another long discussion of uncertainties. It was quite apparent now that we would come to no firm resolution before Rollie and I would have to return to London that evening. Dylan's mind was really quite made up, I felt, and he would come to America against all hazards, but this decision would not be announced until he had conferred with Caitlin and found some means of overcoming her intransigence. I felt in any case that the difficulty in coming to a

195

decision was due only partly to the many troublesome practical considerations that had to be taken into account, and more deeply to some basic disagreement between them for which present issues offered but a new focus. When lunch was over, all three of the children walked with us into the village to have their pictures taken with their grandmother. The most promising background we could find was an old gnarled apple-tree in the kitchen garden of the Pelican. There in the chequered shade of a summery afternoon, with the whole family gathered on or about a green bench, Rollie took a series of group portraits. During the sitting Aeron became cross and irritable, announcing that she was going back into the house. Her grandmother calmed her with a kindly but stern admonition and soon everyone was looking expectantly into the eye of the Leica. Dylan, perhaps momentarily overwhelmed by his position as paterfamilias, was co-operative and interested, yet seemed rather expressionless and had little to say. His notably quiet manner may have been simple deference to Rollie and the family scene she was bent on capturing. Yet one cannot help thinking that there was a solemnity in the event of which he was wholly conscious.

Now it was time for Rollie and me to set off for London. Surrounded by three generations of Thomases, we piled into the little car and drove off to a chorus of good-byes and the excited barking of the dog, Mably, who had had his picture taken, too.

When, according to plan, I phoned Dylan at home two days later, he said it looked as though he and Caitlin would be coming to America, the only thing standing in the way of the trip being the slim chance that the film-script job might at any minute be offered to him. Caitlin was still less than enthusiastic about the venture, he reported, but was willing to come with him rather than put up with a makeshift life in London during his absence. He would hear for certain within twenty-four hours, he expected, and would phone me at once. Next morning I was writing pre-sailing letters in the lobby of my hotel when I was paged to come to the phone. The film deal had fallen through, Dylan said; he and Caitlin would definitely come to New York about the middle of October. He asked me to proceed with the travel arrangements we had discussed, and confirmed our earlier understanding of the range and purpose of the American visit: performances of *Under Milk Wood* at the Poetry Center and perhaps elsewhere, a few readings of his poems at high fees, a month or so with Stravinsky in California, then home by Christmas with hope that the future might be financially easier.

VIII

1953: September—November

When I sailed for home that night my thoughts were ambivalent: if I was sorry that Dylan had not heeded my judgment, I was pleased he had sought my encouragement, especially as it seemed that the decisions he had arrived at were likely to lead to a sweeping change in his financial circumstances; yet his irascible temper and the mental turbulence of which it was a sign left me doubtful and uneasy because I knew that its under-lying stresses would be removed neither by money, mobility, nor public acclaim, and certainly not by the scattering of his talent into purchasable fragments. Nevertheless we had made our commitments. As soon as I was home in Cambridge, I went to a travel agent to arrange passage for Dylan and Caitlin. From him I learned that it would be impossible to obtain berths in tourist class accommodations for mid October—still the 'high' season for westward crossing—without delay and uncertainty. Since the first performance of *Under Milk Wood* was now scheduled to be the opening event of the Poetry Center season on 24th October I had to make a quick decision. I cabled Dylan, asking if he would consider flying over alone, with Caitlin following by the first ship on which I might be able to book passage. He cabled back that he was coming alone. From the meagre phrasing of this answer I could not tell whether Caitlin had altogether given up her intention of coming, or whether Dylan had simply recognized the expedience of his coming by air in order to meet his first engagement.

A plane ticket was forwarded to him by the travel agency; he was due to arrive in New York on the morning of 14th October. Liz was planning to meet him at Idlewild, but when she checked with the air-line, Dylan's name was not on the passenger list. Three days went by without news of him. As we later learned, he was already in London and ready to depart when his ticket was just being delivered in Laugharne. On 17th October I received a cable: 'Pickett [*sic*] arrived couple days too late now catching plane 7.30 Monday 19th desperately sorry Dylan.'

When he finally arrived, complaining of the heat yet wearing a prickly camel's hair scarf and a rug-heavy suit, Liz was there to greet him. He wanted a drink 'right off,' but as they approached the airport bar they found it was being picketed for alleged non-union practices. Dylan's thirst was so great that he was willing to put aside compunctions he would normally have considered binding. But if he was ready to cross the picket line, Liz was not. When he could see that she was adamant, he gave up. 'All right,' he said, 'but only for you and the Rights of Man.' As they got into the taxi for Manhattan, Dylan sank back with a tremendous sigh. His visit in London, he said, 'was the worst week of my entire life.' Caitlin had been with him, and now that his American trip had led to just the makeshift situation she had most wanted to avoid, mutual unhappiness and guilt had caused continual dissension. But he was curiously preoccupied by something that had happened on the flight: an Irish priest from New York, returning from a visit to his homeland, had boarded the plane roaring drunk at Shannon. When he continued to drink and, to the distress of other passengers, became garrulous and increasingly obstreperous, the stewardess had declared the bar closed to his orders. Without liquor, he soon had an attack of delirium tremens, and had finally to be bound and shut in the men's room. He was kept prisoner there until, at Gander, he was taken off the plane in the care of a physician. While Dylan made some grim comedy of his report of the incident, he was perhaps as shaken by it as he was amused.

At the Chelsea, he discovered that the reservations I had made for him had been cancelled because of his three-day tardiness and that, for several days at least, none of the large, bright rooms facing on to 23rd Street would be available. He was given a small room in the rear of the hotel. While he seldom seemed to pay the slightest attention to his living-quarters anywhere, being put into a small dark room when he had become used to the best in the house upset him inordinately and made him sullen. But a drink with Liz at the Silver Rail on Seventh Avenue soon pulled him out of his sudden depression. After they had had a quiet dinner at a Spanish restaurant in the village, he was in a sober and serious mood for a rehearsal of the newly revised and now fairly complete play-script. To the actors, who not only held him in warm affection as a person but who showed an almost awed respect for his ingenuity as a man of the theatre, his presence was magic. Under his direction the new version of *Under Milk Wood* fairly leaped into shape. After the rehearsal, which had put him into the mellowest of humours, Dylan wanted to visit the White Horse; with Liz and a young poet friend of his he stayed there in quiet conversation until two.

On the next morning, as he and Liz were walking toward the Village from 23rd Street, he spotted a billboard poster advertising a new movie, *Houdini*. Dylan called Liz's attention to the sign, remarking that the great magician had always fascinated him—particularly for his fabulous escapes from the many ingenious traps that he allowed to be devised for him. The worst horror in life, said Dylan, the horror beyond horrors, was the sense of being hopelessly trapped. It was a subject he was going to write about—in fact, he said, he was already well along into a prose-piece about an 'escape artist.' 'Autobiographical?' asked Liz, and Dylan smiled as he said: 'You know me too well.'

In the middle of the afternoon, after he had gone to have a few drinks by himself in Julius's, Liz rejoined him. But he said he was feeling unwell, that perhaps he had better return to the hotel to rest. Liz accompanied him, sat with him through the remainder of the afternoon, and later went out to a nearby delicatessen to get him a light supper. After he had eaten he said he felt he could sleep, and she left him in the early evening. Before he closed his eyes, he turned to her and said with a weak smile: 'It looks as though I'm putting you on as nurse awfully quickly.' 'Oh,' said Liz lightly, 'is that what I am?' 'No,' he answered, 'not my nurse, and not my secretary— my friend, my *real* friend.'

201

He slept late the next morning and was sober and professionally concentrated when the next rehearsal of *Under Milk Wood* took place in the afternoon. Later in the day he went to a Yorkville bar with Liz and a British photographer, drank moderately, and shortly announced that he wanted to have a good meal. They taxied downtown to Herdt's, on Sixth Avenue near 14th Street. There he ate an enormous dinner—a dinner which, in the course of events, was to be his last full meal. Continuing in the ingratiating sobriety he had shown through the day, he mentioned repeatedly, yet without explanation, his immense relief in having 'escaped' from London.

Liz met him for lunch the next day at a sea-food restaurant near the Chelsea. But the food so displeased him that he went into a rage—a most unusual thing for him to do under any circumstances—and would not eat a bite. While he sulked and fumed after his outburst, it became obvious to Liz that Dylan was in an acute state of nervous agitation; she walked with him back to the hotel where, ostensibly, he was going to settle down to work further on his script. Two or three hours later she phoned him from her office. Dylan answered in a voice barely audible; apparently he had become stupefied with drink. Alarmed, Liz hurried to the hotel. There she found him with a group of people from Cinema 16 who had come to arrange for his appearance on a symposium they were sponsoring. Also in the room was an eminent literary critic whose work Dylan much admired, and who had simply dropped by to talk with him. But when Liz could see that the critic's visit had only led to heavier drinking, that Dylan was now completely intoxicated and quite out of connection with his company, she asked all of the visitors to leave. She persuaded Dylan to rest, then, and within a few hours he had returned to comparative sobriety and was able to work on new scenes of the play. He dictated to Liz new passages which, in spite of his shaky condition, were composed on the instant. All of these remained as part of the finished work.

Early in the evening, they went together to rehearsal, but by the time they had reached the auditorium Dylan said he felt too ill to participate. Herb Hannum, an architect whose acquaintance Dylan had made more than a year before, and for whom he had since developed a deep affection, had come to the Poetry Center to go out with them afterwards. While Dylan remained in Herb's care, Liz went on stage to read his lines while he rested on a couch in the Green Room. When he had first walked into the auditorium that evening, Dylan had said that he found the place stifling hot; but within a few minutes he said that he was freezing, that he couldn't get warm enough. Herb covered him with overcoats borrowed from the dressing-room, but Dylan said he was still shivering cold. When he dozed off for perhaps fifteen minutes, Herb went out to bring him food— clam chowder and crackers and coffee and, in the hope of making him warm, brandy and hot-water bottles. Dylan accepted these ministrations 'like a baby,' according to Herb, but could not fall asleep or be rid of his spasmodic restlessness. Sitting upright every few minutes, he would say: 'What's going on? What part are they reading now?'

At a rehearsal-break, Liz came back to type up new sections of the script. Dylan told her that he would join the actors, to read 'the new stuff,' when the rehearsal was called. Doubtful, she asked him if he really felt capable of reading. Dylan answered yes, firmly, and went on stage to read with his company through the final twenty minutes of the play. When he returned to the Green Room he became nauseated and had to vomit, retching so violently that he lost his balance and fell to the floor. When Herb had helped him back on to his feet, Dylan, gasping, leaned against the wall. 'I can't do anything any more,' he said. 'I'm too tired to do anything. I can't —, I can't eat, I can't drink…I'm even too tired to sleep.' He lay down on the couch. 'I've seen the gates of hell to-night,' he said. 'Oh, but I do want to go on—for another ten years anyway. But not as a bloody invalid—not as a bloody invalid.' He groaned and turned his face to the wall. 'I'm too sick too much of the time.' After a few minutes of sleep, he opened his eyes and, calmly, sadly, said: 'To-night in my home the men have their arms around one another, and they are singing.'

When Liz and Herb went back to the hotel with him he

203

seemed exhausted, overwhelmed by miseries that had led him beyond despair into fear. Unwilling to leave him alone, they saw him to sleep and Liz stayed with him through the night. Dylan was sleeping soundly when, next morning, she left the Chelsea to go to her apartment.

Herb came to see Dylan later in the morning and they went out to breakfast at the Chelsea Chop House. Shaken by what he had experienced with Dylan the night before, Herb asked: 'Dylan, how long have you been this way?' 'Never this sick,' said Dylan, 'never this much before. After last night and now this morning, I've come to the melancholy conclusion that my health is totally gone. I can't drink at all. I always could, before…but now most of the time I can't even swallow beer without being sick. I tell myself that if I'd only lay off whisky and stick to beer I'd be all right…but I never do. I guess I just forgot to sleep and eat for too long. I'll have to give up something.' 'What do you mean, Dylan,' asked Herb, 'do you mean life?' 'No,' Dylan said soberly, 'I don't know…I want to go on…but I don't know. I don't know if I can. I don't feel able any more. Without my health I'm frightened. I can't explain it. It's something I don't know about. I never felt this way before and it scares me. When I was waiting for the plane this time in London, I found I was drinking in a mad hurry…like a fool, good God, one after another whisky, and there was no hurry at all…I had all the time in the world to wait, but I was drinking as though there wasn't much time left for me…to drink or wait. I was shocked…I felt as though something in me wanted to explode, it was just as though I were going to burst. I got on the plane and watched my watch, got drunk, and stayed frightened all the way here… really only a little booze on the plane but mostly frightened and sick with the thought of death. I felt as sick as death all the way over. I know I've had a lot of things wrong with my body lately, especially the past year or so. Since I was thirty-five I've felt myself getting harder to heal. I've been warned by doctors about me, but I could never really believe them…that I was ever sick seriously or in any real danger. I didn't know how to believe it…or maybe I did believe it, but couldn't accept it. I think I just felt that I might be getting older faster than I expected to, older than I should be at my age. But now I don't know. Maybe I've always been frightened but didn't know it until I couldn't drink when I wanted to.'

When Herb suggested that it would be wise for him to see a doctor, a psychotherapist, Dylan seemed surprised. 'Do you really think that could help me now?' he asked. 'Certainly,' said Herb. 'But I don't know how to help myself any more,' said Dylan; 'how can anybody help someone who can't do that? I've always wanted to be my own psychiatrist, just as I've always wanted everybody to be their own doctor and father.'

Liz, meanwhile, returning to the Chelsea, found a note from Dylan asking her to join him and Herb. When she did, Herb asked her help in persuading Dylan to see a doctor—not a psychotherapist, but a physician who might tender Dylan the immediate attention he needed. While Dylan at first resisted this idea—not vehemently, but with the routine antipathy he showed toward all efforts designed to convince him that he needed help —he was quite easily prevailed upon. Liz made a phone call that resulted in an appointment almost at once.

When they went for a consultation with Dr Milton Feltenstein, Dylan was given an injection of ACTH (cortisone). The doctor, for whom Dylan felt a warm personal as well as professional regard, had months before warned him that only a rigorous and unbroken regime would begin to relieve him of his physical torment. On this new occasion he made clear to Dylan that the injection was but a temporary boost—a prop that would help him get through the next few days, and emphasized again the necessity of his agreeing to a long-range programme of medical care.

As Liz and Dylan strolled up Third Avenue after their visit to the doctor, she asked him if he would tell her more of the nature of his illness. 'I have such a feeling of dread,' he told her, 'a terrible pressure—as if there were an iron band around my skull.' But even as he spoke the injection of ACTH was taking positive effect. Dylan soon remarked that he was beginning to feel much better and, more physically alert than he had felt for days, seemed comparatively outgoing and relieved of self-concern. As they were passing an Army & Navy store, he said that he needed some handkerchiefs. They went in, and Dylan bought six big plain white ones, then wandered about the shop. He especially liked American working men's clothes, he said— he had taken a number of shirts back to Wales in the previous spring, and wanted to take more of them this time—blue ones. Leaving the store, they took a taxi uptown for the final rehearsal of *Under Milk Wood*, which was to be publicly performed that evening.

My only personal contact with Dylan since he had come to New York was a welcoming call I had made from Cambridge on the day he arrived. Having heard nothing of the events of the past five days, I came to the Poetry Center that afternoon to find rehearsal going on in the darkened auditorium. When I discerned Dylan sitting in a front row, from which he was supervising action on the stage, I took a seat directly beside him. When he recognized me, we exchanged a whispered greeting so as not to disturb the actors, then sat in silence for another ten minutes. When the house lights went up and I could see him, I was so shocked by his appearance I could barely stop myself from gasping aloud. His face was lime-white, his lips loose and twisted, his eyes dulled, gelid, and sunk in his head. He showed the countenance of a man who has been appalled by something beyond comprehension. Since there was still another scene to be run through on the stage, I left him, promising to join him and Liz at the nearby Irish bar within the hour. Backstage I sought out Liz. 'What's the matter with Dylan? He looks terrible.' She closed her eyes and slowly turned her head from side to side. 'It's something very strange, John,' she said, 'something new and dreadful. I don't know what it means, I don't think Dylan does...'And briefly she told me of Dylan's agonized talk the night before.

After an hour of desk chores in the Poetry Center office, I went to our Irish bar rendezvous, only to wait in vain for the appearance of Dylan and Liz. When I sought them in other likely places nearby and still could not locate them, I phoned the

Chelsea. There was no response from Dylan's room. Puzzled, and downcast by this defection, I went back to my hotel.

With its original cast, and with final additions incorporated into the script, *Under Milk Wood* was given a third reading before a large audience that evening. While it was a good one, I felt it did not quite succeed in striking the fire of those performances I had seen in May. Conscious of the whiteness of Dylan's sick face as it showed through all the lights focused upon it, I could hear, above the music of his voice: 'I have seen the gates of hell.'

Rollie gave a party for the actors and their friends at her apartment after the performance. Most of the time Dylan seemed rather muted in his talk and general behaviour. One of the guests later told me that during a conversation she had noticed that he refused the drinks offered to him. When she had asked why he was not drinking, he had answered casually, almost brightly: 'It's just that I've seen the gates of hell, that's all.' The words had already become something to say at a party. As a small group of us lingered on into the morning hours, Dylan grew expansive, talkative, laughed boisterously, much like his normal self, and my concern was for the moment alleviated—at least my alarm over the illness that could be read in his face. Still troubled by the feeling that I had been carelessly neglected by Dylan that afternoon, I had no way of knowing that his lapse of consideration was not, as I felt then, a failure of trust, but, as I soon learned, merely a confusion on both our parts of times and places.

He and Liz came next morning to see me at my hotel. There we had a strangely remote and disturbing talk about finances and the necessity of Dylan's having more money immediately. We spoke like strangers. The affectionate intimacy of our long discussions in Wales had entirely disappeared. The tone of our interview struck me as being like that of a business conference between someone who wanted money and someone who supposedly could be made to supply it if sufficient pressure were brought to bear. With a new shock of disillusion, I felt as though I had been used to good advantage over a long period, but that now my term of usefulness was over except perhaps in my ability to rake up immediate cash. Overwhelmed by this impasse, in which disappointment and anger were equally at work, I was barely able to speak. If I had known then that Liz had also found affectionate communication with Dylan abruptly broken off, and that she too was bewildered by this development, I could have viewed the incident objectively. Ignorant of everything but what I had witnessed, I could only retreat.

We taxied to the Poetry Center auditorium, Liz and I silent for reasons of our own, Dylan suddenly chipper and as full of song as a lark. The matinée of *Under Milk Wood*, on Sunday, 25th October, the last in which Dylan was to participate, was by every report its greatest performance. A thousand people were left hushed by its lyrical harmonies and its grandeur, among them Robert Shaw, the eminent choral director, who came backstage and, moved to tears, expressed his admiration. Dylan himself said he had at last heard the performance he wanted to hear.

Unable to explain to myself the curious change in Dylan or to come upon any means of re-establishing a happier sense of ourselves, I spent the afternoon in withering depression. Meanwhile, suffering her own dilemma, Liz nevertheless accompanied him to a party on Sutton Place—a party which, we later learned from Dylan himself, had been 'set up' by the particular friend whose claim for Dylan's attention was now largely his zeal as a procurer. While some of his recent offerings had been refused, he had on this occasion come up with a prize—a refugee countess whose 'sense of comic despair,' according to Dylan, was the most attractive thing about her. The party had hardly gone on for an hour when Dylan broke his abstinence of days by gulping down one tumbler of Irish whiskey after another; he then became boisterous and brawling, and shortly disappeared for hours with her into the upper regions of her large town house.

My own gloomy afternoon, spent with Rollie in her apartment, had made me so lugubrious a companion that she finally drew me out to tell her what was on my mind. When I did, she told me what I had not known—that on the previous afternoon, just when I had been searching for Dylan and Liz, they had been searching for me. When they had phoned Rollie in an attempt to locate me, she had learned that both Dylan and Liz felt I had been neglecting them, that my apparent lack of concern for Dylan had troubled him deeply, and that they were puzzled as to what to make of my behaviour. When even this knowledge could not overcome my sense of disillusion to the point where I would act, Rollie firmly insisted that I not leave the city, as I was about to do, before seeking them out. Under her prodding, I came to realize that I could do nothing but find Dylan in order to confirm or be rid of the burdens of our inscrutable predicament.

When I got to the Sutton Place address only nine or ten people were left, most of them seated on the floor having a lounging sort of supper around a low circular table. I spoke with Liz and greeted Dylan with a feint at cheerfulness. A few tense minutes later, I asked Liz if she and Dylan would join me where we might talk apart from the company. We went up a flight of stairs into a drawing-room and sat down, Liz and Dylan on a couch, I on a chair facing them. The room was semi-dark, lighted only from the hallway and by chequered reflections of lights on the river.

Sick at heart, I began to say words I had rehearsed in the taxi ride down, only to find that, as I quickly came to tears, I need say nothing. Dylan began to weep, and Liz wept. Speaking half-articulate phrases, we learned that each of us had felt shut off, that each had sensed disillusion with the other, and that the clumsy silence into which we had retreated was the consequence of a sensitivity so acute and of a misunderstanding so vast that only now could we begin to comprehend it. Suddenly all the tensions surrounding the last two days seemed to be dissolving into thin air. Holding my face in my hands as I attempted to regain composure, I felt strong arms about me. Standing behind me as he held me very firmly, Dylan spoke the last words I was ever to hear him say directly to me: 'John, you know, don't you?

209

—this is for ever.'

Moments later, feeling absurd and foolishly dramatic as we wiped our tears and blew our noses in the semi-dark elegance of our surroundings, we knew that our paralysing impasse had been broken, and that we had awakened into a new sense of one another as if from a dream in which we moved about like tight-lipped strangers. Free at a stroke from the tensions we had so silently brought upstairs, we went downstairs and joined the party. Liz and I sat on a couch, water-lights and the dim shrieks of tugboats moving on the river behind us. Dylan, having just been served a fresh tumbler of whisky, joined a group gathered about the mantelpiece across the room.

We spoke only of Dylan; not until days later did it occur to me that this was the only time she and I had conversed in intimate confidence about him. Now that the emotional pressures of the day had been lifted, and their causes dispersed, we felt bound by an understanding perhaps possible only to those to whom Dylan had been both a living delight and a living torment. He was, Liz said, without any question, the most lovable human being she had ever known. While she adored him, she knew also that he was a destroyer—that he had an instinct for drawing to him those most capable of being annihilated by him. In the short time in which she had known Dylan, the attentions he demanded, whether these were conscious or unconscious, had caused her to lose all sense of her own existence, and to be attuned only to his. Now she felt she was at a breaking point. To-night she was going to let him know that she could no longer be with him, and that she could no longer take care of him.

This first discussion of the consequences of our having known Dylan was a mutual revelation—our feelings were identical, and the bewilderment we shared was of the same nature and sprang from much the same experience. We both took his poetic genius for granted; and while we could accept—though not wholly comprehend—his genius as a human being, we could not avoid seeing ourselves in some ways as circum-stantial victims of an enchantment Dylan inevitably put upon

210

anyone who came close to him. He knew by instinct who was, and who was not, susceptible to this enchantment. More than once, recognizing his power to exert it, and then to betray those who were subject to it, he had said to Liz that he felt 'like a murderer.' While he persisted in it, his Machiavellian role brought him neither pleasure nor security, but only further self-distrust and a deeper sense of self-degradation. The briefest review of Dylan's emotional life would suggest that no man was ever more adept in killing what he loved, or suffered more in the consequence. While this was an agonizing recognition to make, in meeting upon it we had found a new bond of strength which, all too soon, would be all that we might trust in.

As the evening wore on, Dylan returned to unabashed dalliance with his hostess, while, sprawling on the floor, he spilled liquor and ashes over himself, and seemed to have retreated into that state of loud drunkenness in which babyish self-indulgence overtook all of his lovable qualities and left him a figure of ridicule to strangers and a figure of despair to friends. Resigned to this development and again almost as unhappy as we had been hours earlier, Liz and I decided to leave the party together. We were putting on our coats in the entrance hall when, like a child who fears he has been deserted, his eyes wide and rueful, his little brief-case clutched in his hand, behind us came Dylan. 'Here I am,' he said, and quickly put on his coat and came along with us.

Several others from the party got into our taxi, and I was dropped off at Grand Central where I was to catch a train for Boston. As the taxi proceeded downtown, Dylan asked Liz to come with him to the White Horse; she said no—she wanted now only to go home. As the taxi drew into her neighbourhood, Dylan said: 'I *used* to have a friend who lived near here.' 'You still do,' said Liz, and left him. Dylan went on to the White Horse, stayed out most of the night, and returned to his hotel with a girl 'loaned' to him by one of his drinking companions.

On the next morning, 26th October, Liz phoned him on matters related to the production of his play, then went to her office still determined to leave him, in personal torment from the circumstances into which she and Dylan had come, she was nevertheless fearful that, heedless of his doctor's advice, he would continue to go without food and to abuse himself with drink. In the middle of the afternoon she had a phone call from Dylan; he wanted to see her 'terribly,' he said, and begged her to meet him. When she went to join him at the Algonquin, she found him in conversation with a Dutch business man whose acquaintance he had made just a few minutes before. Dylan, already drunk, ordered one whisky after another. When the conversation turned toward politics and war, without warning he suddenly went into a raving fantasy. His talk, implying that he had been in actual war-time combat, that he had witnessed horrors involving his family, became disconnected, violent, maudlin, and obscene. A waiter came to the table to quiet him, but Dylan, helplessly gripped by his fantasy, ranted on about blood and mutilation and burning and death. In an attempt to calm him, Liz held his hand; he broke into tears and began to sob. The Dutchman, more sympathetic than alarmed, indicated that he understood the irrational nature of Dylan's lapse, and left him in Liz's hands, saying: 'He is a good man, take care of him.'

When they left the Algonquin a few minutes later Dylan continued in drunken behaviour that seemed to be touched frighteningly with a streak of insanity. He made gargoyle faces at people passing by in the street, walked in a tottering and lunging parody of drunkenness, spoke four-letter words loudly with complete disregard for who might hear them. As they stopped for a traffic light, Dylan turned to her. 'You really hate me, don't you?' he said. 'No,' said Liz, 'but it's not for your l ack of trying.' He became less erratic then, and wanted to go to a movie. In one of the crowded 42nd Street houses they sat through a double-feature, Dylan apparently recovered sufficiently not only to give his attention to a Mickey Spillane thriller and to a western, but to indicate that he was absorbed and delighted by both of them. When the movies were over he was sober and wanted to go to Goody's, one of the bars of the Village where he and Liz had often spent quiet evenings together. Now they would go there, he said, in a spirit of 'reunion.' As they sat at the bar, Dylan, apparently overtaken by a new pang of anguish, began to speak of himself. 'I'm really afraid I'm going mad,' he said; 'there's something terribly wrong with my mind. Perhaps it's sex, perhaps I'm not normal—perhaps the analysts could find it out.' A while later, returning from the cigarette machine, he noticed a young couple in a booth, their heads amorously together. 'How filthy!' he said to Liz. Amazed at such an unexpected remark, Liz told him that he spoke like a Puritan. 'Yes,' he said, as if for the first time he had understood something about himself, 'I *am* a Puritan!' As he talked further of his mental confusion, Liz said quietly that he would have to find the answers, that if he were going to avoid despair he would have to find professional help. Dylan agreed, then abruptly ended the session at Goody's by saying that they must leave at once, that he could not stay there a minute longer. As they were stepping into a taxi, a young man approached. 'Are you Dylan Thomas?' Dylan nodded, whereupon the young man launched into an explosive paean of hero-worship, and asked for an autograph. On a small piece of paper, leaning out of the taxi window, Dylan wrote (it was now after midnight) 'Dylan Thomas October 27 birthday,' and gave it to the boy saying that he was really only posing as Dylan Thomas. Liz accompanied him to the Horse, but Dylan was too distressed and ill to stay for more than a few minutes. When they returned to the hotel, she said good night to him with a promise to phone early in the morning.

His birthday began quietly enough, Liz returning to have breakfast with him before going to her office. When she went to meet him at the Horse at six in the evening, she found Howard Moss, who had come to buy Dylan a birthday drink. After toasts to the event, Howard left and Liz, with Dylan and a group who had joined them, went on to the apartment of his friends, Dave and Rose Slivka, who had prepared a celebration in his honour. In a crowd of invited guests Dylan was wretched and nervous, unable, after the first half-hour, to join the conversation or to partake of the elaborate dinner that had been prepared. When he announced that he was sick and would have to return to the

213

hotel immediately, his host drove him and Liz to the Chelsea.

Back in his room he fell upon the bed, saying: 'What a filthy, undignified creature I am,' and remarking upon the 'awful' occasion of his 'wretched age.' Unwilling to let him sink any further into despair, Liz spoke to him firmly, begging him to do something to save himself, to fight against the terrors that were slowly overwhelming him. As she spoke—not gently this time, but out of the grief and impatience to which his alternating gestures of self-destruction and appeals for loving attention had brought her—he shouted for her to stop. Sharply hurt by his response, Liz rose and was about to leave the room when Dylan said: 'That won't help my agony.' He wept then, and as Liz tried to comfort him he spoke of Caitlin. 'I know she's crying too,' he said.

In the late evening I phoned from Cambridge to wish Dylan well on his birthday. From his mere whispers of response I sensed that he was either ill or had had too much to drink. I tried, ineffectively in the circumstance, to convey an affectionate greeting, but he seemed so far away and out of connection that I doubted he knew who was calling.

He read his poems at the City College of New York on the following day and spent hours drinking with new acquaintances he had made there. When Liz went to see him at the hotel in the early evening, he was about to leave for the symposium on film art arranged by Cinema 16 with a delegation of people who had called for him. In his vague greeting to Liz, she had a disturbing feeling that he did not remember that they had agreed to meet. She went with him to the programme, the panel of which was made up of Arthur Miller, Parker Tyler, Maya Deren, with Willard Maas as moderator. Dylan, apparently in fine fettle, was a frequent and serious participant in the discussion, expressing incomprehension and then alarm at some of the sophisticated notions proffered by Mr Maas and Miss Deren, particularly when they spoke of 'levels, conscious and unconscious,' and offering his own simple feelings with the remark that, as far as he was concerned, he 'just liked stories.' The most 'poetic' of films, he felt, were those of Charles Chaplin and the Marx

214

Brothers. When, late in the discussion, Willard Maas remarked that no one had yet introduced a consideration of 'love' as a factor in the art of the cinema, Dylan coyly turned to him. '0 *Willard*,' he said, 'I didn't know you *cared*.' A group accompanied him and Liz to the White Horse afterwards, where Dylan, delighted by a series of caricatures Liz had made during the course of the evening, passed them about for every one to see.

Swearing to Liz, and perhaps to himself, that he would drink nothing now but beer, Dylan headed into another busy day. He met his Sutton Place inamorata for lunch and, while he had intended to work on the cutting of *Under Milk Wood* for publication in *Mademoiselle*, dallied through most of the afternoon with her in her town house. In the evening he and Liz went to dinner with Cyrilly Abels and her husband, Jerome Weinstein, whose other guests were the Indian writer, Santha Rama Rau, and her husband. Happy in this company, Dylan participated warmly in a lengthy political discussion and, later, told ghost stories, in the narration of which he and Miss Ramu Rau were chillingly proficient. For the hundredth time Liz was struck by his ability to be easy and gracious in all the ways that the misery in his face belied.

On the next evening, when she met him at six o'clock to attend a dinner party at the home of Ruthven Todd, she found him with Herb Hannum and his rich woman friend who, she had already learned from Dylan, had asked him to marry her. It was a difficult session for everyone. When she asked them all to come to dinner on Sutton Place, Dylan told her of their previous engagement and indicated that it was now time for them to go. He had, as it turned out, resolved that very day to see no more of her. Rebuffed, his lady suitor left and they went on to Ruthven's. Under his host's subtle and sympathetic insistence, Dylan drank only beer, and talked through the evening with fourteen or fifteen people, among them a young Negro novelist with whom he discussed at length technical points of fiction. When the party broke up, he asked Liz and Herb to come with him to the Horse for a night-cap.

On the morning of 31st October, Dylan had a phone call from a young woman, a close friend of Liz's, whom he had met when he stayed with her and her husband on one of his college visits. Delighted by the opportunity to see her again, Dylan made a date to take her and Liz to lunch. When they met, he said that he wanted their luncheon to be very special—they would have the poshest one they could possibly order and that they would do this at Luchow's. While Dylan himself ate next to nothing, merely picking at the dishes he ordered, this turned out to be a pleasant, even merry occasion, and the party did not break up until it had been moved to Costello's on Third Avenue, one of Dylan's first American haunts. There he was later called for by Harvey Breit and taken off to a dinner party. Before leaving, he promised to rejoin Liz and her friend at eleven o'clock. After going separate ways, they returned to Costello's in the late evening, hut Dylan did not show up.

When Liz spoke with him by phone on the following morning, he said he was in dreadful condition, that his hangover was 'a real horror.' Worse than that, he said, was the memory of something he had done: in the dimly recalled night before, he had taken a sudden dislike to a woman who was riding in a cab with him and had literally thrown her out into the street, simply because he could not for another moment bear the sight of her. He asked Liz to meet him, and about noon they went to the Horse. A number of friends and acquaintances drifted by as Dylan drank beer and raw eggs—a diet which, for days now, had provided his only nourishment—and slowly began to recover equilibrium. Early in the evening, a group of people clustering around his table moved on to dinner at a Village restaurant, and later some of them went on to a small party in an apartment on Central Park West. While this was meant to be a quiet gathering, Dylan became drunk, unstrung, messy in behaviour, made obvious advances to a dancer whom he pursued about the apartment (while his pursuit was unsuccessful, it was so physically awkward that the young woman spent weeks afterwards under medical care for a concussion), and showed every sign that, ill or no, he could still muster the zest of

216

his famous party behaviour.

After midnight, Howard Moss invited a group from the party to come to his apartment for a night-cap. As they were making desultory conversation and listening to music there, Dylan said nervously: 'I just saw a mouse. Did you see it?' He pointed to a door. 'It went under there.' Liz and the others did not see it, and sensed immediately that there was no real mouse to see. But Dylan was obviously so distraught that Liz said yes, she had seen it, and he seemed relieved. Asked by Howard if he would read a poem or two, Dylan said he would like to very much. In a few minutes, leafing through the later poems of Yeats which, to Dylan, were the greatest of all modern poems and which had become increasingly the models of what he himself strove toward, he begun the last reading he was ever to give. Among the pieces he chose were 'Lapis Lazuli,' 'News for the Delphic Oracle,' 'Long Legged Fly,' 'John Kinsella's Lament for Mrs Mary Moore.' Before he had finished his recital, he also read W. H. Auden's 'September 1, 1939.'

It was a warm night. When the reading, which had lasted for more than an hour, was over, he went with Howard out on to the terrace of the apartment to look at a rose-tree which now bore its last blossom of the summer. Approaching in darkness, Dylan went too close and scratched his eyeball on a thorny stem. He winced and cursed as he withdrew, but fortunately the sharpness of the pain lasted only for a moment. Shortly he was back in the apartment and had settled down to drink until the party broke up about 5 a.m.

When he awoke in his hotel after a few hours of sleep, the pain from his bruised eye and the throb of his hang-over was so great that he was unable to leave his bed. Liz nursed him through a long painful day and by early evening he had returned to a semblance of normality. Against her advice he decided that he should not give up a social engagement he had promised to meet that evening: an unveiling of a statue of Sir Thomas Lipton by the sculptor, Frank Dobson, taking place at the Wildenstein Galleries. After this ceremony was over, he and Liz went to the Colony for dinner as guests of Ben Sonnenberg, the publicist, who was in charge of the unveiling. In a soiled shirt, and an ill-fitting bargain suit an acquaintance had persuaded him to buy at a garment-district emporium, Dylan made polite, even enthusiastic, conversation in the opulence of the Colony, at ease with everyone except perhaps himself.

It was an elegant gathering, and while Dylan ate nothing, he did take advantage of the occasion to have his first drinks of the day. As he and Liz were about to leave the restaurant when the dinner party broke up, Dylan spotted William Faulkner and a lady companion at a nearby table. He went over to Faulkner, exchanged brief greetings with him, and returned with the remark to Liz that some day, he hoped, he and Faulkner would really be able to talk.

Dylan wanted to go on to Costello's. As they sat in a booth there, Liz made drawings and caricatures. Delighted by these, Dylan asked for a whole series of eccentric figures, including one of 'the drunkest man in the world.' Liz attempted this but, try as she might, the features of the drunkest man in the world were impossible to get just right. Soon Dylan said he was hungry and that he wanted to go back to the Chelsea. At his insistence they bought quantities of food at a delicatessen; but when the midnight supper was prepared, Dylan would have nothing but a bowl of soup.

On 3rd November, Election Day, Ruthven Todd and Herb Hannum came to the hotel early to visit with Dylan. Liz joined them in a late morning's talk, then said she would have to take leave of them in order to vote. Dylan took a satirical view of this, but could not dissuade her. When she and Ruthven returned from the polls, a young poet had come to join the group, and a new drinking session was soon well under way. To forestall, if she possibly could, the onset of another alcoholic day, Liz prevailed upon them to leave. Dylan slept then, to be awakened only by the arrival of the lecture agent whose offer, made in the previous summer, had been one of his main reasons for coming to America. After a brief conversation with the agent, Dylan signed a contract that would guarantee him one thousand dollars per week for his services. His connection with the agency would begin immediately, and there was a clause in the contract stating that he could withdraw at any time when his earnings did not reach that figure.

When he had handed back the signed contracts and said goodbye to his new agent, he lay down on the bed. While he had made a late afternoon appointment to have cocktails with Santha Rama Rau and her husband, and Cheryl Crawford, the theatrical producer, he said now that he could not go anywhere. He seemed exhausted, self-preoccupied, and morbidly depressed, but after a short nap he awoke saying that he would keep his cocktail date after all. Liz went with him to Miss Rama Rau's apartment, where he drank moderately, played with her little son, and seemed quite his congenial self in conversation with Miss Crawford.

Afterwards they went to visit the sculptor, Frank Dobson, at his hotel. While they had planned to go with him and a theatre party he had organized to see *Take a Giant Step*, Dylan felt that he was not up to it. When they had made their excuses to Dobson, they returned to the hotel. Dylan's exhaustion seemed as much mental as physical as, hardly able to speak, he fell asleep immediately. Liz sat with him through the evening. Fretfully turning on his bed, he awoke to speak, sometimes in tears, of his wife, of the misery of his existence, and of his wish to die. 'I want to go to the Garden of Eden,' he said, 'to die…to be for ever unconscious…' And then, later: 'You know, I adore my little boy…I can't bear the thought that I'm not going to see him again. Poor little ——, he doesn't deserve this.' 'Doesn't deserve what?' asked Liz. 'He doesn't deserve my wanting to die. I truly want to die.' Speaking of Caitlin, then, he said: 'You have no idea how beautiful she is. There is an illumination about her…she shines.' As Liz attempted to comfort him, telling him that he did not have to die, that he could get well, he began to weep uncontrollably.

In fitful sleep, broken only by disconnected and further agonized snatches of talk, he kept to his bed until 2 a.m. Then, suddenly, he reared up with a fierce look in his eyes. 'I've got to have a drink,' he said, 'I've got to go out and have a drink. I'll

219

come back in half an hour.' Liz pleaded with him, but he ignored her entreaties and left her. Alone in the room, she waited as half an hour went by, then an hour, then an hour and a half. Dylan opened the door, walked to the centre of the room, and said laconically: 'I've had eighteen straight whiskies. I think that's the record.' He sank on to his knees, reached out his arms, and fell into her lap saying: 'I love you...but I'm alone,' and went to sleep.

When he awoke in mid morning he said he was suffocating, that he had to get out into the air right away. Liz went with him for a walk that led, inevitably, to the White Horse, where he had two glasses of beer, chatting meanwhile with a truck-driver acquaintance. But he was too sick to stay for long. When they returned to the hotel, and without allowing him opportunity to object, Liz said: 'I am going to call the doctor.' Dylan resigned himself to this, and Dr Feltenstein was summoned and arrived within the half-hour. The doctor gave him medications that would relieve his sufferings, temporarily at least, and instructed Liz in procedures for taking care of him. Dylan slept, off and on, through the afternoon, and when he awoke with another severe attack of nausea and vomiting, Dr Feltenstein was summoned again. Without equivocation, he told Dylan that he would have to begin immediately on a regime of medical attention. In response, Dylan was evasive, pointing out that he had engagements to fulfil at Wheaton College, at Massachusetts Institute of Technology, and at Mt Holyoke, and declared that he felt he would soon be all right. The doctor dismissed his arguments, gave him a shot of ACTH, and told him that the new regime would begin at once. Restive, Dylan protested again, whereupon the doctor made a slight compromise: he would allow him to fulfil just one of his engagements, after which he would have to return to New York immediately for continuance of treatment. As Dylan, still reluctant, fretted and showed his impatience by groans and sighs, the doctor asked forcefully: 'Do you want to go on being sick?' Quietly, firmly, Dylan said: 'No.' When the interview was over, Liz stepped into the hallway with the doctor. When she returned to the room, Dylan asked: 'What did he say to you? Did he say I was going to die?' 'No,' said Liz, 'he didn't say that . . he simply said that you will have to accept the fact that you're very ill and that you'll have to begin to-day to do something about it.' 'I will,' said Dylan, 'I'll do whatever you wish.' 'But,' said Liz, 'is that what *you* wish?' 'Yes,' said Dylan, 'I truly, truly do.'

After another vomiting spell—a consequence of his alcoholic gastritis—he became drowsy and fell asleep. Liz had meantime phoned me in Cambridge to say that the plans for the week-end, when Dylan was to spend a leisurely five days with me after his engagement at Wheaton College, would have to be cancelled. In the late afternoon she went out to buy supplies the doctor had recommended for Dylan's new diet. He slept for a couple of hours, awoke to vomit and, when this subsided, lay down again, but not to rest. As Liz almost instantly recognized, Dylan was beginning to go into delirium tremens. He indicated that he was 'seeing' something, that it was 'not animals... abstractions.' As perspiration broke out on his face and he began to retch again, Liz phoned Dr Feltenstein, who came to the hotel immediately. As Dylan, raving now, begged to be 'put out,' the doctor gave him a sedative. Fearing that delirium tremens might make Dylan uncontrollable, the doctor advised Liz to call in some friend to stay with her, insisting that it be a man. After several attempts to locate friends of hers and Dylan's by phone, she was able to get the help of Jack Heliker, the painter, who arrived within a few minutes. By this time Dylan had become a little more peaceful. As Heliker came into the room, Dylan held out his hand: 'This is a hell of a way to greet a man, isn't it?' and very soon he fell into a restless sleep. Liz and Heliker sat by his bed as Dylan waked and dozed intermittently. 'The horrors' were still there, he said— 'abstractions, triangles and squares and circles.' Once he said to Liz: 'You told me you had a friend who had D.T...what was it like?' 'He saw white mice and roses,' said Liz. 'Roses plural?' asked Dylan, 'or Rose's roses with an apostrophe?' Then Liz said: 'You know, Dylan, one thing about horrors—just remember, they go away, they do go away...' 'Yes,' said Dylan, 'I believe you.' As she sat beside him holding

221

his hand in hers, she suddenly felt his grip stiffen. When she looked at Dylan his face was turning blue. A quick call to Dr Feltenstein brought an ambulance that took Dylan to St Vincent's Hospital.

At home in Cambridge I was asleep when, at two-thirty in the morning, I was awakened by the insistent ringing of the phone. It was Liz, calling from New York. Her voice shrill, barely controlled, she told me that she was speaking from St Vincent's Hospital where Dylan had been received into the emergency ward. Quickly filling in details of the dreadful evening since her talk with me by phone in the late afternoon, she said that Dylan had passed into a coma, that he had been given oxygen, that a spinal tap was being made to ascertain whether he had sustained a cerebral haemorrhage, and that his name was on the critical list. As she spoke quickly, disconnectedly, she broke down. I could hear her weeping, for a time unable to speak at all. And then, dismissing all details, she said with an anguished sob: 'John, he may be dying...he may be dying,' and implored me to come at once.

Three hours later, on the first plane available, I was flying over Long Island Sound in the pink-and-orange sun of a windless morning. In this numb suspension I sat sick and chill, attempting to sort out thoughts and feelings that had gripped me since Liz's call. While my mind would not work, I knew that I was stunned—as if I were leaning against a wall of apprehension that would give way if I moved so much as an inch. I had made the flight between Boston and New York hundreds of times, yet the memory of that one passage remains with me precise in every detail from the moment I boarded the plane until I left. It was as though my attention would fix on anything but the one fear that obsessed it.

Liz had asked me to phone her apartment on Charles Street —just a few steps from St Vincent's—as soon as I reached New York. When I phoned from the airport Jack Heliker answered. Liz was still at the hospital. Since she would have phoned him with news of any critical change, and since she had not, he assumed that Dylan's condition was at least no worse.

I took a taxi to the hospital, which is located on 11th Street at Seventh Avenue. As I hurried in by the front entrance, I could see Liz, comforted by Ruthven Todd, being led in the direction away from me down the corridor. I called out to them. By their dazed expressions I believed at once that Dylan was dead. I put my arms around Liz, and she wept on my chest. Ruthven embraced both of us, saying: 'No, we haven't lost him, John, he's still with us.' We retired to a waiting-room. Barely able to speak from the shock and grief of the night's events and her long vigil, Liz told me that Dylan's condition was so critical that any moment might bring word of his death. While the spinal tap had shown no evidence of the cerebral haemorrhage doctors had first suspected, there was some evidence that Dylan had sustained a diabetic shock, and this clue was being followed up. Minute by minute, as we sat in a ghastly apprehensive embrace in the dim waiting-room, we watched for a word or sign from the emergency ward. As she tried to tell me of the events that had led to this moment, Liz faltered and had only breath enough to say: 'Oh, John, why didn't I call the *police?*' No one calls the police, I told her, no one calls the police.

Within an hour, the swinging doors of the adjoining corridor were pushed open. Dylan, outstretched under sheets, was wheeled to an elevator and taken to the third floor, where he was put in a room in the St Joseph's division of the hospital. Doctors and nurses surrounded him as he was rolled past the waiting-room; we could see only that he lay inert, his face in an oxygen mask, his wild hair limp and wet, his face blotched with fever. We grasped at one small hope: since the physicians had allowed him to be removed from the emergency ward, he was at least not sinking.

Dr Feltenstein came to us shortly and, in medical terms, impressed us anew with the minute-by-minute balance upon which Dylan's life depended. When he questioned us about any knowledge we might have had of a recent fall, and about the diabetic condition that the doctors now suspected, we had nothing to offer. In 1950 Dylan mentioned to me that he believed he had cirrhosis of the liver, but had never spoken of diabetes, or

223

ever again of the suspected liver condition.

Within half an hour we were allowed to go upstairs to see him. He was breathing heavily through the oxygen mask, attended by doctors and nurses while a blood transfusion was being administered. Since there was nothing to do but look on helplessly, soon we returned to the waiting-room. There we found Ruthven's wife, Joellen, and shortly came Rose and Dave Slivka, who were particularly close friends of Caitlin's. When Liz and I went to the third floor again we were not allowed at Dylan's bedside. Activity around him continued without respite. Standing at the door of his room, we could observe only that he was still alive and that ceaseless effort was being made to save him.

Later in the morning I made local and long-distance calls to people who were close to Dylan, and arranged to have Caitlin notified. Our vigil was joined now by Herb Hannum, Rollie, and Howard Moss. We spent the endless afternoon waiting, Liz and I conferring at intervals with Dr Feltenstein and Dr James McVeigh, the staff physician who had been put in charge of Dylan. When we learned that it was now established that Dylan had sustained 'a severe insult to the brain,' and that this was due to direct alcoholic poisoning of brain cells and brain tissue, we made arrangements with Dr Feltenstein to call in a brain specialist for consultation. Dr Leo Davidoff was our choice, since we had learned of his reputation as one of the world's leading specialists, and we set about securing his services.

By early evening we had to accept two seemingly contradictory statements: on the one hand, Dr Feltenstein informed us, the longer Dylan remained in coma the less were his chances of recovery, since the long duration of the coma indicated the severity of injury to the brain. On the other hand, Dr McVeigh pointed out, the longer Dylan remained alive, the more evidence did we have of his basic strength to endure and perhaps overcome the violence of the shock he had sustained. Physicians had spent the whole day attempting to restore basic somatic balances. By evening this had been achieved. But there was no sign that the coma was any less deep than at the very beginning.

Just before midnight, at the request of the nurse who was attending him, Liz and I spoke to Dylan a number of times, saying the same words and phrases over and over again. At moments we believed we saw flickers of response, and the nurse encouraged us to continue. But to almost every observation Dylan remained wholly unconscious, only his eyes moving now and then, sightless and without focus. Half an hour later, when Rose Slivka and I were at the bedside, I tried again, saying softly to Dylan that he was not alone, that Caitlin was coming to him, that Liz and I would stay with him, and attempting otherwise to have him recognize me if only by my voice. While I spoke there was a sudden, definite reaction. The rhythm of his breathing became slightly agitated, and he uttered a sound that seemed to indicate that his whole body was straining toward speech. This seemed a miracle, yet I doubted the evidence of what I saw and heard. A few minutes later I spoke to him again, and again came the same response, an effort so agonized and instantaneous, and yet so inconclusive that I could hardly bear to watch. Whether Dylan had heard and somehow understood, or whether his reaction was but a muscular spasm, was impossible to know. While I took hope in the thought that, whatever its nature, his response was immediate and unmistakable, doctors later told me that his coma was of such depth as to leave him utterly senseless to any influence.

Through the hospital dimness I could now discern new faces in the doorway. John Berryman, the poet and critic, had come from Princeton and, along with a number of people whom I did not know, David Lougée, one of Dylan's first American friends. Strangers came and went through the long night. One was an elegantly dressed young woman who simply appeared at the door of the room, stared at him for half an hour, and departed without speaking to anyone. Many others came only long enough to look in, or to speak to the nurses, and so confirm for themselves the rumours of Dylan's plight. About 4 a.m., Sister Consilio, who was in charge of the St Joseph's division, came to us and advised us to go home to bed. She assured us that

225

Dylan's physical functioning had been restored, that his condition had become much less critical, and that he was now out of immediate danger. While most of us tended to accept the truth of this, we were still reluctant to leave the hospital. Gaunt, mesmerized by her unbroken vigil of more than twenty-four hours, Liz would not accept the nun's word or her advice. Sister Consilio then became adamant, changed her counsel into an order, and led us away from Dylan's room toward the main entrance of the hospital. Liz, as adamant as she, and too distraught now to comprehend the situation, refused to leave. But, finally prevailed upon, she was taken away from the hospital by friends who stayed with her through the night.

Back in the hospital just before eight o'clock, I found the only response I could elicit was 'no change.' The oxygen mask was still on Dylan's face, his eyes, spasmodically turning, fluttering, were open, but their unseeing gaze only confirmed his unfathomable sleep. Liz returned shortly and we waited together through the morning, moving from Dylan's bedside to the waiting-room in turns, retreating only when we felt our presence might be an annoyance to the doctors and nurses who continually came and went. In the early afternoon we learned that Dr Leo Davidoff would not be available, but that he had unqualifiedly recommended to us Dr C. G. de Gutierrez-Mahoney, a brain specialist and brain surgeon. He arrived shortly, and Dr Feltenstein escorted him to Dylan's bedside. When the two physicians returned after an hour's consultation, Liz and I were asked into an ante-room to speak with them. We found Dr de Gutierrez-Mahoney to be an elegant, soft-spoken man who knew Dylan's work and understood its worth, and who seemed to understand by instinct not only every nuance of our concern but the circumstances that had given us the responsibility of providing for Dylan's care. Confirming the earlier diagnosis of 'direct alcoholic toxicity in brain tissue and brain cells,' he said that in the nature of the case there was no basis for undertaking surgery. Everything that could be done to make possible Dylan's survival had already been done, but it was likely that his condition was not reversible. He had been on the phone to London, where friends of Dylan's, having read of his illness in the newspapers, had found a physician who offered facts pertinent to Dylan's previous physical condition. Among these were points of information we ourselves had never known: that Dylan had suffered 'black-outs' on several recent occasions in Wales and in London, and that in a visit to his Swansea physician he had been specifically warned that alcoholism had brought him to the threshold of an attack such as had now overtaken him. Observing that Liz and I were unable to accept the notion that nothing further could be done, Dr de Gutierrez-Mahoney asked if there were unresolved questions in our minds. I inquired whether Dylan's ability to have sustained the initial shock that led to coma (it was now more than forty hours in duration) might give us hope—whether he might already have shown unexpected reserves of physical strength that might point to some chance of his survival. The doctor's answer was that, somatically speaking, Dylan had been restored to comparative normal functioning; the 'X' factor, and the crucial one, was the still indeterminable degree of 'insult to the brain.'

Our bedside vigil continued into the evening. By now the hospital staff, plagued with telephone calls by the hundreds, bewildered to find its waiting-room continually overflowing with visitors bent on seeing Dylan or having direct news of him, had ordered that only Liz and I be allowed to visit Dylan. Passes to this effect had been given to us. About ten o'clock we could see, by the increased activity of doctors and nurses, that Dylan was undergoing a change. At three o'clock that afternoon we had conferred at length with Dr McVeigh who had predicted a probable change, for better or for worse, within twelve hours. We knew now that the change had come, and had little hope that it would be for the better. For the first time, Liz and I were asked to leave the bedside and return to the waiting-room. There we found a whole new group of people, a few of whom were our friends. In the appalling hospital silence of late evening we sat without speaking. Just before midnight Sister Consilio approached us, her face grave. 'Mr Thomas's condition is now highly critical,' she said. 'Would any of you care to come with me to the chapel to pray?' Three of the group accompanied her. Liz and I, with the others who stayed, shared a silence that was itself a prayer.

Yet this crisis passed. When we were allowed to make a brief visit to Dylan, we found that a tracheotomy had been performed. Mucous and other impedimenta had obstructed his breathing to the point of suffocation. Swift surgery had removed the obstructive matter; now there was a tube inserted into his nose and another in his throat. While he breathed more freely and with more regularity than earlier in the evening, his body now seemed hopelessly ravaged, as though he were not a man but some organism kept alive by invention. When we spoke to this pathetic body that now seemed to have given all of its will to the accoutrements sustaining its life, I felt finally that I was no longer speaking to Dylan, and knew that the remote hope I had come upon the night before was gone.

When a cable containing a tender message to Dylan from Caitlin had been delivered in the afternoon, we had put it on his bedside table in the meagre chance that it would be the first thing he would see should he come out of coma. But as we looked upon his expressionless face that lay mere inches away from her message, the distance between became immeasurable. Dylan was now beyond all love, even Caitlin's. When we spoke to him now, our words formed no question because we knew there could be no answer.

This was the longest night of all, when every clock stood still, and we sat in a desert of hopelessness. Still we made our alternating vigils, waiting for the only end we could now contemplate. Just before dawn Sister Consilio came to us. Dylan's condition remained critical, she said, but she would like to have us accept her assurance that he was not likely to die within the next few hours. The tracheotomy had successfully relieved the crisis of the late evening; he had gained strength since then and was now breathing peacefully. We left, then, and I slept for two hours.

Again on Saturday morning the report was 'no change'— and we knew by this simply that Dylan's enormous physical strength was continuing to resist the 'insult' to his brain. But by early afternoon we could see that he was sinking. His breathing was troubled and irregular; his temperature rose and fell in sudden changes that left his face alternately red and perspiring, blue and pallid. Now we had to find strength to act upon a new development. We learned that in London efforts were being made to find a seat for Caitlin on a plane scheduled to take off for New York at 3 p.m. If, as seemed certain now, Dylan would die within the next few hours, her coming might be a compounded misery for herself and for others. While Dr McVeigh confirmed our observation that he was now sinking rapidly, there was still the possibility that Dylan might continue to confound prognosis. If there was any chance that Caitlin might share Dylan's last hours of life, that chance would have to be made possible. Yet, should she arrive in New York too late, it would likely be worse than if she had never come at all.

A phone call was put through to London, where Caitlin, awaiting her plane, was being cared for by David Higham, Dylan's literary agent and long-time friend. The imminence of Dylan's death was impressed upon Higham, who at once said he would convey the facts to Caitlin. Higham was uncertain about what she would do and felt it unlikely that she would be able to leave on the three-o'clock plane, since it was now less than two hours from flight time, and no seat was yet available. In any case, Higham said, he would cable as soon as Caitlin had made up her mind.

While Dr Feltenstein remained as attendant physician, Dr de Gutierrez-Mahoney had now assumed complete supervision of Dylan, had subsequently called in other specialists, and had himself been a constant visitor to the bedside during the past two days. His failure to give us any sign that might feed a last flickering hope had slowly brought us to resignation. When we conferred with Dr Feltenstein, we learned that Dylan's death was not only next to inevitable, but that it was now also to be desired: should he somehow manage to survive, the damage to his brain was so great that he would be a permanent invalid, physically as well as mentally. When we comprehended this, when we could grasp the idea of Dylan's mind brought into some half-articulate and crippled distortion of itself, we could only wish that death would come soon. While we had been assured from the first that he was conscious of no pain, it was impossible to look upon that struggling body as it fought for breath, its eyes roaming without rest, and not suffer the conviction that Dylan was embroiled in speechless agony.

E. E. Cummings and his wife came to the hospital that afternoon, and scores of strangers, some of whom were now in the habit of making daily visits. In our conversations with them, we became aware that, while our intimate knowledge of Dylan's worsening condition had led us to accept the reality of his death, others, completely unprepared to accept it, listened to us with faces showing scepticism or outright disbelief. On Friday morning the *New York Times* had carried a brief report of his having been taken ill, but otherwise, except for rumours that had run about the city—one reporting that he had had a cerebral haemorrhage, one that he had fallen downstairs while intoxicated, another that he had been mugged by unknown assailants, still others too repulsive to mention—there had been no public report of his true condition.

Visits through the evening showed no change in Dylan's now high and constant fever that at times reached 105.5°. Higham, meanwhile, had sent a cable saying that Caitlin had found a place on the three o'clock plane from London. Now that she was *en route*, the only thing to do was to pray that she would not come in vain, and to set about insuring that not a moment be lost between her landing at Idlewild and her arrival at St Vincent's. I phoned first the British Consulate and then the headquarters of the British Delegation to the United Nations. The former was taken quite by surprise, having had no previous word of Dylan's illness; and the latter was all but closed up. I was promised assistance from both offices should the proper individuals in authority be reached; but since it was Saturday night it would be difficult to locate those with power to act. In view of this, I phoned Washington and got a friend there to work directly through the British Embassy. He, in turn, phoned an attaché who promised to make arrangements through the Consulate in New York, and assured us that everything would be done to see that Caitlin would not be impeded by customs or other immigration formalities. The business of arranging this, with intermittent visits to Dylan in between, had taken more than three hours. Half blind and useless from fatigue, I was taken away from the hospital at 2 a.m. by Howard Moss, who gave me sedatives and put me to bed. Against all advice, Liz remained at Dylan's side through the night.

When I awoke just after eight I hurried back to St Vincent's. Entering by the main door, I caught sight of Caitlin, escorted by Rose and Dave Slivka, who had gone to Idlewild to meet her, coming in through the emergency ward corridor. We embraced, kissed, and she said: 'Why didn't you write to me? Is the bloody man dead or alive?' I led her upstairs to Dylan's room, but a nurse asked that we wait for a few minutes before entering. As we stood outside while the nurse finished bathing Dylan, I could see Liz sitting alone at the far end of the corridor. Caitlin and I went in. Dylan was now in an oxygen tent, his breathing much less forceful and steady than it had been on the night before. Caitlin took his hand and spoke to him. I left her, and went to Liz. Within fifteen minutes Caitlin came from the room. As I approached her I could see that the reality of Dylan's condition had registered its whole truth. Silently, she circled about, her hands uplifted, as if she were under a spell; then she moved with a sudden lurch to a window and pounded her head against it in an attempt to smash it through. But the window, reinforced with a netting of wire mesh, did not break. She became calmer then, and I escorted her back to the waiting-room, where Rose and Dave Slivka took her away to their apartment near by. Returning to Liz then, I found her calm, resigned to a circumstance too complex to unravel and, as she had determined days before, ready now to remove herself from a scene where, by all official and conventional canons, she had no place.

When Liz left the hospital I was alone for the first time in four days. In the magnified stillness of Sunday morning the waiting-room was empty. When I went upstairs to see Dylan, wintry-bright sun streamed into his room and made a prism of the transparent oxygen tent covering the upper part of him. He breathed easily, quietly, his eyes closed, his face calm. I sensed the resignation of each of his faculties, the composition of all of his will. The dark night of his soul was over, and the long day of his dying. At his own pace, in his own time, Dylan was approaching his own good night. When I spoke to him, I knew I spoke only to myself.

Back in the empty waiting-room, I sat down in a misery of recognition so piercing that it was as if I had just that moment come upon the scene I witnessed. Until then I had never really believed, in spite of the evidence of the doctors and of my own eyes, that Dylan was doomed. When at last I knew, not with my mind—since it would accept only what had happened and still stubbornly resisted what might happen—but with all of my being, that Dylan would die, I wept away the disbelief that had somehow held me together since the moment of Liz's call to Cambridge. There had never been a lonelier hour of my life, but by the time grief had run its term and found the limits of the expression I could give it I had come upon new strength.

In our responsibility for Dylan which, in the absence of any other authority, Liz and I had had to assume, we had naturally proceeded with no caution for expenses, either in regard to hospital fees or to those of physicians. Had we known that St Vincent's Hospital would eventually cancel all costs for Dylan's care, the problem of money would not have forced itself upon us as acutely as it then did. But now we felt the time had come to prepare for medical fees quite beyond our private means, to provide ready money for expenses that would come at Dylan's death, and to raise funds for Caitlin and her three children. After I had spent two hours in making phone calls, first to James Laughlin, Dylan's publisher, who said he would fly in from his home in Connecticut immediately, and then to other individuals who I thought might give money to take care of immediate expenses, Caitlin returned in the company of Dave and Rose Slivka.

She was wearing a striking, close-fitting black wool dress;

232

her tawny yellow hair was loosely done up; she looked radiantly beautiful, and she had had too much to drink. Before we went upstairs, she embraced me, a bit unsteadily, and held me to her for fully a minute. She stayed at Dylan's bedside for about twenty minutes, and then she was asked to leave the room by distraught nurses who could not keep her from lighting cigarettes in the danger zone of the oxygen tent, or from pressing herself upon Dylan in such a way as to obstruct his breathing. When she was led to an adjoining room—which the nuns had made available to her as a private waiting-room—I joined her there with Rose, David Lougeé, and Rollie. Someone had brought whisky at Caitlin's request. She drank from the bottle and was very soon in a state of distraction in which, suddenly berserk, she wildly assaulted me and then turned fiercely on those who tried to pull her away. As she still fought and wrestled with the others through the length of the room, I went dazedly into the corridor and tried to come upon some perspective through which to view a development that now threatened to overwhelm us all. Entering Dylan's room, I stood in the dim blue light of his bedside and watched his sleep for perhaps ten minutes. As I stepped back out into the corridor and was about to return to Caitlin, the sister in charge of the floor approached me in great agitation. Caitlin's behaviour, she reported, had become uncontrollable. She had torn a crucifix from a wall and smashed it, demolished some pots containing plants set on a wall-shelf, and splintered to bits a statue of the Virgin. Fighting off nuns and nurses, as well as the friends who tried to calm her, she was now in a state of hysteria. Rollie, who had witnessed all of this, came to me and suggested that a physician be called, since Caitlin was now impervious to any entreaty. The nun in charge sent for one of the doctors on duty in the emergency ward. Within a few minutes he had come with an attendant and a wheel-chair. Caitlin was led from the ante-room; her face was flushed, but she was momentarily docile. She refused the wheel-chair with a burst of profanity, and was escorted into the elevator and down to the emergency ward. There she flared up again, biting an orderly on the hand, attacking the doctors attending her, and tearing the habit of a nun. When I went downstairs a few minutes later I learned that she had finally been restrained in a straitjacket.

We phoned Dr Feltenstein, who said he would come immediately. Meanwhile James Laughlin had arrived. Liz, who had come back to the hospital for this purpose, went out with him and me so that we might present our ideas for the establishment of a fund to take care of Dylan's expenses now and in the future. When we returned, Dr Feltenstein was just coming from an interview with Caitlin, who was being kept in a room adjoining the emergency ward. He impressed us with the extremity of her hysteria, warned us that she was a menace not only to herself but to others, and told us that on no account could she be allowed to go free. When we made clear our refusal to be party to any action that would commit Caitlin to Bellevue—the municipal psychiatric hospital to which a staff physician was attempting to send her—Dr Feltenstein offered to bring in a psychiatrist. This man, Dr Adolf Zeckel, came within half an hour, examined Caitlin, then conferred with Dr Feltenstein, Rose Slivka, and myself. This was the dilemma: since Caitlin was not rational and would have to be cared for, and since St Vincent's refused to keep her, the only recourse would be to have her sent to a private hospital. He recommended that we authorize him to send her to Rivercrest, an institution in Astoria, Long Island, just across the river from Manhattan. When he could see that we were still hesitant and unhappy, Dr Zeckel pointed out our only two other alternatives—either to commit Caitlin to Bellevue, or to assume personal responsibility for her care. After all we had witnessed, we had to admit—even against the press of circumstance that might cause anyone to take leave of his senses—that Caitlin's need was not the ministrations of well-intentioned friends but of professionals. An ambulance was arranged for. Dr Feltenstein took two hundred dollars from his pocket to be used as a deposit at Rivercrest. With Rose, and Ruthven Todd, attending her, Caitlin was taken away to the Long Island institution. When the ambulance arrived there, I learned later, she had become calm and rational enough to assess her situation, and to commit herself.

When James Laughlin returned with his friend, Philip Wittenberg, the well-known literary and theatrical attorney, the three of us sat down to a brief conference during which we devised initial steps for putting the machinery of a fund into operation. This would be named the Dylan Thomas Memorial Fund. The first letters of the appeal, containing the names of literary sponsors who would be approached by telephone that very evening, were to be ready for mailing on the following day. Philip Wittenberg would serve as treasurer, and cheques would be received at his mid-town office. Our talk was brief and to the point, no one now indulging in any sentimental hope that a memorial fund would prove premature.

All through that day and on until after midnight, as he slept far from the grotesque violence and grief that surrounded him, Dylan had shown little change. But on Monday morning, 9th November, my first glance told me that, somewhere in the night, he had gone into his final phase. His fever had subsided; his breathing had become so slight as to be almost inaudible; and now and then there would be little gasps and long breathless intervals that threatened to last for ever. His face was wan and expressionless, his eyes half-opening for moments at a time, his body inert.

When I phoned Rivercrest in the hope that I might speak with Caitlin, I was told that she had spent a quiet night, but that no one could yet speak with her or come to visit her. When I inquired into the possibility of her being released, I was told that this would not be considered until Dr Zeckel came to see her on Monday evening. This seemed an intolerably long time for her to be alone, no matter what professional assistance might be available to her. I then phoned Dr Zeckel and obtained his permission for an afternoon visit by her closest friends, Rose and Dave Slivka. As to the possibility of her being released, the psychiatrist felt that we would have to accept the likelihood that she would be confined for at least two or three days.

Dylan's life simply ebbed away, without any further sign of struggle, through the long morning. With Liz, who had returned to the hospital late the night before, I made frequent visits; we sometimes took his hands in ours, sometimes spoke softly to him in the last hope that some small word of love and comfort might penetrate the limbo in which he lay.

When a British physician who was visiting in New York recommended to Ruthven Todd that Dr James Smith of Bellevue, an alcoholic specialist, be called in, Liz and I went to see Dr de Gutierrez-Mahoney in order to secure clearance for the consultation. While Dylan's doctor welcomed this development, we sensed that, while he carefully said nothing that might deepen the despair we felt, he regarded Dylan's condition as terminal. When we returned to inform Dr McVeigh that Dr Smith would be coming to see Dylan in the early afternoon, he advised us to phone Dr Smith and urge that he come at once. We did this, and he arrived at the hospital within fifteen minutes. After his examination of Dylan and his report to the physicians, he conferred with Liz and me. He told us that he had made certain recommendations, that these were 'purely a matter of chemistry,' and that it appeared to him that Dylan's condition was not reversible. Now there was suddenly increased activity at the bedside, with an anaesthetist constantly in attendance.

A few minutes after one o'clock in the afternoon, Liz and I sat with a group of people—some of whom we had never seen before—in the shuffling dimness of the waiting-room. When someone asked Liz to come out for a cup of coffee, I urged her to go along. Before she left, I said, I wanted to go upstairs to Dylan just one more time. Liz said she would wait until I had come down. As I stepped from the waiting-room into the corridor, I saw John Berryman rushing toward me. 'He's dead! He's dead! Where were you?' I could not believe him but I did. 'When?' 'A few minutes ago. I just came from the room.' I turned and walked slowly back through a group of strangers toward Liz, took both her hands in mine, and nodded. She rose instantly, her hand fiercely gripping mine, and we rushed to the elevator.

In Dylan's room nurses were dismantling the oxygen tent and clearing away other instruments. He had stopped breathing, one of them told us, while she was bathing him. As she was about to turn him over on his right side she had heard him utter a slight gasp, and then he had become silent. When the nurses left us alone, Liz sat down in the chair in which she had watched all the nights of his dying. Dylan was pale and blue, his eyes no longer blindly searching, but calm, shut, and ineffably at peace. When I took his feet in my hands all warmth was gone; it was as if I could feel the little distance between his life and death. Liz whispered to him and kissed him on the forehead. We stood then at the foot of his bed for a few very long minutes, and did not weep or speak. Now, as always, where Dylan was, there were no tears at all.

APPENDICES

APPENDIX I

There is no such thing as the one true Dylan Thomas, nor anybody else; but, necessarily, even less so with a kaleidoscopic-faced poet. He is conditioned by the rehearsing need to withhold from the light his private performance till it is ready for showing.

I am not quarrelling with Brinnin's presentation of Dylan. It is impossible to hit back at a man who does not know that he is hitting you, and who is far too cautious of the laws of libel to say plainly what can only be read between the lines.

I want only to make clear that an intensive handful of months, at divided intervals, over a comparatively short number of years do not, however accurately recorded and with whatever honest intentions, do justice to the circumference of the subject.

And, though I have tried very hard to keep off this painfully tricky, already overwritten subject, I think it is only fair, after reading Brinnin's one-sided, limited to Dylan's public and falsely publicized life version, that I should try to show what went before. To give some dawning idea of the long-growing years, with none of Brinnin's skill, but with a longer and, I hope, deeper understanding of the changing man hidden inside the poet.

I feel that I should (that it is an Augean duty, pushed on to me against my will) do my best, with a still hot shovel of overloaded feeling and a lot of windily winding words, to vindicate first Dylan, then me, then both of us together. And hope that the truth that I am trying blindly to say, to find out for myself, will come out through all the literary muddles and faultily *not* detached attitude. And I hope it is a better truth than Brinnin's.

CAITLIN THOMAS

APPENDIX II

This disclaimer and the reason for its placement here have been widely misunderstood, perhaps because developments leading to both were obscured in the emotional stress of the time. When I sent the newly completed manuscript of this book to Caitlin Thomas, I made two requests: first, that she excise anything she might consider offensive, incorrect, misapprehended or otherwise troubling; second, that she grant me permission to quote from, or publish verbatim, letters of mine from Dylan which alone would lend my account an essential degree of authenticity. Long months of silence ensued, ending, finally, with a note to the effect that she had no objections and that permission for use of the letters was granted—with one proviso: that the book be prefaced by a personal statement of her own.

Delighted by what I took to be an act of generosity, I thanked her, even though I was convinced that she had not turned so much as a page of the manuscript. This conviction remained unshaken through years saddened for me by interviews, on the air and on the page, in which she railed against what I had written, then against America and the whole procession of diabolical bartenders, ravening Bacchantes and lascivious widows for whose assaults upon Dylan's person and integrity I was judged responsible.

Fifteen summers after the book was published, I was sitting one morning at a sidewalk cafe in Palma, waiting to be joined by Ruthven Todd, a lifelong friend of Dylan's and for many years of mine. Ruthven, who had kept with me the deathbed vigil in

242

New York, now made his home in Majorca. Arriving on the run, he gave me a hug, sat down and, waving a packet, told me to open it. Inside were a dozen photographs he'd picked up en route—Kodachromes of Caitlin and the Italian companion with whom she lived in Rome and who would later become her second husband.

"What a bloody shame," said Ruthven. "The two of them left just two days ago. You'd have been in for the surprise of your life."

"Surprise?"

"Caitlin found my copy of *Dylan Thomas in America* in the guest room. One morning, book in hand, she came to breakfast. Know what she said? 'Dear funny old John,' she said, 'his fucking book isn't nearly as bad as I thought.' Can you believe, all these years, she'd never *read* it?"

The happy truth—more than thirty years since the first publication of this "fucking" book—is that I have lived long enough to remember the moment in 1950 when, through the raucous turmoil of a pub in Laugharne, I first laid eyes on the savagely beautiful woman whom Dylan adored; to have survived the years of an estrangement which, on my part, never existed; and to hear, like an echo that will not diminish, words from our last conversation: "Brinnin, can you forgive me? In my heart, I always knew that you were the best thing that ever happened to me and Dylan."

APPENDIX III

AFTERWORD to the 1988 edition by John Malcolm Brinnin

The memory of those few seconds when Dylan's baby-like feet —"me little trotters," he called them—began to turn cold in my hands has remained with me now for thirty-five years. Quitting his deathbed, I took with me all that I knew of him and had shared with him into an impenetrable privacy of grief. That was where it would stay, I thought, a possession of no value to anyone but myself.

When, in the aftermath, memorial gatherings and tributes began to take place in New York and elsewhere, I kept apart, unwilling to rehearse my memories or to make my own homage in anything but silence. Apparently, this reluctance sparked the determination of reporters, interviewers and others in the media to pursue me for "the *real* story" of Dylan's death, and for details of the widely bruited-about scandals of his life. Beleaguered by their importunities, I took haven in a ramshackle hotel in the Bahamas. There one morning, perusing shelves of mildewed books in an old public library open to the weather, I came upon the *Journals of Dorothy Wordsworth*. While this was hardly the kind of assuaging literature I must have been seeking, I began to read with, largely, a technical interest which made even the most pedestrian accounts of Dorothy's stewardship absorbing. The result was a poem, an attempt to come to grips with what had happened and, incidentally, perhaps bitterly, to send up the sedulous, self-stricken practice of daybook keeping which I had myself been "at" for more than two decades.

JOURNAL ENTRIES

"*It is all over.*" I cut out.
An island takes me out of season.
Palm trees, dreamy as giraffes,
munch the dead air.
My room is shuttered, small, pistachio.
A rainy old mirror tries, but I
have given my last interview.
"*Let him die!*"... Why? asks the light bulb,
rocking the dim room. "*Because he's dead.*"
Skin I shred from a raw
knuckle tastes of salt.
Has that smashed body on the rocks got home?
(Someone wipes the inside of a kettle.
Someone straightens a chair.
The whole house aches,
getting the story right).
I down a toothbrush tumbler of warm scotch.
Weightless as a moth, I saunter out.
I hear my own hard heels on the swept racks
of the straw market.
I watch a turtle put its football stitch
across the civic beach.
"Shu-gah," says a girl in skin-tight cherry,
"You want good lovin', shu-gah?"
My room is as I left it.
I've been everywhere.
Three o'clock. Another page
of faithful Dorothy's dank daybook:
"July 28th, 1800. Intensely hot.
I made pies in the morning. William went
into the wood and altered his poems."

Meanwhile, what would become known as "the Dylan industry" had begun, and I wanted none of it. Importunity now took the form of hundreds and hundreds of invitations to tell what I knew of "the hottest poet since Byron" on national television talk-shows, university lecture programs and ladies' literary societies from New Jersey to Idaho. Turning down all of them, I shared what I could only with a few British friends, acquaintances of Dylan's—among them T S Eliot and Louis MacNeice—who had appealed to me in the hope of picking the truth from a tangle of rumors that showed no sign of ever being unsnarled.

As the first anniversary of Dylan's death approached, I was aware of, but paid little attention to, notices of commemorative broadcasts and other programs of that nature. One November evening in Boston, I attended a dinner party, after which the company retired to an upstairs sitting room. There, my host flipped on a radio for an hour-long series of reminiscences, beginning with Dylan's recital of "And Death Shall Have No Dominion." Stunned by the sound of his voice (I had long since put away every reminder of him, including his recordings), I sat down and listened in a kind of mute turmoil as one individual after another spoke his recollections of the man and retailed anecdotes already as famous as they were false. So much of what I heard was mistaken, distorted, careless of fact or unconsciously malicious that I found myself close to panic. "*No! No!*" My shout stuck in my throat. "*You've got it all* WRONG!" Even more dismaying was a feeling that, bit by bit, Dylan was being taken away from me and, with it, a fear that, brain-washed into submission, I'd come to believe what I heard and so muddy or replace memories that were mine alone.

Next day, set upon breaking the thrall of other peoples' versions of what I knew first-hand, I went to my desk and turned out seventy-five typewritten pages. Syntax, sequence, exactitude—all went by the board under an overwhelming compulsion to begin my own reclamation project. While memory still served, I would test it to the limit and so repossess what was subtly being taken away.

The stages by which that first sheaf of scattered memorabilia came to be a book were guided less by me than by others free to look ahead while I looked back, among them my publisher, Seymour Lawrence, who saw what I could not. When the story of my years with Dylan was ready to come into print, I had two hopes: that its irrefutable veracity would squelch for good the endless rumor and surmise threatening to turn a gentle genius into a drunken clown; that, salvaging "my" Dylan, I would be so much at peace in the security of a shared affection that I could let the world make of him what it would. The first of these hopes was dashed, irretrievably, when the sensationalized reception of *Dylan Thomas in America*, especially in England, gave a totally unexpected boost to just those aspects of the Dylan legend I had tried to quash. The second produced an irony. While I had made the ultimate effort to dispel the legendary Dylan and reclaim a friend so dear that he often fell asleep on my shoulder, I now sought ways to be free of him, public *persona* and good companion alike.

Nothing quite worked—as I recognized one Sunday after-noon when, strolling with a friend through Greenwich village, I found our steps leading inevitably to "the horse," the White Horse Tavern where, to this day, the ghost of Dylan presides. "When are you going to let Dylan go?" she asked. "Isn't it about time you said goodbye?" The first opportunity to do so was of my own devising; the second, and final, was provided equally by history and the good offices of ex-President Jimmy Carter.

A few years after Dylan's death, I went to Laugharne by myself with nothing more in mind than to follow Dylan's Walk to the Boat House, have a pint in Brown's Hotel with his beloved Ivy Williams, and to sit for a while by his graveside. Approach-ing the cemetery, I recalled talk I'd heard of a cairn and other kinds of monument deemed appropriate. But, no; the modest wooden cross I knew from photographs was still there, slightly askew, incised with the innocent simplicity of a child's lettering in a copybook. If, I thought, it had ever occurred to Dylan to design his own grave marker, this is what he would have produced. In a silence broken only by the streak of a jet fighter

247

across blue sky, I picked a handful of the wildflowers growing about and laid them at the foot of the little cross.

But even this most private of farewells was not conclusive. When *Dylan*—the play based largely on my book—made its Broadway debut, with Alec Guinness in the title role, there we were again, figures resurrected from these pages and thrust into a drama straining to make tragedy of an episode which, for me and for Dylan, was never more than a circumstantial encounter rifted, even in its most congenial exchanges, with black humor and dominated by a sense of plight.

For the capstone to a relationship publicized out of all proportion to Dylan's life and, in a lesser degree, to mine, I had to wait twenty-nine years. In 1982, living in Key West, I learned of the "unveiling and dedication" of a memorial to Dylan in Westminster Abbey on March 1st—the day on which Wales honors St. David, its patron saint. From the moment I'd seen this notice, I knew that neither love, however ambivalent it had come to be, nor money, however short in supply it was, would prevent me from being there, and so booked a weekend's round trip to London. When, on my return, I wrote details of the occasion to a friend, he took my letter to the editor-in-chief of *The New Yorker*. And there, expanded and revised, it was published—anonymously—within the month:

"I was ushered into the first pew of that part of the North Transept designated North Lantern, which allowed me a close view of the High Altar, on my left, and of hundreds of Welsh men and women—each wearing a single yellow daffodil—in the pews directly across. Members of the Thomas family were seated catercornered from me, in one of the choirs stalls to my right. 'Not many souls under this roof not from Wales,' said a small gray woman next to me. Her voice had the pretty lilt I remembered from talks I'd had with villagers during summertime visits to Dylan in Laugharne. 'Do you know if your Jimmy Carter will be coming?' I did not think that likely, I told her. 'Jimmy Carter got the ball rolling on this whole thing,' she said. 'That time they brought him to Poets' Corner, he looked around and asked the high hats with him why there was no sign of Dylan Thomas.' A man's voice over my shoulder joined in—'And you know what *they* said? "Who's *that*?" they said'—just as Bach's Toccata and Fugue in D Minor from the organ brought the congregation to attention. The service began with a white-cassocked procession of members of the Collegiate Body, followed by what the program called 'representative clergy,' along the nave and up into the sacrarium. As these men took their places, the organ played Daniel Jones's musical setting of Dylan's 'A Refusal to Mourn,' which seemed to me a good beginning to a memorial service for a man who spent his life denying precisely those ordinary sentiments which never failed to bring him to tears.

"Welcoming the gathering of fifteen hundred or so, the Dean of Westminster provided a fact that did not seem entirely pertinent: while Keats, Shelley, and Byron each had to wait almost a hundred years to be honored with a stone in Poets' Corner, Browning and Tennyson came by theirs 'almost instantaneously'. As I calculated that Dylan, were he alive, would be sixty-seven years old and younger than perhaps a third of those who'd come to do him homage, the woman next to me touched my elbow. 'I should venture waiting twenty-nine years is *quite* long enough,' she whispered. Then came a brief reading, from Revelation 10, by the Abbey's Precentor and Sacrist, which included, 'I saw another mighty angel come down from heaven, clothed with a cloud: and a rainbow was upon his head, and his face was as if it were the sun, and his feet as pillars of fire: and he had in his hand a little book open.' This was followed by an oddly perfunctory address given by a layman friend of Dylan's, and by 'Hymn 372 A. M. R.,' in which the Welsh delegation across from me, unanimously and without a glance at the printed text, embraced its chance to out-sing the organ by many decibels. While this was going on, those of the Thomas family present, followed by Michael Foot, the leader of the Labour Party, and other dignitaries, were ushered out of their choir stall and into the aisle leading to Poets' Corner. There

249

television crews under high floodlights were waiting to photograph the unveiling. Since both Caitlin, the poet's widow, and Llewellyn, his elder son, had decided against coming to the ceremonies, Dylan's only daughter, Areonwy Thomas-Ellis, with her husband, and Dylan's son Colm and three grandchildren made up the familial procession. For a few moments, they were visible to almost no one but the crews manning cameras. Then, over a loudspeaker, came Aeronwy's clear, strong, and mellow voice: 'May I ask you, Mr. Dean, to receive into the safe custody of the Dean and Chapter, here in Poets' Corner, this Memorial Stone in honor of Dylan Thomas.' With this, she removed from the stone a Welsh flag, with its claw-footed dragon, and the Dean replied, 'To the greater glory of God, and in memory of Dylan Thomas, we dedicate this Memorial in the Name of the Father and of the Son and of the Holy Spirit.' Two of the grandchildren then laid a wreath on the memorial, and for a half hour or so afterward there were hymns, prayers, and readings of 'Poem in October' and 'Fern Hill.'

"Everything was well paced and liturgically stylish, and moved along more or less as expected until the Dean, rising to give the concluding blessing, suddenly interrupted his own speech and lowered his voice. 'I have just been handed a letter from former President Jimmy Carter,' he announced, 'which I should like to read.' As a little frisson of surprise seemed to run through the Abbey, the woman next to me nudged my arm and sent me a glance at once steely and satisfied. Mr. Carter's letter thanked everyone who had anything to do with the occasion, and recounted his own introduction to Dylan Thomas, in 1953, when he came upon 'A Refusal to Mourn' in an anthology; his immediate purchase of all the available poems; the sessions with his family in which Dylan's techniques were studied; and his subsequent readings of biographies of the poet. A high-pitched metallic burst from the organ—Mathias' Toccata Giocosa—summoned stewards, who directed us, pew by pew, down the aisle to Poets' Corner. There floodlights made

Dylan's 'conifer green Penrhyn stone' stand out sharply from the stones surrounding it—Byron's on its left, George Eliot's on its right, Henry James's and that of Gerard Manley Hopkins below.

"Outside, a bit stunned by the actuality of it all, the discrepancy between that radiant stone and Dylan's often expressed wish never to be anything but 'lost and proud'—and I must admit, having a few valedictory thoughts of my own—I was buttoning my overcoat against the cold sunlight when I found myself next to a man holding a little girl. Amber-eyed, with fair hair cut in the demure permanent-wave manner of the nineteen-twenties, she stared at me over his shoulder for a few seconds, then reached out a small white hand. As I brought my index finger to within an inch of hers, she took hold, tightened her grip, and would not let go until the man, shifting the weight of her to his other shoulder, turned around. 'This is Dylan's granddaughter,' he said. 'Her name is Hannah.'"

John Malcolm Brinnin died in 1998.